The Politics of
Antisocial Behaviour

Routledge Advances in Criminology

The Politics of Antisocial Behaviour

Amoral Panics

Stuart Waiton

Routledge
Taylor & Francis Group
New York   London

First published 2008
by Routledge
270 Madison Ave, New York, NY 10016

Simultaneously published in the UK
by Routledge
2 Park Square, Milton Park, Abingdon, Oxon OX14 4RN

Routledge is an imprint of the Taylor & Francis Group, an informa business

Transferred to Digital Printing 2009

Typeset in Sabon by IBT Global

Library of Congress Cataloging in Publication Data
Waiton, Stuart.

The politics of antisocial behaviour : amoral panics / Stuart Waiton.
p. cm. — (Routledge advances in criminology ; 3)
Includes bibliographical references and index.
ISBN 978-0-415-95705-2 (hardback : alk. paper)
1. Deviant behavior—Great Britain. 2. Moral panics—Great Britain. 3. Fear of crime—Great Britain. I. Title.
HM811.W39 2008

302'.170941--dc22   2007025255

ISBN10: 0-415-95705-2 (hbk)
ISBN10: 0-415-87272-3 (pbk)
ISBN10: 0-203-93837-2 (ebk)

ISBN13: 978-0-415-95705-2 (hbk)
ISBN13: 978-0-415-87272-0 (pbk)
ISBN13: 978-0-203-93837-9 (ebk)

Dedicated to Penny Lewis

Contents

Foreword

British and American sociologists who study deviance and social problems have been talking with—and sometimes past—one another for more than forty years. In the 1960s, Americans developing the so-called labeling approach to deviance inspired British sociologists to establish their own National Deviancy Conference. Perhaps the most influential concept to emerge from that work was *moral panic*—first used by Jock Young and then Stanley Cohen, both active in the NDC.

But labeling faltered in the 1970s, after it came under attack from several directions. In particular, radical criminologists—particularly in Britain, and including Young and others prominent in the NDC—challenged labeling's political assumptions. British studies of deviance and moral panics took a turn that was both political and cultural—heavily theorized interpretations of skinheads, punks, and muggers flourished.

Meanwhile, in the U.S., some sociologists associated with labeling began to shift their attention to the social construction of social problems. By the early 1980s, there were already dozens of constructionist case studies, and the approach continued to expand. Constructionism offered advantages. Whereas labeling confronted rival—sometimes quite hostile—interpretations of deviance, there was no other, theoretically coherent approach to the study of social problems, so constructionists had the field to themselves. In addition, constructionist analyses permitted a range of interpretative stances: one could debunk one set of claims, while celebrating the successes of another set of claimsmakers. Constructionism did not require analysts adopt particular political or ideological assumptions.

By the 1990s, constructionist analysis had spread to Britain. In *Intimate Enemies: Moral Panics in Contemporary Great Britain* (1992), Philip Jenkins (educated in the U.K., but now based in the U.S.) demonstrated how several claimsmaking campaigns that had been launched in the U.S. had spread across the Atlantic. By the end of the decade, there was a substantial body of work examining British claims by such British sociologists as Frank Furedi (1997, 2001), Adam Burgess (2004), Ellie Lee (2003), and Stuart Waiton (2001).

This new volume by Waiton should prompt another round of cross-Atlantic conversation. British and American analysts have always made rather different uses of the idea of moral panic. Americans tended to emphasis the quality of *panic*—the sense of heightened, exaggerated alarm that characterized many social-problems claims. In contrast, British sociologists put more weight on the *moral* qualities of moral panics. In keeping with British sociology's tendency to emphasize politics and ideology, analysts in the U.K. understood moral panics as conservative efforts to denounce threats to the established moral order.

But, by the turn of the millennium, it was hard to identify many successful social problems campaigns mounted in either country solely by conservative claimsmakers. Increasingly, for instance, moral conservatives in both the U.S. and the U.K. found themselves allied with at least some feminists in campaigns about such issues as pornography, child sexual abuse, and satanic ritual abuse. This required rhetorical shifts, so that, for example, instead of emphasizing pornography's immoral qualities, advocates now charged that it led to sex crimes, the exploitation of women doing sex work, and the objectification of women generally. Morality was downplayed, and victimization emphasized.

Further, as Waiton demonstrates, a growing body of other alarms is framed in terms of risks, rather than morality. Fetal alcohol syndrome, secondhand smoke, avian flu, road rage, climate change, the digital divide, and countless other phenomena are constructed as threats by physicians, scientists, and other expert claimsmakers who avoid the language of morality, in favor of claims about endangerment and victimization. To describe these new campaigns, Waiton has coined the fabulous term *amoral panic*.

At least to an American reader, one of the most interesting aspects of this story is the realization that some social-problems claims travel better than others. Road rage made the transition from the U.K. to the U.S., but claims about workplace bullying and antisocial behavior haven't really caught on over here. Similarly, Waiton builds an elaborate argument that British politics has been transformed by a rhetoric of risk that permeates discussions of many aspects of social policy. This is, I think, less evident in the U.S., where recent discussions of the American federal government's role in social policy have tended to revolve around just a few key issues—welfare reform, education, immigration, and health care. While the rhetoric of risk appears in some of these debates, its role seems less central in the U.S. Hopefully, American scholars will take up Waiton's challenge, and explore the similarities and differences in how our two societies go about both claimsmaking and policymaking.

Joel Best
University of Delaware

REFERENCES

Burgess, A. 2004. *Cellular Phones, Public Fears, and a Culture of Precaution.* New York: Cambridge University Press.

Furedi, F. 1997. *Culture of Fear.* London: Cassell.

Furedi, F. 2001. *Paranoid Parenting.* London: Penguin.

Jenkins, P. 1992. *Intimate Enemies.* Hawthorne, NY: Aldine de Gruyter.

Lee, E. 2003. *Abortion, Motherhood, and Mental Health.* Hawthorne, NY: Aldine de Gruyter.

Waiton, S. 2001. *Scared of the Kids?* Sheffield: Sheffield Hallam University Press.

Preface

> The demand for law and order, which at first sight appears to attempt a restoration of moral standards, actually acknowledges and acquiesces in their collapse. Law and order comes to be seen as the only effective deterrent in a society that no longer knows the difference between right and wrong
>
> (Lasch 1977: 187).

In Britain over the last two decades, the move towards using laws and regulations to resolve society's problems has developed at a relentless pace. Often narrowly understood within public debate, as the actions of authorities to genuine issues of concern about rising crime, or of violence and abuse, relatively little is said about the extent to which this way of running society has come to dominate ahead of all others. In the UK an acceleration of new laws took off under the Conservative leadership of John Major in the early 1990s and has subsequently been accelerated further under the Labour governments since 1997.[1] In the UK it has recently been observed that almost unbelievably there have been over three thousand new laws introduced since Labour came to power—one for every day they have been in office. The purpose of this book is to attempt to explain this development by examining the 'politics of antisocial behaviour'.

Discussing *Why Americans Hate Politics*, E. J. Dionne Jr., in 1992, observed that at the moment when democracy is blossoming in Eastern Europe, it is decaying in the United States. For over three decades, he continued, 'the faith of the American people in their democratic institutions has declined, and Americans have begun to doubt their ability to improve the world through politics' (Dionne 1992: 9). It is the proposition of this book that a similar loss of faith in politics has developed in Britain and that it is this development, perhaps above all others, that helps to explain the rise of *The Politics of Antisocial Behaviour* and indeed of *Amoral Panics*.

The above quote in *Haven in a Heartless World* by Christopher Lasch is a good starting point for this book. His argument was that in the United States the move towards a tough law and order approach by the political elite did not, as it was understood, indicate a shift to the right with a subsequent restoration of 'moral standards' in society. Rather it indicated the reverse. The move by the elite to enforce standards of behaviour through law—rather than through moral or political arguments, campaigns and movements—indicated that in fact, the elite had given up. They had lost the capacity and even the will to lead—now the best they could do was regulate and control a society that felt increasingly out of their control.

There is a belief within key strands of social thought that in the late twentieth and early twenty-first centuries we have moved 'beyond'. We have entered a 'late' (Beck 1992) or 'liquid' form of modernity (Bauman 2000a); we have moved 'beyond left and right' (Giddens 1994, Furedi 2005), or witnessed the *End of Utopia* (Jacoby 1999). The profound change to society, and for the elite, in Jacoby's writing for example, relates to 'the end of ideology'—an understanding that first emerged with Sartre in 1946 and has been resurrected a number of times since. The issue of right and wrong, raised by Lasch above, is related here to the issue of right and left, and of the demise of these conflicting ideologies. Whether the above authors are correct in their varied understandings about society, they all sense a profound change has take place within Western society in the past two decades, one that necessitates a new approach to understanding social problems and the reaction to them by the political elite.

One, and arguably the most significant, change has come in the nature of politics itself—a change triggered by or that can at least be represented by the collapse of the Berlin Wall in 1989. This change had huge international ramifications, with the end of the Cold War and the collapse of the Soviet Union and the belief in socialism. More generally however there appears to have been a certain collapse in the belief in politics itself. Frank Furedi in *The Politics of Fear*, for example, argues that this collapse has resulted in a 'profound sense of fatalism', which suggests that 'politics is a pointless exercise' (2005: 2). This collapse for Russell Jacoby has resulted in a declining political imagination and a loss of 'a sense that the future could transcend the present' (Jacoby 1999: xi). Within the UK Alan Finlayson's *Making Sense of New Labour* perceptively notes that with the transformation of politics—and of the once solid political organisations, and loyalties—today's political elite no longer has the capacity to engage the 'energy' of the public (Finlayson 2003). The international ramifications of these changes are not the subject of this book. However, the implications for national and indeed local politics are—as the grand narratives of the past become replaced with the personalised focus of the 'politics of behaviour'.

The underlying argument presented in *The Politics of Antisocial Behaviour* is that politics has changed, not just changed, but has been transformed. It is no longer politics as we knew it in the past, but is something with little meaning, coherence or constituency. It does not engage with what C. Wright Mills (1968: 355) described as the *public*, or take place in what Jürgen Habermas (1992) called the *Public Sphere*. It appears difficult for all sections of the political class to define what they represent. In Britain, the party of government for the last decade has apparently been following a Third Way. But even this name is more an attempt at describing what the Labour Party is not—neither left nor right—than what it actually is. This more confused state of politics and political identity is coupled with the growing disconnection of all the major political parties in the UK—and arguably across the Western world—from the public—a process that further confounds the capacity of today's leaders to direct social processes.

The 'crisis of confidence' that grips the Western elite is partly masked by the fact that 'There Is No Alternative' to capitalism today. But that the market is now the only accepted way of organising society does not necessarily mean that the politics of the right has a coherence and dynamic behind it. Within the 'politics of crime' the trend towards more laws, policing, incarceration and surveillance is often understood as a consequence of society's 'shift to the right'. However, this idea of politics being dominated by a purposeful outlook or belief system—an aggressive form of neo-liberal authoritarianism—and a dynamic enforcement of order over society is questionable. The *Culture of Control* (Garland 2002) that has emerged most significantly in Britain and the United States is perhaps not the result of an aggressive elite attempting to enforce their rule on society, but rather as Lasch suggests—the mass of legislation, new laws and regulations has emerged, not as a way to enforce the authority of the elite, but because of the lack of authority within the elite itself.

Zygmunt Bauman, the British based sociologist, in his description of today's *Liquid Modernity*, depicts not only a society, but an elite that have lost their way, that are no longer grounded, that lack the ability to rule 'the waves and tame the seas' (Bauman 2000a: 182). If he is right, what implications are there for understanding what social problems emerge and engage the imagination of the elite and society? Perhaps political preoccupation with 'antisocial behaviour' in the UK, of 'spitting yobs', noise, graffiti, litter and myriad offences that have become 'social problems' resolved within the new framework of 'community safety', can best be understood as an expression less of 'real' problems than of the political elites' sense of their own loss of control—their inability to engage the public or direct society.

Britannia it seems can no longer 'rule the waves' but it can make everybody *safe*. Fortunately perhaps for the elite, the more fragmented public appear to also often understand their *troubles*[2] in terms of the behaviour of those around them and of the need for safety. As Bauman observed,

> It is perhaps a happy coincidence for the political operators and hopefuls that the genuine problems of insecurity and uncertainty have condensed into the anxiety about safety; politicians can be supposed to be doing something about the first two just because being seen to be vociferous, tough-tongued and keeping busy about the latter (Bauman 2000b: 35).

The question of crime and the myth and reality of the extent of this social problem has been an ongoing discussion for decades, and today perhaps more than ever before there is a general acceptance of the significance of the problem of crime in society. However, the argument being made here, is that to fully understand the significance of crime and more particularly antisocial behaviour, as key issues for society, we need more than statistics that show the 'real' rise and fall of these problems. We must also understand why crime and antisocial behaviour at certain times capture the imagination of both the public and most importantly the political elite, and why in particular it captures their imagination today.

To reiterate—what Lasch was alluding to in the 1970s was that crime became an issue for those running society when they lost the capacity to lead people morally or politically—or to engage the 'human subject' in transforming society. When you no longer feel you can transform individuals' hearts and minds, indeed when your own heart is no longer in it—you lose the sense that society can be changed, and seek instead to regulate it.

The 'collapse' of politics, in this respect, can perhaps help to explain why politicians are more inclined to attempt to regulate the 'behaviour' of children, than to influence the 'beliefs' of adults.

Christopher Lasch described the present period as an *Age of Diminishing Expectations* (Lasch 1979), an age that has similarly been depicted as one in which the culture of society has embraced a *Morality of Low Expectations* (Furedi 1997). In this period a declining view of human possibilities has meant that cynicism and irony appear to be two of the few universal characteristics of our time (Calcutt 1998). In this 'culture of limits,' safety and 'risk' have become fundamental organising principles for society. And again the question of how these developments have impacted upon our 'obsession' with crime and antisocial behaviour needs to be addressed; our sense of the dangerousness of other people. At a time when our belief in human progress is 'diminishing', we appear to be more inclined to attempt to regulate than free up, to control rather than liberate.

Recent criminological discussions have attempted to compare the rise of private 'monied police' and the active public involvement in crime and safety initiatives today as being similar to these developments at the end of the eighteenth century (McMullan 1996). Zedner, for example has argued that 'Contemporary calls for "community engagement", "active civic partnership" and "local capacity building"—might just signal a renaissance of this classical notion of civic virtue' (Zedner 2006). However, these comparisons do not sit comfortably with what has been described as the modern day *Fall of Public Man* (Sennett 1986), or with the description of the vibrant creation of the 'public sphere' in the eighteenth century (Habermas 1992). The 'age of enlightenment' was, for example, a period when there was a dynamic sense that 'anything was possible'. Even for those engaged by problems of crime and public safety, like Jeremy Bentham, there was a sense of optimism and a belief in the possibility of creating a perfect, well-ordered society; with the development of the British police force being seen within the context of extending the freedom and liberty of the public. Where the goal for society then was the extension of liberty, something that was actively pursued through a new kind of public spirit, today this spirit has been sapped and the meaning of liberty has been transformed—and is now discussed within the context of the 'freedom' from fear.[3]

Within today's representation of 'liberty', the goal for society is no longer freedom as such, but safety. Society appears to be developing a new 'morality' of safety, based not upon a strident sense of purpose and belief in the benefits of social control, but within a new form of *anxious authoritarianism* where liberty has come to mean the right to be protected.

In the 1970s the loss of belief in positivism, or planning and intervention, to resolve the problem of crime led to the famous understanding that when it comes to addressing the issue of crime, 'nothing works'. Today in comparison Braithwaite observes, 'evidence clearly no longer sustains a 'nothing works' conclusion (Braithwaite 2000: 53). However what Braithwaite has missed is the extent to which the idea of something 'working' today has been downgraded. In the past the belief that things 'worked' in terms of crime was largely underpinned by a sense of progress at a social and individual level. The idea of rehabilitation embodying both of these elements—a belief in the capacity to change individuals—indeed for individuals to change themselves—and also a belief in society, its improving dynamic, something positive that people would increasingly want to be rehabilitated into. However, today the idea of the robust individual—the subject—has itself been questioned, as has the very idea of progress as a positive thing. The idea of what 'society' is or should be is no longer clear, nor, within the framework of crime and punishment, is the social process of rehabilitation spontaneously obvious. What is this thing called 'society' that people are to be rehabilitated into? In this context when we talk about something 'working' we are discussing something very different from the past—often more of a number-crunching exercise in risk management—than a positive sense of individual and social progression in any meaningful sense. The understanding of individual responsibility and of the relationship between the individual and society are, today, both confused and confusing. Where 'treatment' in the past was predicated upon a sense of both the individual and society, today the therapeutic treatment of offenders increasingly engages the self with the self rather than with any socially defined moral points of reference (Nolan 1998: 3). Rehabilitation in this respect is off the agenda, while thoughts of what ultimately causes crime and deviance must be tossed into the waste bin of history.

When politicians and criminologists talk about things working today, the sentiment being expressed is more one of relief rather than optimism—a sense that we have managed to hold back the impending tide of disorder across society and disorders within individuals: at least for the time being.

In different historical periods, since the enlightenment, there have been differing views about crime, however, there has until relatively recently been a certain belief that this was a problem that could be overcome, through rationality, or planning and social change. This is no longer the case. In a recent discussion about Shearing's understanding of a new 'regulatory state', by Braithwaite, we find an example of today's diminished expectations of how people approach the issue of crime and safety (Garland and Sparks 2000).

Exploring Shearing's work around crime and policing in South Africa and the role of the free market within this process, Braithwaite notes that,

> For Shearing, the market mentality engenders deep inequalities in security, especially in his beloved South Africa. Yet it is a global mentality that has colonized all our sensibilities. This leads him to conclude that there is no alternative but to work with these sensibilities and seek to harness them in a transformative way.

For Braithwaite, Shearing, like many other criminological critics, 'is no utopian dreamer; he is a Foucauldian schemer' (2000: 59). His scheming for the South African blacks, post apartheid, is limited to a hope that they will receive state-aided funding and become established as 'powerful customers with the ability to control their security' (Braithwaite 2000: 59). There is here, perhaps typically, no comprehension, let alone discussion about overcoming the problem of crime. Now the idea of equality that captured the imagination of black South Africans for generations has been reduced to the promotion of 'equality of security'.

In a world of limited expectations, safety is god.

The decrease in expectations of today's Western elites, and indeed many of their critics, has led to safety becoming a predominant framework of governance. Richard Williams notes in *The Anxious City* that we can see how Trafalgar Square, historically London's site for imperial celebration, and consequently a site for protest, has been transformed in the reconstruction project, 'World Squares for All' which reformed 'the old ideology of Empire', and replaced it with, 'the architecture of civility' (2004: 134–35). Influenced by the Labour governments' interest in regulating public space:

> [A] place that was built originally to monumentalise the past, to celebrate the achievements of empire, in particular its military prowess, has been reinterpreted as a site of bourgeois pleasure, with its promenades, its café, its 24-hour security presence, and one of its monuments, the empty fourth plinth, reinvented as an entertainment for gallery goers. The logic of empire in summary, is replaced with the logic of civility (2004: 141).

Trafalgar Square, in a sense, has changed from a site of imperial pride and radical resistance, to a safe space for all. The empty plinth—a plinth that in the past would have had a 'Great British' statue on it—faces the 200 foot tall Nelson's column and is perhaps the best expression of the modern elite contrasted to the assertive leaders of the past. Today the plinth may change its statue to entertain the tourists, but its general emptiness reflects the elites' inability not only to present a modern-day hero to the public, but also to imagine one for themselves. It appears that today there is no one who embodies the 'difference between right and wrong'. Civility may sound good, but the image depicted by Williams is a new Trafalgar Square that is somehow more hollow—a cosy café—but no society.

Today we find few who are competing to promote what is 'great' and 'good'—we are rather more likely to be encouraged to 'get real'. Realism has become an influential outlook in society as it has within criminology, on both the right and the left, both outlooks expressing in their own way the growth of pragmatism—or pessimism—following the declining belief in 'utopias' or ideals. One consequence of this development is that our more limited horizons have impacted upon how we understand social problems and indeed how we understand people. Our gaze is rarely raised by the aspirations of society, but is drawn downwards into a world as seen through the eyes of characters like the *Taxi Driver* Travis Bickle. The 'real' world it appears is becoming ever more dangerous, more damaged and 'antisocial'.

The 'politics of antisocial behaviour' has emerged at a time when left-wing idealism has largely disappeared, but has also been accompanied, somewhat paradoxically, with the decline of conservative reminiscing or sense of moral purpose. In Pearson's book *Hooligan*, written in the early 1980s, a time when conservative celebrations of the 'good old days' was still going strong, he notes how for over a century British conservatives have been harking back to the golden days of twenty years hence. Since the nineteenth century he observes, changes within society led to a certain conservative reaction about the state of society, within which almost invariably the days of proper moral standards were to be found two decades previously. But what of today? Rarely do we find conservatives harking back to the 1980s as a model for citizens and society. Indeed the past is something that appears to be less of a resource for conservatives than it used to be. Christopher Lasch observed this development in 1970s America, noting that the lessons that had been taught by the 'American past' were increasingly becoming understood as no longer relevant and even as dangerous. Formerly Lasch notes, historians assumed that men learned from their previous mistakes, but now that 'the future appears troubled and uncertain, the past appears "irrelevant" even to those who devote their lives to investigating it' (Lasch 1979: xiv).

Rereading Pearson's book I am struck by how distant it feels, a book written in another time. Whatever the explanation for the 'authoritarianism' of today, it cannot be found in the conservative impulse described by Pearson. If the present and future look bleak in the cultural imagination, it seems the past is less than ever before a resource to help lead us out of our current malaise.

The way society is presented in often desperate terms by politicians has become so commonplace we hardly notice it any more. The killing of the young child James Bulger by two other children in 1993 was an early example of this trend, where 'Jamie' became a symbol for a number of politicians, including the then Labour leader Tony Blair, of what was wrong with British society. But this understanding of children killing children as somehow being representative of British society and the British people actually tells us very little about the general state of society, and an awful lot about the more degenerate and pessimistic mindset of the British political elite.

New laws are introduced today, and old freedoms lost with almost casual political statements or bills that nonchalantly drift through Parliament. Before the 1990s for example the type of countries that were understood to have curfews were either authoritarian communist regimes, unstable states that were constantly under threat, or what were termed 'tin-pot dictatorships'. For a nation like Britain to introduce curfews on the streets at this point in time would have been unthinkable. By the end of the decade however, curfews had become not a source of embarrassment to Western leaders but something that both Bill Clinton in the United States and Tony Blair in the UK promoted. Blanket regulations of the nighttime activities of young people were no longer a reflection of authoritarianism—but simply one of myriad initiatives to help improve 'community safety'.

1 Introduction

Antisocial behaviour is important because it is the newest horseman of the apocalypse

(Field 2003: 64).

INTRODUCTION

Twenty years ago antisocial behaviour did not exist as a significant social problem nor was it a political issue. Today, it seems, it has become the 'newest horseman of the apocalypse'.

The term 'antisocial behaviour' has the advantage of flexibility. It can refer to the behaviour of infants, of young people and adults. It can relate to behavioural issues, to crime and even incivility. Perhaps most importantly in today's use and understanding of this issue, it connects the everyday nuisance behaviour of people with a wider sense of disorder and social breakdown. In a general sense, 'antisocial behaviour' is a political term, and it is this wider understanding of antisocial behaviour that is examined here.

The problem of antisocial behaviour has not been dreamt up by politicians. Indeed as is often pointed out, for 'local people' it is a major issue of concern. However—as with the question of 'youth' in the 1960s or 'mugging' in the 1970s—the question of why 'antisocial behaviour' has become such a prominent issue should not simply be taken at face value as an expression of an objective 'real' problem in society. The problems of litter and graffiti for example have been an annoyance for 'local people' for decades but not until recently have they been grouped together under the banner of 'antisocial behaviour' and promoted as a key problem for government and society itself.

What politicians do and do not respond to depends on many things—not least of all their own understanding of society and the problems they themselves face in dealing with social changes. It is the proposition of this book that 'antisocial behaviour' can only be fully understood as a social problem by understanding the changing nature of politics and the changed relationship between the public and the institutions of society. Perhaps 'antisocial

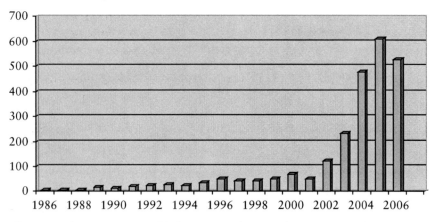

Chart 1.1 The term 'antisocial behaviour' in the *Guardian* newspaper.[1]

behaviour' has gotten worse in the last two decades—but this cannot explain why it is now understood to be perhaps *the* greatest problem that British society faces.

APOCALYPSE NOW?

If the above chart gives an indication of the stark rise in the concern with antisocial behaviour we can perhaps add to this by observing that if we look at all British newspapers just in the month of January 2006 we find over 1500 articles that relate to this problem—that's around 17,000 articles a year. Turn on the television in the UK and almost every week, and sometimes every day, there is a new documentary looking at this issue—often with camera teams following young 'gangs' around the street and using undercover cameras to unearth the 'neighbours from hell' who are 'destroying neighbourhoods'. The term antisocial behaviour itself has become part of everyday vocabulary in the UK to describe activities that include what used to be called the 'mischievous' behaviour of children and young people. More recently the debate about antisocial behaviour has itself branched out even further to be incorporated into a discussion about 'respect', civility and manners.

As Burney notes, 'the concept anti-social behaviour has come to dominate Britain's law and order discourse' (Burney 2005: 3). It has also become a significant issue within the workplace—teachers' unions have campaigned against antisocial behaviour and the 'rising tide of pupil indiscipline', while public sector workers have similarly been encouraged to watch out for and report signs of antisocial behaviour amongst the public. Almost all 'community' buildings now are adorned with posters warning the public about their antisocial behaviour, while community workers applying for grants for local initiatives are encouraged to incorporate a section explaining how their youth work program, play park, neighbourhood centre or swimming club helps to 'reduce antisocial behaviour in the local area'.

The problem of antisocial behaviour is often located in what are described as 'sink estates', however it is also associated with far wider concerns about the general behaviour of people across society: It is something that affects us all. For Labour MP Frank Field we face a problem of *Neighbours from Hell* (2003); the best-selling author Lynne Truss' latest book, *Talk to the Hand*, describes *The Utter Bloody Rudeness of Everyday Life* (2005); and for the Conservative Alexander Deane:

> Britain is a depressing country to live in. An atmosphere of depression, despondency and pessimism reigns, one more suitable for a poor nation with high unemployment than for a large, successful one with low unemployment. This is largely because of antisocial behaviour (Deane 2005: 99).

Perhaps these authors have a point, and there are certainly issues to address regarding how people in the UK—and arguably across Western societies—relate to one another today. However there is a sense of doom within this debate—indeed, as Deane accurately describes, there is an atmosphere of pessimism within the UK more generally—but is this really being caused by people being 'antisocial'?

Antisocial behaviour relates to many forms of behaviour from dropping litter, to vandalism, drunkenness and so on. It is also interconnected with the issue of crime—indeed we are more inclined to discuss crime itself today with reference to 'crime and antisocial behaviour'. Antisocial behaviour is directly associated with crime—and arguably is understood today to be even more of a problem than crime itself. This is a change in how antisocial behaviour was discussed even in the mid-1990s. At this time the problem of antisocial behaviour that was beginning to become important within politics—and especially within the Labour Party and Labour leadership—was often given significance by connecting it with serious crime. The 'broken windows' theory was used at this time to explain how areas that experienced petty forms of antisocial behaviour could become areas of more serious crime: If a broken window on an estate is not fixed, more windows will be broken, more antisocial behaviour will develop until the estate is riddled with crime. Thus we must have a zero tolerance attitude to antisocial behaviour, to stop this spiral into chaos. Here *the* problem was understood to be serious crime—while antisocial behaviour was of significance because of its association with this more serious problem. Today this situation has to some extent been reversed. Antisocial behaviour, while being connected to crime, can today stand on its own as a major social problem.

Elected prime minister in 1997, Tony Blair and the now Home Secretary Jack Straw had helped to substantially change the 'New' Labour Party image away from the 'old' welfarist party of the past. One key element in this transformation was the creation of the Labour Party as the new party of law and order. 'Tough on crime, tough on the causes of crime' was Blair's now famous slogan, and crime has remained a significant issue for all of the political parties. However, over the past decade it is the issue of antisocial behaviour that has become increasingly important for the government. In 2002 for example Blair used the Queen's Speech—where the priorities for the government are set out—to explain that antisocial behaviour, and specifically vandalism, graffiti and fly-tipping, were 'probably the biggest immediate issue for people in the country' (*Guardian* 1 November 2002).

So seriously has the British government taken the problem of 'antisocial behaviour' that immediately following Labour's victory in the General Election in 2005, Prime Minister Tony Blair launched the 'Respect Agenda'. This agenda is part of the government's growing interest with what has been described as the 'politics of behaviour'—an agenda that opens still further the public debate about antisocial behaviour and incorporates issues of politeness and manners. A *Respect Action Plan* was published by the government's Respect Task Force—coming after the setting up of the various Antisocial Behaviour Task Forces around the country. To emphasis the seriousness of this new Action Plan, it included a note written by each member of the cabinet—from the health secretary to the secretary of state for work and pensions to the then minister of respect himself, Hazel Blears—explaining what contribution their departments would make to the battle against antisocial behaviour.

It appears that the government is doing everything in its power to 'stem the tide' of this new horseman of the apocalypse.

THE FEAR FACTOR

Alongside the rising concern about antisocial behaviour has come the engagement by politicians, the police and local authorities with the 'fear of crime'. An 'issue' that was of limited if growing importance in the 1970s has today become a thing addressed to a large extent within its own terms. We no longer have to fight only against crime—but also against the fear of it. Once again the issue of antisocial behaviour has grown in significance within this framework of challenging fear in society, as the understanding of public insecurities regarding crime has developed to focus less upon the one-off serious crimes that people occasionally suffer—and more onto what could be described as 'problems of everyday life'. It is within this understanding of fear in society that the problem of antisocial behaviour has become understood as a greater problem than even crime.

As early as September 1995 the then Shadow Home Secretary Jack Straw launched a campaign against 'aggressive begging' and against disorder on the streets. As the *Guardian* noted, 'He concedes that much of what he calls disorder—loutishness, graffiti, people hanging around streets being aggressive, intolerable noise—are not in themselves crimes, but says disorder as much as street muggings contribute[s] to the fear of crime which send neighbourhoods into a spiral of decline' (*Guardian* 9 September 1995).

The question of antisocial behaviour, while relating on the one hand to petty acts by people in public, has also within politics been addressed as a major issue for rebuilding communities and society more generally. Antisocial behaviour for New Labour is not simply about tackling crime—it is also about re-creating civil society and a 'sense of community'. A housing executive in the Labour council of Manchester explained this 'socialist' approach to the politics of antisocial behaviour.

> We're dealing with the children of people who grew up under Mrs Thatcher, and were brutalised. We're recreating society. Putting back some of the social glue. We have nothing—nothing—to be ashamed of as socialists. If you're rich, you can buy yourself out of it, but these things take place among deprived communities. They want social glue and that's what we're trying to give back to them (*Guardian* 24 July 2004).

Also in 2004 the then Home Secretary David Blunkett explained the government's approach to civic republicanism, arguing that

> People say that actually feeling safe to walk down the street, is the first and primary goal that they want us to achieve. That way, they'll come out to public meetings, they'll go down to their local school, they'll join in in being part of the solution.[2]

The problem of antisocial behaviour is here both understood as a problem caused by a minority of 'brutalised' people and, more significantly, connected to the wider sense of fear in society. It is this sense of fear that David Blunkett feels is at the root cause of public disengagement and a solution to this problem.

If Blunkett's vision of an active public reenergised by resolving the problem of fear appears somewhat fanciful, the question of the actual causes of fear in society is also debateable. The fear of crime became a debate in the United States in the 1960s and was understood in part to relate less to the experience of crime than to the wider understanding people had about the 'broader fabric of social life'. Research in the US and also later on in the UK itself found that incivility in communities added to the fear of crime. However, this was also linked to the views people had about these problems, their own attitudes to issues like law and order and to major issues to do with trust and social cohesion within society more generally. Insecurity is also something that at least in part relates to people's economic circumstances. As Burney observes, 'poor people do suffer more from crime and disorder but they also have more things to worry about and are more likely to feel things are out of control'.[3]

Fear and insecurity in society can be understood in relation to many different factors—it can relate to economic circumstances. It is arguably also connected to wider social and political changes. A more fragmented society for example and one that has low levels of trust between the people and its institutions may well experience higher levels of fear than a society with strong bonds between people and key institutions. However, the question of insecurity and of social cohesion and public trust that has often been understood as most centrally a moral and a political issue has today been transformed through New Labour's approach, which has focused more narrowly upon the fear of crime and antisocial behaviour. In so doing wider social questions have been sidestepped and reduced to the issue of behaviour and crime.

Today the fear and concern about antisocial behaviour can perhaps best be understood as one fear among many: an issue that is framed by a wider *Culture of Fear* (Furedi 1997), or what Burney calls a 'risk consciousness'. Discussing 'antisocial behaviour' as a potential moral panic, she notes that

> Risk consciousness besets modern society and anti-social behaviour is only one among many of the issues which seize public attention. Pollution, paedophiles, food scares, medical errors and many more threaten our peace of mind as ever-present dangers which from time to time throw up peaks of alarm triggered by fresh events or 'expert' reports (Burney 2005: 11).

This approach is useful because it takes us away from the focus on 'sink' estates and 'yobs' to studying the culture of society itself: It also leads us to ask different questions about the social problem of antisocial behaviour. For example, if we are living in a 'culture of fear', can this explain to some extent why antisocial behaviour has become such a major issue, and by engaging with people through their fears have politicians actually encouraged this fear?

At the risk of being one-sided, the suggestion being made here is that *it is not antisocial behaviour that creates fear—but rather, fear is today expressed through the issue of antisocial behaviour.*

ANTISOCIAL

The term 'antisocial behaviour' has a long shelf life and articles can be found about this issue from the start of the twentieth century. The specific word 'antisocial' stretches even further back in time—its first use being located by the *Oxford English Dictionary* in 1802. The original definition of 'antisocial' in this dictionary printed in 1885 reads:

Antisocial: opposed to the principles on which society is constituted
(Oxford English Dictionary in 1885).

The first use of the term 'antisocial' in 1802 and then a later use in 1844 both related to concerns about radical republicanism, firstly during the French Revolution and latterly in relation to the rise of republicanism in Ireland. In 1802 a Parisian is noted to have described 'A collection of all the rebellious, *antisocial*, blasphemous books published during the Revolution'.

Interestingly a revised definition of 'antisocial' in 1989 had changed to:

Antisocial: Contrary to the laws and customs of society; causing annoyance and disapproval in others: children's antisocial behaviour
(New Oxford English Dictionary 1989).[4]

The first use of the term antisocial emerged at the time of the French Revolution, when the political framework of radical revolutionaries on the *left* and conservatives on the *right* was first established. It is perhaps no accident then that the new definition of antisocial emerged in 1989 at a time when the *left* in the form of communism and socialism was collapsing. When the term antisocial was first used it was highly political and related to major competing ideas about politics, morals and society. The radical Republicans were understood to be 'opposed to the principles on which society is constituted'. By 1989 in comparison the term antisocial incorporated, 'causing annoyance and disapproval in others: children's antisocial behaviour'. This addition was not an alternative definition to 'contrary to the laws and customs of society', but was part of this understanding—which means that here the antisocial behaviour of children was equated with the undermining of societies laws and customs.

That the behaviour of children can be linked to the undermining of society perhaps tells us more about the fragile nature of that society than about the behaviour of children itself. It may indeed be no accident or mere linguistic fate that the declining significance of left and right within politics and of competing *macro* approaches to society resulted in a the word antisocial being changed to relate more specifically to *micro* issues of an interpersonal nature—of 'annoyance' and of children's bad behaviour.

HARM

The original use of the term antisocial was used to denounce the activities, writings and beliefs of radicals. Today it has a wider meaning that relates to the 'annoyance' being caused to others. Within the definition of 'antisocial behaviour' in the Crime and Disorder Act 1998, being antisocial relates to this annoying behaviour, specifically that behaviour that is 'likely to cause harassment, alarm or distress'. Burney notes that when looking at the issue of antisocial behaviour the government has come to understand that 'repeated offensive behaviour can be as bad, or worse, than being a victim of a one-off more serious crime'. However, the government's extrapolation from this in presenting a picture of 'generalised thuggery and harassment affecting the whole country' is highly questionable (Burney 2005:9).

The criminalisation of behaviour that was previously not seen as worthy of legal sanction has developed alongside the growing importance of the 'victim' within the criminal justice system. With the growth in legislation and initiatives to deal with antisocial behaviour an ever wider net has been cast that has helped to redefine more things as being 'antisocial' and to equally see more people as victims of this behaviour. What is seen as being harmful to people has expanded—as has the government's attempt to prevent harm happening.

Preventing harm by monitoring and limiting antisocial behaviour has become an institutional framework for local authorities. In youth work, as we have observed, preventing antisocial behaviour has become a key target and basis of attracting funds to projects. This can be seen as simply a practical attempt, and arguably a more positive attempt to resolve this problem—it can however also be seen as a more negative basis on which to justify this work in the first place. Rather than an approach to young people that is centred around the positive experiences they can have, the actual aims and objectives of projects have become framed around and legitimised in relation to the reduction of antisocial behaviour. Much youth work (and arguably much school work) in this respect has become less about transforming young people than crime prevention—a form of damage limitation.

Protecting people has become an industry. Private security is one example of this, as is the growing surveillance of public spaces. However within workplaces, universities and schools, protection from harm and offence has developed apace, with codes of conduct regulating people's behaviour and health and safety initiatives increasingly influencing people's day to day activities. Safety, as Furedi argues, has increasingly become not simply a practical matter but a more significant organising framework for institutions and for government. 'Child safety' is perhaps the best example of this development, with safety issues overhanging how children's activities are understood and indeed how we understand children themselves.

The growing significance of safety within society—and with the 'harm' done to people—can perhaps best be understood as a new approach within society based on what in science is called the precautionary principle. The influence of this approach within politics is not simply a technical matter but suggests a profound change in the way that society is engaged with by the political elite. This development that has occurred alongside the major changes within politics itself has resulted in the transformation of politics away from any attempt to *create* towards an approach based on trying to prevent *harm*. The result has been that where previously politics attempted to engage with the 'energy of the people' to change society in a positive way, today the mindset of politicians—the social problems they recognise and engage with—and the way solutions to problems are understood is now framed by an outlook based on attempting to limit the damage that people are doing to society, to one another and indeed to themselves.

'Community Safety'—a new core strategy adopted by local authorities to direct their services and policies—is one illustration of this harm prevention approach to society. Community safety is new and did not exist as a term let alone a key principle for local authorities until the late 1980s and mid-1990s respectively—and it is a good example of the wider cultural mindset that is structured around harm reduction.

Preventing harm is not a novel development. Insurance for example could be seen as a development over the last century that attempts to do just that. Within politics itself the idea of a 'Conservative' Party clearly relates to the conserving of something that is perhaps seen as being damaged by modern society. Indeed for John Stuart Mill preventing harm to others was seen as the only legitimate use of power in society against the liberty of individuals. However, harm reduction, damage limitation or 'risk management' were not previously the central organising principle of politics or of society's institutions more generally. Today this has changed—and it is within this context that the growth of 'antisocial behaviour' must at least in part be understood.

The question of harm appears to be more significant today than previously and incorporates an ever increasing variety of issues and forms of behaviour. What would have been considered as harmful in Mill's day—indeed to people only a few decades ago—is very different compared to the expanding range of 'harmful activities' today.[5]

Forms of justice are also shifting towards a preoccupation with 'harm'. One of the promoted benefits of restorative justice for example is that it 'repairs the harm' that has been caused by an offender.

Within criminology itself even radical criminologists are attempting to repose the study of crime and move to study 'harm'. These criminologists suggest that we need to go *Beyond Criminology* (Hillyard, Pantazis, Tombs and Gordon 2004) by *Taking Harm Seriously*. In *Beyond Criminology* everything in life—capitalism, the state, immigration, the workplace and poverty, to name but a few—is understood within this framework, and our focus becomes on the harm being done by and to people. Where previously radicals would challenge issues of poverty and capitalism in their own terms with alternative political arguments, today it appears they are engaged by these subjects less with a sense of a creative alternative than with a more negative engagement with harm in society.[6]

The issue of harm is not simply one that engages criminologists and community safety officers but is an issue—or rather an approach to social problems that is ingrained within the culture of modern British and perhaps modern Western society. Minimising harm rather than creating good influences how we relate to the global environment and to the local environment, to how we understand our children's lives and our own; it impacts on how products are advertised and how we think about consuming them; it is perhaps the new organising principle for society and more especially for politics itself.

In relation to the rise of the social problem of 'antisocial behaviour', the argument being presented here is that this 'problem' could only emerge in the form it has at a time when the role of government was being transformed to one that is systematically organised around the issue of *harm* and *safety*. Within this context the activities of individuals and communities are no longer engaged with in terms of the positive, active and creative potential within them, but instead are engaged with more negatively, in terms of the potential 'harassment, alarm or distress' being caused by antisocial behaviour.[7]

THE BOOK

The aim of this book is to shift the discussion about antisocial behaviour from the myopic focus on 'yobs' and 'neighbours from hell' onto a wider sociological study of the *Politics of Antisocial Behaviour*. This is done in part by adopting aspects of the social constructionist approach to social problems that has been developed by Joel Best and Philip Jenkins, and is also influenced by the ideas of Frank Furedi in *Culture of Fear* (1997) and *Therapy Culture* (2004), and also Christopher Lasch in *Culture of Narcissism* (1979). The book also attempts to address a number of criminological debates—especially in understanding the nature of what Garland has described as a *Culture of Control* (2002); more generally, the sociological understanding of moral panics is addressed here. To summarise the argument, it is the belief of this author that we do live in a culture of control—and in a society that is in a panic. This culture, however, is not being driven by a purposeful moral or political ideology, but is rather the consequence of the collapse of morals and politics: *Today society does not face the occasional moral panic, but is rather in a permanent state of amoral panic.*

In the following chapter the new 'moral' absolute of safety is examined with reference to one of the first major local initiatives set up to deal with antisocial behaviour. The Hamilton curfew as it came to be known was an initiative introduced shortly after the Labour government was elected in 1997 and is a useful illustration of how safety—and the prevention of harm—had become the basis upon which the relationship between the public and the authorities was framed. The significance of this is not simply in terms of the changing role of the state, but also in the changing and diminishing expectations of individuals that developed from this approach.

In the subsequent chapter these developments are situated within what is described as the 'collapse of politics' that occurred in the early 1990s and which led to a more systematic use of laws and regulations to control areas of life that had previously not been seen as necessary. Rather than seeing this as a continuation of Margaret Thatcher's politicisation of crime in the 1980s, the approach adopted by John Major in the 1990s and subsequently by Tony Blair is understood to be a reflection of the declining significance of Politics (with a big P), and the move towards a politicisation and micro-management of behaviour in everyday life.

The changing nature of politics and the growing 'politics of behaviour' is founded upon what is discussed in the next chapter as an outcome of 'diminished subjectivity'. In this chapter the centrality of the victim within the discourse of crime and within society more generally is explored to help unearth some of the broad cultural themes that underpin the development of antisocial behaviour as a social problem. The more universal engagement in society with this 'victim' is seen as significant not simply in terms of the changing nature of individual subjectivity, but more importantly as a cultural framework that influences the way the diminished expectations of society impact upon how the individual is engaged with and constructed.

The penultimate chapter takes the arguments thus far and attempts to repose the question of moral panics. Having started with an understanding of the 'politics of antisocial behaviour' as a form of moral panic in society, we found that this understanding of an old conservative form of moralising no longer explained the nature of the 'panic' around the issue of antisocial behaviour. The nature of panics themselves and indeed what are seen as 'moral panics' today suggests that there is a more all-encompassing 'culture of fear' that is being engaged with and promoted by both traditional conservatives—but more importantly by 'radicals' in society. This form of panicking is 'amoral' in the sense that it is not grounded in any wider moral (or indeed political) ideal, but rather within the more vacuous prism of safety—and it is the very loss of these ideals that lay the basis for the myriad panics that exist today.

Finally an attempt is made in the concluding chapter to repose the question of 'antisocial behaviour' and of an antisocial society. Many of the problems of behaviour in society—but also the exaggerated fear of them—can be better explained by the more disconnected nature of society and of the individual from society. One of the tragedies of the myopic focus upon antisocial behaviour as a social problem is that it is making things worse. The problems we face today must be answered within the realm of morals and politics, for *we are not living in an antisocial society—we are living in an asocial society*.

2   Safety—The New 'Absolute'

> Safety has become the fundamental value of the 1990s. Passions that were once devoted to a struggle to change the world (or keep it the same) are now invested in trying to ensure that we are safe
>
> (Furedi 1997: 1).

INTRODUCTION

On the 21st October 1997 the dark and empty streets in the Hillhouse estate of Hamilton in Scotland were temporarily filled with journalists and cameramen keen to get the first image of a 'curfewed child'. One young lad, about 12 years old, duly obliged with a bit of cheek to a policeman, who himself obliged the cameras by grabbing the boy, whereupon the bulbs flashed and the headline story for the mornings papers was guaranteed.

In October 1997 the Hamilton curfew was launched in three estates within South Lanarkshire Council—Hillhouse being the largest of these three areas and the one discussed here. Intended to create 'safer communities', the curfew, officially named the Child Safety Initiative (CSI), was targeted at young people under the age of 16 who were to be moved off the street if they did not have a 'good reason to be out after dark'. This initiative was one of the first significant attempts by a local Labour council to deal with the 'social problem'[1] of antisocial behaviour following the election of the Labour government in 1997. The Hamilton curfew has subsequently and repeatedly been discussed as a key example of Labour's new approach to crime and disorder.[2]

The Hamilton curfew was an example of an early Labour council initiative that attempted to promote the idea of 'community' by tackling various forms of problem behaviour. The concern with antisocial behaviour of young people had influenced the development of this initiative, however, wider issues were raised through this 'Child Safety' initiative'—issues that sat within the broader framework of *community safety*. It is in this respect that the Hamilton curfew is a useful starting point for examining the changing nature not only of policing but also of the political shift towards an engagement with the public around the issues of fear and safety. It is also useful as an illustration of the more limited political objectives being pursued and the more extensive development of the micro-management of everyday life as a new framework for the developing 'politics of behaviour'.

In this chapter an analysis is made of the way the Child Safety Initiative was presented and promoted by the authorities. From an analysis of newspaper articles on the curfew, the speeches given about it, the statements made by politicians, councillors and police chiefs, the 'elite voices' that justified the Hamilton project are examined to identify the underlying 'values' that lay the foundation for its legitimation. What were the key arguments used to support the curfew, but also what were the key arguments used to oppose it—and what if anything connected these ideas? Following the approach adopted by James Nolan, an attempt is made here to illustrate the core ideas, assumptions and understanding that lay the foundation for the 'authority' behind the curfew initiative (Nolan 1998: 24).[3]

The idea of 'rights and responsibilities' that were promoted by the Labour government at this time, and that have become part of today's political vocabulary, is also explored here to illustrate the transformation of these ideas at a time when a more 'risk conscious' approach had emerged.

THE 'NEW' PARTY OF LAW AND ORDER

In 1997 Clause 1 of the Crime and Disorder Bill was being discussed by the Labour government. A new power to reduce disorder was contained within this clause, a power that was to challenge the 'menace' of antisocial behaviour, a power that has become as famous—indeed infamous—as perhaps any other: the Antisocial Behaviour Order or ASBO.

As we have seen, the social problem of 'antisocial behaviour' emerged in the 1990s, and at least in terms of newspaper articles became a hugely reported issue in the new millennium. Despite the exponential increase in articles about antisocial behaviour from around 2004, it would be a mistake to assume that this is when this problem 'took off'. In fact the political interest in antisocial behaviour was already becoming well established at the time of Labour's election victory in 1997. From this point on new antisocial behaviour legislation has been developed, and it is the implementation of these new laws—and in particular the growing number of 'ASBO' stories—that has led to the huge increase in the newspaper coverage in the last few years. By 1997 antisocial behaviour was already developing into a significant political issue around which national and local government initiatives were being established. Indeed as the chart below indicates there had already been a significant increase in the number of articles that related to the problem of antisocial behaviour—an increase that is somewhat masked by the more profound increase that took place later. From being a term of little or no significance in the 1980s, from the early 1990s the recognition

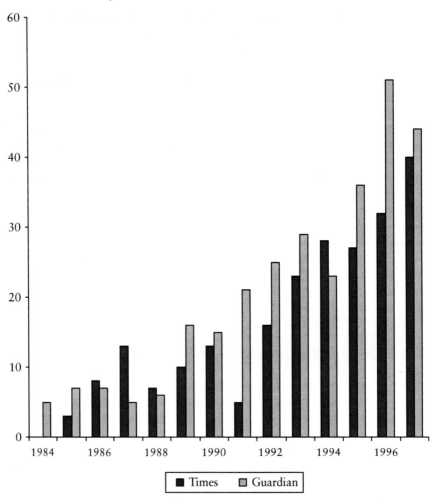

Chart 2.1 Times and *Guardian* searches for 'antisocial behaviour' up to 1997.[4]

of this 'problem' and the use of the term 'antisocial behaviour' in the news-papers grew.

The Hamilton curfew was introduced by a Labour council only a few months after the first Labour government for 18 years had been elected, and was understood to be an important development not simply in terms of this particular initiative but in terms of what it said about 'New' Labour's approach to crime and disorder in general. The Hamilton curfew itself also became significant, winning a number of national and international com-munity safety awards.

This 'pioneering' initiative also set 'the blueprint' for curfew powers to be spread across the whole of Britain as the local newspaper proudly explained,

> The Government's Crime and Disorder Bill, which came into force yesterday, allows local authorities to introduce curfews on under 10s in their area. . . . Prime Minister Tony Blair backed schemes similar to the one pioneered in Hamilton during his keynote address to the Labour Party conference on Tuesday (*Hamilton Advertiser* 1 October 1998).[5]

The Crime and Disorder Act was the Labour government's first major piece of law and order legislation and included a provision for local authorities across England and Wales to introduce a curfew for under-10-year-olds between the hours of 9 pm and 6 am. The Hamilton experience was directly connected to the development of this legislation, and was used as an example of how curfews can have a positive impact upon areas (*Independent* 28 September 1998).

This focus on under-10-year-olds replicated much of the rhetoric surrounding the Hamilton curfew which had promoted the need for the initiative with reference to young children wandering the streets at night. This was related to both the issue of child safety but also to a concern at the time with 'child criminals' and 'irresponsible parents' as illustrated by an article in the *Sunday Times* about 'a seven year old thief, who had been arrested more than ten times':

> The seven year old is just one of hundreds of problem under-10s across Britain who police and local authorities are considering placing under curfew using the new law. Such children cannot currently be prosecuted for their crimes as they are below the age of criminal responsibility (*Sunday Times* 6 September 1998).

The issue of criminal children was promoted here as a significant problem—although even if the 'hundreds' of such children existed in a country of 60 million people a certain perspective on the problem was clearly missing at this time both in this article and in the governments approach to it. The issue of child criminals terrorising communities and the need for curfews to control them soon faded away, and was replaced by the perhaps more realistic concern about young teenagers hanging around the streets. Home Secretary Jack Straw who had been at the forefront of promoting the concern about these problem under-10-year-olds later changed the curfew legislation, increasing the age range of those who could be moved off the street to include any young person under the age of 16. This new curfew legislation was once again promoted with reference to the success of the Hamilton initiative (*Guardian* 7 December 2000).

For many people the election of a Labour government after almost two decades of Conservative rule was a cause for celebration. It was recognised that the Labour Party, now promoted as 'New Labour', had changed; however there remained the hope, for some, that once in power the authoritarian approach of the Thatcher and Major governments would be reversed. As it turned out, the subsequent Labour governments introduced more laws and regulations than even the previous Conservative government—which itself had set a record for the amount of legislation passed.

The drive towards more law and order initiatives should however have come as no surprise as a significant part of the reinvention of the Labour Party was through the promotion of New Labour as the new party of law and order. Indeed the Labour Party and its leader, Tony Blair, had become synonymous with the slogan, 'tough on crime, tough on the causes of crime'. From around 1993 the Labour Party had matched, and at times 'out-toughed', the Conservatives in their promotion of new law and order initiatives with their own 'zero tolerance' approach to antisocial behaviour and the call for 'aggressive beggars' to be moved off the streets. Crime was no longer a right-wing issue, or one addressed by Labour as a secondary issue related to wider social questions like unemployment, it was now a 'working-class issue', and one that Labour took to the polls with great success.

The denunciation of young criminals and antisocial youth encouraged critics of the government's law and order drive to see within it a 'right-wing' form of authoritarianism. However a key focus within Labour's developing approach was not with the 'criminal' so much as with a concern about fear in society, and with the public that was seen as being vulnerable to the 'anti-social' adults and especially the young people who hung about the streets. Individuals and communities, the government believed, were being damaged and undermined and it was this concern with preventing harm being done that lay the foundation to their approach to antisocial behaviour.

COMMUNITY SAFETY

The idea of community safety is today so well established that it is hard to believe that before the mid-1990s it was a rarely mentioned idea. Indeed, at least as far as one can tell from newspaper coverage, the term 'community safety' didn't even exist until 1987. Within a decade it was to become a central framework around which the Labour government developed its policies regarding crime, policing and communities. Today local authorities include 'community safety' as one of the core strategic objectives that directs council policy.

Gordon Hughes and Adam Edwards, discussing the changing nature of crime prevention in the UK, note that officially, crime prevention is about crime (and increasingly disorder) reduction. However, from the late 1990s, this objective has increasingly been in competition with the issue of 'community safety', an issue that relates more directly to the insecurity of private citizens. Despite both objectives relating to reducing crime, Hughes and Edwards note that community safety has other, far broader goals.

The goal of community safety reflects an aspiration to construct a new public good of safety in response to a range of actual and perceived risks and harms. The attainment of such a 'public good' aspires to contribute to a 'quality of life' of citizens and consequently is associated with identifying and addressing community needs for safety rather than a narrower obsession with targeted crime reduction (Tilley 2005: 20).

This community safety approach not only related to genuine issues of concern within communities, it also tapped into a broader insecurity amongst the public and perhaps most importantly was moulded around the developing framework of politics to 'support' and manage the relationships between people within these communities around the issue of safety and fear. The 'well-being' of the public was now measured at least in part with reference to a feel safe factor and protecting communities became part of this more therapeutic micro-political process. Incidents and occurrences that may previously have been seen as important for the police or the social work department were consequently politicised and became more central to how the community as a whole and indeed society itself were understood.

The Hamilton curfew was a 'community safety initiative'—a policing initiative—but more than that it became a prism through which all relationships within the targeted areas were understood and engaged with. Relationships between adults and young people, adults and children and between young people themselves were all addressed in relation to the issue of safety.

SAFETY CLAIMS

Launched in October 1997 the Hamilton curfew—or the officially named Child Safety Initiative (CSI) was promoted at a press conference by John Orr,[6] the Chief Constable of Strathclyde Police and Tom McCabe,[7] head of South Lanarkshire Council. The initiative, they explained, was not a curfew, but a safety initiative that would keep both children safe who should not be out alone at night, and keep adults safe from antisocial young people.

A police flier at the time, promoting the CSI, explained that 'The aim of this initiative is not to force young people off the street: rather it is to make sure that our communities are safer for everyone'. The Scottish Home Affairs Minister, Henry McLeish, also promoted the community safety agenda, arguing that 'This initiative fits in with the Government's push for partnership between families, the people and local authorities to create a safer society' (*Scotsman* 3 October 1997).

The initiative was a collaborative venture that included the council's social work department. Sandy Cameron, the director of this department, argued that, 'this is not a curfew, but an issue of safety and in particular the safety of young people'.[8] Its aim, he argued, was to both prevent young people from becoming criminals, and to ensure the safety of young children. In this way, even the potentially criminal actions of young people were reposed as safety issues. The chief constable added to this understanding by explaining that

> The [principal] aim of the patrols is to ensure that vulnerable youngsters aged under 16—and particularly those aged 12 or less—are not exposed to dangers or tempted to become embroiled in crimes associated with being out alone too late in the dark or with equally vulnerable company—crimes such as vandalism, creating disturbances and minor violence.

Chief Constable John Orr was a well known figure in Scotland at this time, most significantly for his promotion of zero tolerance police initiatives and 'Stop and Search' schemes that had resulted in over 60,000 people being searched as part of a crackdown on carrying a knife in public. The initiatives promoted by Orr can be seen as a 'heavy-handed' form of policing—or what would in the past have been described as a form of 'police harassment'. However the framing of these initiatives were very much in tune with the engagement with public fears and the representation of the problem in terms of the vulnerability of people in public places. In Hamilton John Orr's emphasis was on this representation of local people as vulnerable—even concerning young people who caused trouble—young people that Orr had previously described as 'doped up spitting yobs' (Orr 1997: 110). The police officers who were to police the initiative were themselves, Orr explained, 'specially selected for their experience, skills and empathy'. Moral outrage, or the aggressive assertion of authority, was here replaced by the more empathetic concern about young people who were 'at risk'.

While the general understanding of the 'so called Child Safety Initiative' was that it was a curfew targeted at 'antisocial kids', there was, for the officials promoting the initiative, a significant attempt to stress the child safety aspect of what was labelled the 'Hamilton curfew' by the press and also by local people. National politicians continued to emphasised the 'yobbishness' of the young people on the streets, while the social work department, local politicians and also the local police far more systematically promoted the idea of children and young people as being victims rather than villains.

Discussing the vulnerability of the young people in the curfew target areas, council leader Tom McCabe and head of social work Sandy Cameron portrayed the intervention in Hillhouse as a form of support for young people themselves. During a television interview about the initiative, McCabe for example explained that 'We are trying to give people their liberty back—especially teenagers who through peer pressure may be led into acts that they will regret for a long time afterwards'.[9]

Young people who commit antisocial or criminal acts were here seen, not simply as 'trouble', but also as 'troubled'. The head of social work Sandy Cameron noted that

> It is important to take young people back home into dialogue with their parents—to help them avoid getting into criminal activities. . . . We must also recognise that the misuse of alcohol by young people is a serious problem in our communities, and is something that sets patterns that affect us all.[10]

Here, both McCabe and Cameron portrayed young people, especially those young people committing offences, as potential victims, victims of their peers or victims of alcohol, and in need of protection from these peers and even from themselves and their 'set patterns'. In this respect, at least rhetorically, it became the job of the police not only to control the antisocial behaviour of young people, but also to monitor the unsafe interactions between young people themselves.[11]

The issue of young people drinking that was and indeed is still across the UK an issue of concern regarding disruptive behaviour of teenagers was more generally understood here as a potentially problematic form of behaviour for all young people—something that could be framed and understood as a 'risk'. The Child Safety Initiative in this respect was able to couple the seemingly contradictory concern about 'yobs' with a 'caring' approach to young people. Young people needed to be kept safe and to be aware of the risks they faced, while adults also needed to be kept safe from the disruptive behaviour of these young people.

CHILD SAFETY

The most significant 'claim' made to promote the Child Safety Initiative— was logically enough—child safety. For local officials, this was 'not a curfew', it was an initiative set up because of safety concerns regarding children who were out alone at night. For the local police, in their weekly reports to the *Hamilton Advertiser*, the message that the initiative had been introduced to improve child safety was reiterated time and again. In his speech promoting the CSI, John Orr gave a *typical* example of the problem the initiative was set up to resolve when he spoke of a nine-year-old girl found in a stairwell only in her underwear whose mother was 'dead drunk'.[12] Another story was told of a nine-year-old boy found on the street whose mother was at the bingo parlour and father was in the pub. These examples of unsupervised children, Orr stated, 'beggared belief', as, 'Yet—and what a paradox—paedophile court cases hit the headlines regularly and there is controversy about the issue of the rights of communities to know where convicted offenders are living'.

Following John Orr's speech at the launch of the CSI, the South Lanark-shire Council leader, Tom McCabe, spoke, echoing many of the comments made by John Orr. McCabe challenged the idea that this was a curfew:

> This is a nonsense notion! Such a notion has no place in Hamilton, no place in South Lanarkshire. It has no place in a society heading for the new millennium. The Hamilton child safety initiative is about improv-ing the quality of life for the people of Whitehill, Hillhouse and Fairhill. It is about the safety and the protection of our children—today, now—and in the future.[13]

The question of child safety was directly connected to the idea of irre-sponsible parents whose lack of care was resulting in children being put 'at risk'. John Orr concluded his speech by noting that 'Views on people's rights are many and varied but there can be no argument surely against the right of all people—including and perhaps even especially the young—to live in safety in the community, safe from crime and neglect too'. Safety was something that Orr felt could 'surely' not be questioned, especially the safety of children. No specific dangers in the Hillhouse area were mentioned, although paedophiles, or at least the high media profile of paedophiles, was mentioned. Rather, the very existence of 'unsupervised' children being out on the street was presented as a problem—the message was clear—respon-sible parents must keep their children off the street and keep them safe: A good parent is a safe parent. The issue of 'child safety' was, in this respect, directly linked to the concern about 'parenting', and John Orr promoted the positive nature of the police officers involved in the initiative by explaining that, 'Some of the officers are parents themselves'.

During the initiative the main opposition to the curfew came from chil-dren's charities and a civil liberties groups, all of which raised the question of children's rights, and questioned the authoritarian nature of an approach to young people that resulted in them all being pressured to get off the streets. In response to this, somewhat defensively, the police responded by arguing that the initiative was actually for the young people—it was an initiative to keep them safe. A survey was also carried out by the authorities to question young people about their concerns—which the police used to illustrate that young people also felt that community safety was a major issue for them.

Despite the opposition to the curfew by a variety of groups, there was no questioning of the child safety message promoted by John Orr, Tom McCabe, the head of social work, Sandy Cameron, or the local police. The only questioning of this safety issue was whether or not the representing of the 'curfew' as a child safety initiatives was a reality or simply a gimmick being used by the police to force young people into their home. Little was said about the dangers that John Orr had promoted in relation to 'unsu-pervised children', nor were there any doubts raised about the way young people were said to be 'at risk' from 'peer pressure' and from their own risky behaviour. The issue of 'child safety' was not up for debate. Rather, those groups opposing the curfew attempted to show that in fact, the curfew was making these young people less safe.

In relation to this issue of child safety the only difference between those opposing and supporting the curfew was where the greatest danger was located. For the police this was an issue in terms of children and young people being out on the street. In comparison, as a number of the 'children's campaigners' argued, the greatest danger was not to be found on the streets—but in the home.

For the Scottish organiser of Save the Children, one of the dangers of the police taking people home was that children may face 'the possibility of domestic violence or other forms of harm'. Similarly for Play Scotland, safety was less of an issue in public in relation to 'stranger danger' than the concern that 'children are most often abused by people well known to them in the family or close friends'. Whereas 'children walking aimlessly' was not a positive thing, could the home, with 'the technology of video, computer and internet', have a worse impact on the 'future of the human race'? For Gerison Landsdown, the director of the Children's Rights Office, 'many children may be out in the evening in order to avoid abuse or violence at home. The imposition of a blanket curfew which forces them home would place them at a greater not lesser risk of harm'. Finally, Roger Smith of the Children's Society added his voice of concern, asking, 'Will children be forced into their own homes to suffer violence and abuse silently?' (Waiton 2001: 170).

Child safety was a 'claim' that both sides in the curfew debate attempted to use to their advantage; it was the strongest claim and one that was never in question. However, as we will see, the issue of children wandering the streets at night was more of an urban myth than a reality, and upon examining the actuality of 'child safety' there was very little evidence to suggest that the Hillhouse children were 'at risk'.

FREEDOM FROM FEAR

As well as the concerns about safety for children and young people, the curfew initiative was clearly also about the safety of adults, not so much from crime, but from the emerging problem of antisocial behaviour and from the 'fear' that it was believed was created by this behaviour. Despite the safety rhetoric, it was this aspect of the CSI that was seen as central for the press. This was not something the police and local authority denied, but was rather seen as being part and parcel of the overall approach to community safety, whereby all the members of the community, young and old alike, and indeed the 'community' itself, were seen as being strengthened through the increased safety provided by the police action. Safety for adults was in particular related to their feeling of security as much as the actuality of it, and overcoming the assumed problem of fear was a major aim of the curfew.

Orr explained that the initiative had been 'drawn up in response to local households and young people about vandalism and the presence of unsupervised or unruly children on the street after dark'. Here the CSI, was presented not as an initiative that was coming from above, an assertion and promotion of authority, but was rather something that stemmed from the concerns and fears of private citizens living in the Hillhouse estate. Concern about antisocial behaviour, despite falling crime figures in the area, was an issue for the chief constable, who explained that even if crime had fallen, 'if people remain anxious and concerned, then we must respond decisively'. Here John Orr was not only relating to the problem of crime, nor indeed to actual 'safety' issues as such, but to the *feeling* of safety.

This issue of fear within society was also a more general concern for politicians and was something that the Labour Party itself had prioritised as being of significance for the country as a whole. In the run-up to the 1997 general election, the then leader of the opposition Tony Blair for example, had made the, 'freedom from the fear of crime', one of his 'seven pillars' for the creation of a decent society (*Times* 17 April 1997).

From the outset, the CSI was labelled a curfew by the press, partly because of the nature of the initiative itself, but also due to the idea of curfew legislation being promoted at the time by the Labour government. Especially for the tabloid press, the 'Hamilton curfew' was simply another crackdown on 'juvenile crime', where kids would be 'nicked' for being out at night. Frustrated by the curfew label the local police chief, Jim Elliot, argued that the police were a 'caring organisation' not an 'oppressive one' (*Daily Record* 3 October 1997). However the image of the 'curfew' remained and a year on from the launch of the initiative, Allison McLaughlan, a freelance journalist for the *Daily Record*, summed up what many of her colleagues thought about the police safety-first PR campaign: describing it as 'bollocks, it's about cutting down on crime' (*The Face*, June 1998).

The curfew was also discussed by the authorities in relation to another New Labour slogan at the time, that of 'rights and responsibilities'. Communities, it was argued, were being undermined by the irresponsible behaviour, of bad parents, and young people who were being antisocial, vandalising, drinking on the streets and undermining the well-being of local communities. The issue of responsibility was here seen through the prism of harm— being responsible meant being aware of the potential damage that you and your children's actions may inflict upon others. And in this respect the understanding of rights was represented in terms of being *free* from fear. As Orr explained:

> It is about responsibility. It is about civil liberties and freedom—the freedom of everyone in the community to live without fear or intimidation. Each of us has responsibilities to other people within our communities.

We have to recognise that when some people chose to ignore their responsibilities—to their children, to their neighbours, to their community—to society—it leads to an erosion of community. It leads to people becoming fearful and distrustful of each other.

Challenging the civil liberties arguments that had been made in relation to children's rights, McCabe argued:

The initiative we are launching today is not about an increase in powers at the expense of the freedom of children and young people. . . . It is in fact about returning liberties to communities—about removing fear. The truth is that our children and young people's safety initiative has at its core the rights of children.

The safety initiative, McCabe argued, was a development from a wide process of consultation with young people, adults and Scotland's first Citizens' Jury—a community participation initiative involving a group of local people—which, 'showed that for all ages the number one priority was community safety'.

Both John Orr and Tom McCabe explained that the three areas targeted for the CSI were not high crime areas, and indeed that crime in Hamilton in general was substantially lower than it had been a few years previously. However, there were still some issue of disorderly behaviour that needed to be addressed—and there remained the problem of the sense of fear and the desire for greater safety—something of concern to the authorities and the local people alike.

During the initiative, a contradictory aspect of this sense of fear was referred to by Campbell Thompson, a local senior police officer in Hamilton. Describing the insecurities felt by many adults, Thompson explained that

It's modern society. There's a fear of crime among the elderly that's very seldom justified. A youngster is more likely to be assaulted than the elderly folk, but that's not the old folks' perception. They're taken aback by a bunch of boisterous youngsters in high spirits (*The Face*, June 1998).

Fear, Thompson recognised, was subjective and did not necessarily relate to the reality of any real threat or danger. However, fear was another 'claim' within the promotion of and indeed opposition to, the safety initiative that was rarely challenged and appeared to carry with it an assumed need for action. Fear, like safety, was a powerful claim that justified the curfew. Indeed John Orr, in his discussion about 'paedophile court cases' that hit the headlines, was not suggesting that parents should stop their children going out at night because of the reality of this threat, but rather was pointing out that if there was a fear in society about paedophiles, it appears contradictory for parents allow their children to go out at night. He was in this respect, promoting the curfew with reference to parental fears, rather than to real dangers on the streets.[14]

RECONNECTING THROUGH SAFETY

Fear and safety were both clearly becoming, at this time, warrants, or values, that it was felt were significant and a framework around which both local and national politicians and institutions could engage.

An example of this can be seen more generally with the case of a conference that was being held elsewhere within the Strathclyde region, organised by Strathclyde police, and entitled 'Bridging the Gap between Young and Old'. The conference, while being held at the same time as the Hamilton curfew, was not directly related to it, but was another illustration of the attempted engagement at the time that was being made by the authorities with local people through the issue of safety.

The conference, as the name suggests was predicated on the idea that relations between the generations had broken down, the aim being—to find 'something in common', between young and old. Understood as a form of awareness-raising, the conference focused upon promoting the 'mutual understanding of each other's concerns and fears'. The conference was set up to challenged the idea, which it was understood elderly people had, of young people as '"yobs" . . . only interested in drugs, alcohol and loitering on street corners'. Similarly the conference wanted to challenge young people's apparent understanding of the elderly as '"killjoys" with nothing worthwhile to contribute to society'. These caricatured views, it was felt, 'can lead to unnecessary fear, apprehension, intimidation, aggression and provocation'. As Strathclyde police were keen to tackle not only the issue of crime, 'but the fear of crime', finding something that young people and elderly adults have in common was seen as a way of overcoming this fear and reconnecting the generations.

The common ground around which solidarity could be built, the conference believed, was safety. As the conference promotion paper explained, 'Surely the seed is there. The young care about the safety of their grandparents, and granny and granddad worry about drugs, not for themselves but for their grandchildren'.[15] That young and old not only have fears of their own but also have fears for others was thus understood to be the basis for a common ground between the two. Fear and the need for safety was seen as the framework around which generational divisions and therefore divisions in communities could be overcome. Like the Hamilton curfew, this conference took the fear of crime and the issue of safety as the basis of connecting with people and indeed of reconnecting people with one another.

Speaking at the first Labour Party Conference since the general election victory, Tony Blair rallied the faithful with a speech in celebration of their landslide victory. On May 1, 1997, it wasn't just the Tories who were defeated, he said, 'Cynicism was defeated. Fear of change was defeated. Fear itself was defeated. Did I not say it would be a battle of hope against fear? On May 1, 1997, fear lost. Hope won. The Giving Age began' (*Times* 1 October 1997).

The 'battle against fear'—or the engagement with it—had in reality only just begun, and one month after this speech the Hamilton curfew was launched. Fear reduction was a clear aim and framework around which the chief constable of Strathclyde police felt successful policing should be measured. And community participation around the issue of community safety was something South Lanarkshire council had already been developing through a number of consultation initiatives and the first Citizen's Jury, which had highlighted to the council the need to engage with the issues of fear and safety in the community.

Safety and the desire to feel safe was represented as a community issue, rather than one being adopted and promoted by the authorities themselves. During the CSI, surveys, consultation documents and focus groups, as well as opinion polls, were set up and systematically referred to in an effort to show that the curfew was not only supported by the public, but that the idea of a curfew had itself come from the public.[16] Both the adult opinion of the curfew,[17] and more particularly the 'youth voice',[18] were constantly referred to as evidence of the support for the Child Safety Initiative.

The local MP George Robertson, relating to the 'misery' of those not able to 'live in peace and quiet', was the first person to claim that the idea for the curfew had come from the Citizens' Jury set up in Hillhouse. This was not the case—but the claim was repeated many times throughout the initiative to indicate that this was a community initiative, a 'partnership' based on 'community participation' (*Scotsman* 3 October 1997).[19]

Rejecting the critical attack on the council and the police for being heavy-handed or for taking away young people's rights, the authorities kept relating their initiative to the support from the public, its desire for a safe society, and its support for increased police action in the areas targeted. The curfew itself was clearly justified in relation to the issue of safety—with all groups in the targeted areas being represented in terms of the improved safety the CSI would bring to them. The initiative in this respect, not only aimed to tackle problems of safety and fear, but to *include* the public in this process. On the one hand fear was something that the authorities wanted to overcome to help strengthen communities, while at the same time fear and safety were becoming new organising principles through which the same authorities engaged with the public.

RIGHTS AND RESPONSBILITIES

The well-worn term promoted by New Labour of rights and responsibilities was a central basis for promoting the values of safety throughout the life of the Hamilton curfew. Within criminology, there is also an understanding of recent social policy developments as a form of 'responsibilisation', whereby the public themselves are actively involved in attempts to resolve issues of crime and safety. However, the idea of what a right and indeed what responsibility meant in the context of the CSI was very different to the liberal notion of the past—indeed in contrast to John Stuart Mill's understanding of liberty as the freedom of the individual from the state, the new idea of rights was very different. With the centrality of safety over-hanging every relationship and experience of the adults and young people in Hamilton, the understanding of rights as freedoms was replaced by one of rights as protection. Freedom itself was understood to be the freedom from fear, and from putting yourself and others 'at risk'.

In the summer prior to the introduction of the curfew, Chief Constable John Orr had explained that his approach to policing was based on the 'highest possible' level of protection, especially of children. 'Every single member of the public', he argued, 'has the right to be safe . . . and feel safe' (*Scottish Sunday Mail* 15 June 1997). A month, before the CSI was introduced, Scottish Home Affairs Minister Henry McCleish likewise argued that, 'People have the right to be safe and at peace in their homes. This is at the cornerstone of our vision for a better, safe and more prosperous Scotland' (*Herald* 13 September 1997). In chief constable John Orr's speech that launched the CSI he reasoned that, 'there can be no argument surely against the right of all people—including and perhaps even especially the young—to live in safety in the community'. Council leader Tom McCabe, like Henry McCleish, had also spelt out the significance of this *right*—a right that if neglected led to an increase in fear and the 'destruction of communities'.

Rights were understood here in terms of the freedom to live in safety and without fear—something that local people needed to take more responsibility for, but equally something that could be institutionalised through police initiatives like the Hamilton curfew. Indeed, through the prism of safety, 'liberty' was described by McCabe as something that could be *given* back to young people by the actions of the police, while the most positive thing that politicians could *give* to communities in Hamilton and indeed across Scotland was the 'right' to be safe and the 'freedom' from fear. The principle of the right to be safe and to 'peace and quiet' was, for local MP and Defence Secretary George Robertson, fundamental to a democracy (*Herald* 3 October 1997).

The rights being promoted through the CSI were rights to protection from others or from yourself. While adults were given the right to a quiet life, young people were given their liberty back by regulating the peer pressure they faced that could lead them into acts that they would regret for a long time afterwards.[20]

With newspaper polls suggesting that the people of Hamilton were heavily supporting this initiative, and with the understanding of communities being undermined by fear because of the antisocial behaviour of young people, those arguing for freedom in terms of 'young people's rights' or the rights of local parents to decide when and where their children went at night were depicted as being out of touch.[21] Rights as protection appeared, in this example, to have largely replaced the understanding and desire for rights as freedoms: Freedom itself being seen less in terms of the absence of restraint and freedom from coercion than the coercion of others who undermine the freedom from fear. Rather than the curfew being understood as an extreme measure, it was those who argued for civil liberties who were seen as extremists.

As Dolan Cummings has argued, in terms of the battle for rights as freedoms against the growing use of surveillance and regulation of public space in the name of rights,

> Concerns about civil liberties, in as much as they represent opposition to surveillance, are now considered anachronistic and even damaging, the preserve of 'apologists for the criminal element'. Instead the important thing is that people are safe and that they feel safe (Cummings 1997: 4).

Indeed, whereas the rights of young people were understood to be in conflict with adults' sense of safety, the right to be safe itself was presented as a universal human right that was fundamental to all the different groups of people within the curfew areas: *equality being the equal right to be and feel safe.*

RESPONSIBILISATION

The process of responsibilisation, or what Garland calls a responsibilisation strategy, describes a process whereby techniques and methods are used in society that incorporates an ever increasing number of organisations in crime control practices, while transforming the behaviour of the public accordingly: for example, publicity campaigns that target the public as a whole—rather than engaging simply with deviants—to raise the consciousness of everyone in relation to issues of crime and safety (Garland 1996: 452). Fundamentally having been developed as an adaptation to the failure of the welfare state,[22] this process, Garland believes, aims to create a 'sense of duty' and to develop 'active citizens' who become involved in their own crime prevention strategy as individuals and through partnership work, a process that results in the 'reordering of the conduct of everyday life' (Garland 1996: 453–54). Part of this process, Flint notes, has come with the communitarian attempt by governments to 'attribute responsibility for community problems back onto individuals': this has developed, Gilling believes, within a New Labourite version of Margaret Thatcher's 'authoritarian populism' (Gilling 1999: 11).[23] Governing would now occur through 'regulated choices made by discrete and autonomous actors', human beings governed as 'individuals—who are to be *active* in their own government' (Rose 1996: 328–30; my italics).[24]

The idea of rights and especially responsibility, leading up to the 1997 election, was being forcefully presented by New Labour as a way to, as Labour leader Tony Blair put it, 'reinvent community for a modern age, true to core values of fairness, co-operation and responsibility' (*Guardian* 29 January 1996). The neo-liberal emphasis on 'choice, personal responsibility [and] control over one's fate' matched a similar focus by communitarians upon 'self-responsibility and self reliance in the form of active citizenship within a self governing community' at this time. As Rose observed, despite the ideological differences of these outlooks, both 'utilize similar images of the subject as an *active and responsible agent* in the securing of security for themselves and those to whom they are or should be affiliated' (N. Rose 1996: 335; Flint 2002: 624; my italics).

The process described here usefully indicates the issues and sentiments that the political elite and state institutions have prioritised, and the more generalised connection with the population as a whole around the issue of crime and safety. However this process of responsibilisation does not represent an engagement with 'responsible agents', who are 'active in their own government'—or at least not in terms of how the idea of the individual subject and active citizens was previously understood. Rather, through the prism of risk and harm and the elevation of safety, the individual has been recast as more vulnerable than previously—consequently the expectation of what an active individual is has become diminished.

The idea of responsibilisation and responsibility are not identical.[25] However, both stress, to some degree, the role of the individual within this process, often with reference to neo-liberal and 'market' phraseology. However, despite the rhetoric of community and individual responsibility in the case of the Hamilton curfew the meaning of responsibility had changed. Rather than individuals being encouraged to be 'autonomous' actors, they were responsibilised through a mediating 'third party'. Responsibility was subsequently widened and weakened at the same time.[26]

Examining the 'responsibilisation' process in housing management strategies in Edinburgh and Glasgow, Flint identifies a contradictory development with this process—and one which is similarly noted in respect to the curfew. Despite housing association attempts to make tenants more responsible for the behaviour of themselves and other tenants by involving them in vetting potential tenants and organising meetings to help parents develop strategies for regulating the behaviour of their children, rather than 'individual responsibility' developing, tenants appeared to become increasingly reliant on the housing professionals. In this way, more trivial incidents were reported and issues that were seen as best resolved between tenants themselves were handed over to housing officers and the police to resolve. As Flint notes, one housing officer said that, 'In certain areas the first point of contact is often the police or housing association, even for trivial issues. These disputes should be easily resolved [between neighbours] but aren't' (Flint 2002: 632).

The curfew, like a number of subsequent antisocial behaviour initiatives developed under New Labour, was largely understood and indeed presented as something that would make people more responsible—where individuals were held to account for their actions with regard to others and themselves. However, while on the one hand there was an expansion of what being responsible meant, what was meant by responsibility was diminished at the same time. Here we explore the claims made by those promoting the curfew in relation to the idea of responsibility and responsibilisation to give an indication of the more fragile and risk averse ontological understanding of and relationship being developed by the local authority and police to the targeted population in Hamilton.

WIDER AND WEAKER

Responsibility was *widened* in relation to young people, who were now expected not only to refrain from criminal acts, but from behaviour that was understood to be creating fear amongst adults on the estate. Young people needed to be made *aware* of their responsibility for the anxieties of elderly adults, and become *self-aware* of the risks they and their peers faced from their own and one another's actions. At the same time parents were now expected to internalise a greater awareness of risks posed to their children at night, and to likewise be aware of the fear their teenage sons and daughters could instil in others. In this respect, both young people and parents were 'responsibilised' based on an understanding of themselves and those around them as being fundamentally vulnerable.

Within the 'at risk' framework rhetorically promoted by the police and local authority, individual autonomous action was presented as being somewhat problematic, as the activities of especially young people were understood to involve what could be describe as 'unforeseen circumstances'. In essence a kind of precautionary principle regarding actions between people was adopted and promoted through the CSI, a principle that placed limited expectations upon the actions and responsibility that individuals were expected to take.

The representation of adults on the estates under curfew was of potential victims whose 'right to a quiet life' was being undermined by rowdy youngsters. Understood as being both fearful and vulnerable, the expectation of autonomous action by these adults to resolve the disputes they had with these young people was noticeably missing from any statement by the police and the local authority. In this respect, rather than examining the claims *made* by those promoting or even opposing the curfew, in a sense what is being examined here is what claims were *not made* and what expectations did not exist regarding the people in Hillhouse—indeed what action that may previously have taken place was actively discouraged.

Within the prism of vulnerability, risks were understood to be best avoided rather than confronted, and the responsibility of adults to play a wider role in their community, indeed of taking individual autonomous action to resolve any problems they had—outside of developing personal forms of household security and phoning the police—was actively demoted by those supporting the CSI. Rather a relationship of reliance was encouraged, where a more regular police presence replaced the possible activities of local people to deal with the largely non-criminal nuisance behaviour of young people. This process encouraged the formalisation of previously informal relationships and adults were advised to contact the police regarding the fears they had about young people—regardless of the nature of the activities the young people were involved in. Rather than 'communities' developing a certain independence and 'responsibility' regarding the young people of this area a more systematic relationship with the 'community police' offices was promoted.[27] There was little sense of not only an active community, but even of the active free individual within this process—instead a more passive, risk-averse individual was both promoted and engaged with within the Child Safety Initiative. This can be seen most clearly with regard to the issue of child safety.

Examining the claims made about the CSI, based as it was upon the importance of child safety, typified with examples of young children 'wandering the streets at night', it is significant to note that in no speech or press release, nor in any newspaper article, did any of the individuals or groups promoting the curfew (or indeed opposing it) suggest that the adults in general within the community itself could or should play a more *active* role in ensuring the safety of children who were on the street at night. Within a more fragmented and individuated climate, the responsibility demanded of adults was to themselves and their own security and sense of anxiety. The safety of children was both generalised as a concern for the whole community, and at the same time fragmented—with only the individual parents of children being encouraged to take an 'active' role and being held 'responsible' for the safety of their own child.

In respect to the concerns about young people being disorderly, a similarly passive role for adults was promoted. The image of the adults on the curfewed estates presented by the council, police, politicians and the media, was that of not only being under siege, but also being unable to deal with the antisocial behaviour of children. Despite a recognition by some of the police that elderly adults' fear of crime and young people was sometimes exaggerated, this was not challenged within the campaign. Rather, this initiative encouraged local adults not to deal with young people but instead to phone the police. Fear in this sense was treated as an objective condition that was not contestable. Fear was understood to be a risk in and of itself, responsibility for adults being in relation to their own physical and emotional well-being—something that was best protected through risk avoidance and the limiting of contact with young people at night.

This approach was reflected in a Strathclyde police advertising campaign at the time, which stated: 'If you think there *may* be trouble, pick up a weapon'. The weapon in question was a telephone and the message not to intervene yourself was clear. Also, during the curfew, following complaints by adults about rowdy teenagers in another area of Hamilton, the police put out a statement to the public explaining that adults should, 'Call us and we will come round and deal with the situation. Do not engage them yourself, call us' (*Hamilton People* 12 December 1997).

It is worth reiterating that the social problems being addressed in Hamilton were not related to serious violent criminal incidents but to 'antisocial' young people and their nuisance activities. Phoning the police was encouraged based on the fear that something 'might' happen, and as such the police were being called into action not in relation to criminal acts themselves, but based on the fear that individuals felt about nuisance behaviour of children and young people and the potential risks they face when confronting young people. Rather than having any active engagement with these young people, the adults of Hillhouse were encouraged to hand *responsibility* to the police, who would intervene on their behalf.

The image of adults as vulnerable and in need of support was equally applicable to the representation of young people in the Hillhouse estate, and helped to transform the nature of 'responsibility'. Through the prism of risk and safety, young people were simultaneously held responsible for the fears of adults, while being represented as ultimately incapable of being responsible for themselves and their dealings with peers. Within this framework, a diminished sense of expectations similar to that which was noted above in relation to adult responsibility was promoted in relation to young people as well. Young people were represented, especially by the tabloid press, as 'trouble-makers'. However, through the language of risk, young people were also portrayed by those both promoting and opposing the curfew as 'troubled'—and in need of regulation in the form of support and protection rather than punishment.

PARENTAL RESPONSIBILITY

Of all the groups in Hillhouse, the main one targeted in terms of the need for greater responsibility was parents. However, while a responsibilisation process did occur, in terms of encouraging an individual awareness of risks and dangers for children on the streets and from young people misbehaving, again the informal idea of individual responsibility was transformed. In its place a more contractual and enforced notion of responsibility was promoted, while at the same time the idea that parents should have personal responsibility for decisions regarding their children was diminished. While denouncing irresponsible parents, there was also a sentiment expressed by those promoting the curfew that parents were not capable of controlling their children and that the police, in this respect, could act as a parent support agency. Parents were therefore responsibilised in terms of their awareness and need to restrict the independent activities of their children, while being encouraged to understand this form of responsibility with reference to the police, whose role was to provide advice and action in the form of a surrogate parent.[28]

In Hamilton, 'responsibility' was more of a pressure put on parents than something that they were expected to take and develop for themselves. This more communitarian sense of responsibility—or more accurately this post-liberal understanding of it (Reece 2003)—to some degree actively undermined the more classically liberal (or neo-liberal), idea of individual responsibility. One commentator noted that, 'Another objective [of the curfew] is increasing awareness of parental responsibility. Yet paradoxically, they seem to be taking decisions, and the authority to enforce these decisions, out of the hands of parents'.[29]

While promoting the idea of good responsible parenting in Hillhouse, parents were seen as being responsible for their children's behaviour in a way that broadened the meaning of responsibility within the framework of risk and safety, while also diminishing what responsibility meant. Children and young people who were 'unsupervised' and potentially at risk, and adults who were made to feel at risk from the presence of teenagers were all, to some extent, part of the problem of 'irresponsible parents'. A responsible parent was a risk-averse parent, who was *made* aware by the local authority and police.

Part of the reason given by the council and Strathclyde police, for the implementation of the Child Safety Initiative was a need to make parents more responsible. However, one of the basic responsibilities of parents—the decision about when and where to allow their children to go at night—was in part taken from parents by the activities and promotion campaigns of the police during the CSI. An example of how this responsibility became something decided by the police rather than parents was demonstrated on Halloween night. For this night parents and children were informed by officers going to all the schools in the area that it was OK for children and young people to go out for Halloween. But this relaxation of the curfew came with a warning from a Strathclyde police spokesman: 'We would like all parents to make sure that their kids are supervised and go out that bit earlier in the evening' (*Scotland on Sunday* 31 October 1997). The reason for this 'advice' from the police was that 'parents should be aware, whether it's Halloween or not, of the dangers of allowing their children out after dark without proper supervision' (*Hamilton Advertiser* 30 October 1997).

Discussing the use of curfews in the UK and USA, a *Sunday Mail* reporter noted that the use of curfews was a useful tool not only for the police but also for parents, as 'It allows them to tell children what they should do—not because they want to lay down the law but because it IS the law' (*Sunday Mail* 15 August 1999). Rather than parents using their own authority to take responsibility for their children, here the authority of the law was *borrowed* by parents—the enforcement and ultimate responsibility for the 'in-time' of children becoming that of the police.

The population of Hillhouse as a whole was encouraged through the promotion of the CSI to change its behaviour, become more aware of the dangers and anxieties that existed in its community, and to understand itself and its children in relation to the risks it faced. Responsibility for the social problems addressed by the authorities was understood in relation to parents and young people, whose 'risky' lifestyles and activities undermined the security of the entire community. This process of responsibilisation both widened and weakened the meaning of responsibility. Through the precautionary framework promoted, responsibility was to the generalised risks portrayed by the authorities; awareness of this responsibility to others meant adopting a risk-averse approach to situations and experiences; with a greater understanding of the insecurities of others and the self leading to an expectation of caution and precaution. Within the rhetoric surrounding the curfew, therefore, the notion of being 'streetwise' was problematised—both in relation to children and young people—but equally in relation to adults themselves. Being *aware* meant being more fearful and replaced an expectation of individual *initiative*. Understanding of 'risk' replaced *action*, contact and confrontation between people. In essence, the promotion of the CSI sponsored a form of responsibilisation that would *formalise informal relationships*, by developing an internalised form of responsibility based on the doctrine of safety and caution, and by encouraging individuals to permanently mediate their relationships with others through the activities of the authorities.

THERAPEUTIC LEGITIMATION

This idea of 'feeling' safe related to the issue of the fear of crime, something that had slowly become an issue in its own right in the UK through the 1980s and accelerated in the 1990s. As we have seen, by the time the curfew was launched, the reduction of fear was central to both politicians and the police. In a sense the role of the police was now far more significant than previously as they were not only there to reduce crime—but also to reduce public insecurities and so, it was believed, help to strengthen, perhaps even rebuild, communities. As Garland argues, fear—'once regarded as a localized, situational anxiety, afflicting the worst-off individuals and neighbourhoods, has come to be regarded as a major social problem and a characteristic of contemporary culture' (Garland 2002: 10). With the shift in concern towards fear of crime as a thing in itself to be addressed, both at a local—but more significantly at a national, or even universal—level, policing has changed accordingly: 'The police now hold themselves out less as a crime-fighting force than as a responsive public service, aiming to reduce fear, disorder and incivility and to take account of community feelings in setting enforcement priorities' (Garland 2002).

In the Hamilton example, the emotion of fear was understood to be central to the problems of individuals and to the community as a whole. By engaging with the problem of crime at this level, the authorities were taking on a more therapeutic role in their attempt to *manage the anxieties of the public*. The question of public insecurity was taken for granted, everyone on the Hillhouse estate was represented as either living in fear, or—like young people drinking at night—at risk, and needing to be made aware of the danger they were in. The message in this respect appeared to be that the people of the area were living in fear—and those who are not—should be, or least should be more 'risk conscious'. Also as we have seen, most starkly in the case of child safety, there was no expectation placed on people in the area to put themselves out and take an active role in engaging with, even young children, who were understood to be out late at night. The people of Hillhouse were either treated as if they were vulnerable and at risk or a risk to others.

Ultimately, the success of the initiative itself was understood by the police and politicians in relation not to the reduction of antisocial behaviour itself, but more directly in relation to the fear of the public. Fear in this respect was understood as a universal emotion felt by the people of Hillhouse—something that had a sense of permanence, that was undermining the 'sense of community', but that was also the foundation upon which a connection could be made between the authorities and the public. Fears for and of children and young people were both related to and validated in the development of the curfew, and it was this generalised sentiment of fear—rather than the specific anxieties regarding particular activities of young people and children—that was being engaged with.

The notion of a therapy culture relates not to the specific activities of therapists, but to a cultural elevation of the significance of the emotional aspect of individuals—and in particular to an acute orientation to the public as being vulnerable to emotional damage. Through this therapeutic framework, an orientation towards the people of Hillhouse was established, within which previously understood social problems were reinterpreted as emotional ones and new social problems—like antisocial behaviour—were understood to be problematic with reference to the emotional reaction of others.

Through the therapeutic gaze of the authorities, social problems were reformulated and the meaning of *freedom* was redefined to mean the freedom from feeling fearful. 'Removing fear' was the way to 'return liberties', and the 'number one priority' of the curfew was to ensure the entire community felt safe. At the same time, the responsibilisation process attempted to engage with the fear that parents had for their children—and specific threats, like the threat of paedophiles, were promoted as an issue that should be of concern for those parents who allowed their children out at night. Similarly young people themselves were engaged with and encouraged to support the curfew, based on their own potential insecurities regarding themselves and other young people.

Crime and antisocial behaviour were understood to be, and projected as, social problems with reference to the individual's sense of 'well-being' and the community sense of confidence established through a generalised mood of safety. The basis and reconstitution of the community in this respect related to the emotional self—something to be engaged with and reformed by the authorities. The understanding of 'community' was therefore predicated less upon the commonality felt and developed between people—or their economic or political connections—but with reference to the more individualised sense of insecurity and feelings of fear. Consequently there was an 'anti-social' component within this understanding that encouraged the idea that the rebuilding of 'community' was predicated upon people being left alone, to live their 'quiet life' in peace.

The 'common' 'value' engaged with through the CSI was the fragmented individual's feeling of anxiety.

Moving young people away from areas where adults are concerned about their behaviour may not be a new development. However, the heightened significance given to the insecurities of adults—and indeed to the community as a whole—reflected a qualitative elevation adopted by both politicians and the police to the concern with the emotional reactions and fears of adults.[30]

Transformed from individual cases of criminal or antisocial behaviour into a concern with a general sense of anxiety on these estates, the 'social problem' of, as one newspaper labelled it, 'streets of fear', was engaged with (*Herald* 21 October 1997). This existing understanding of communities, indeed of society more broadly, meant that any example of nuisance behaviour of young people was interpreted as the basis for this universalised sense of fear and indeed helps to explain the newly developing category of 'antisocial behaviour' that transformed occasional incidents of misbehaviour into a permanent problem that was understood to be undermining the 'confidence' of communities.

The fear of crime has been an issue in criminology and politics in the UK from the 1980s. However, this fear was both contested and less central to the concern about crime and social problems affecting communities. There were unquestionably issues regarding youth drinking and vandalism in the Hillhouse area, and as the police explained the curfew had been introduced in part because of complaints by adults. The question addressed here, however, is not the myth or reality of the antisocial activities of young people in the targeted areas—although as the police admitted, Hillhouse was not an area of particularly high crime rates—but rather the justificatory basis of the initiative, which was in large part focused upon the sense of anxiety felt by the public.

Fear was itself constituted as a risk.[31] Fear and safety became essential in understanding the targeted communities and the individuals within them, and regardless of the objective basis of this fear, its very existence was the social problem that was seen as needing to be addressed.

In Hillhouse this fear was understood to be a problem for the whole community, each member of it subsequently being seen as a potential victim of crime but also an existing 'victim' of behaviour that created a dark cloud of fear.

In April 1997, shadow Home Secretary Jack Straw had described the fear of crime as something that 'hangs like a dark cloud in the air'. Elaborating, Straw believed the extent of this problem meant that

> Two thirds of women pensioners are scared to leave their house at night. Our pensioners are prisoners in their own homes who only want to live in peace. Surely the prisoners should be those who commit the crimes, not those who are the victims of crime. It cannot go on (*Guardian* 26 April 1997).

With this permanent and fundamental sense of fear, which was understood to be hovering above communities, the basis for police intervention related to criminal acts was transformed into a more subjectively constituted defence of the public's emotional well-being. This engagement with the sense of vulnerability of the public thus provided the justificatory basis for the curfew.[32]

In a sense the community being engaged with was a community of vulnerable individuals, a community victimised by fear. This perceived sense of victimhood was understood to be the potential common bond between individuals—and the basis of state engagement and legitimation. As Garland explains:

> The symbolic figure of the victim has taken on a life of its own [and has become] . . . a new social fact. The victim is no longer an unfortunate citizen who has been on the receiving end of a criminal harm, and whose concerns are subsumed within the 'public interest'. . . . The victim is now, in a certain sense, a much more representative character, whose experience is taken to be common and collective, rather than individual and atypical (Garland 2002: 11).

HILLHOUSE

The ideas developed above are a continuation of work that was carried out in Hillhouse in 1997 that led to the book *Scared of the Kids?* (Waiton 2001). Thus far the claims made about the curfew have been examined rather than the 'reality' of the problems on the targeted estates. Below the 'myth and reality' of the social problems in Hillhouse are briefly explored.

Despite some genuine issue regarding crime and the behaviour of young people in the area—Hillhouse—considering the nature of the curfew initiative and the national notoriety it received, was a surprisingly ordinary estate.[33]

From police reports, media coverage, and interviews with adults and young people in the areas of Hamilton targeted for the curfew, there were clearly some problems of crime and disorder. There was in Hillhouse, like many areas, a certain problem of crime, drunken behaviour, graffiti and vandalism, while some children and young people were out on the streets at night 'after dark'. In this respect there were some 'real' problems that were being related to by the police and local authority that led to the introduction of the Child Safety Initiative.

The curfew was presented as something that the community wanted, not only because of concerns about antisocial youth, but also, as council leader Tom McCabe had argued, because local people were also concerned about the safety of young people. The couplet of safety for children and safety of adults from children was central to this initiative. The police had similarly presented the CSI as an initiative that was largely introduced because of concerns about young children 'wandering the streets late at night', putting themselves at risk and potentially getting up to 'no good'. However, in the Scottish Office research *Evaluation of the Hamilton Child Safety Initiative*, a research document based on an examination of the impact of the curfew on the Hillhouse estate in its first six month trial period, it was noted following three group discussions with adults and young people that:

> All three groups questioned the justification for deploying resources into the HCSI [Hamilton Child Safety Initiative] when they felt there was no real evidence that under 10s were causing crime or disorder problems on the streets, especially not in Hillhouse (McGallagly et al 1998: 60).

One of the groups also questioned whether the CSI could be expected to tackle problems such as 'bad parenting' and change the attitudes of 'one or two irresponsible parents who let their children out on the streets late at night' (McGallagly et al.1998: 60).

The research with children and adults discussed in *Scared of the Kids* also raised questions about the necessity of a curfew based upon the 'social problem' of young children 'wandering the streets at night'. Hillhouse Community Council chair Joe Parfery, for example, was unaware of any great safety problem, especially from strangers and paedophiles. He was equally unaware of any great number of young children wandering the streets at night. He explained: 'There are a few children who stay out, especially during the summer, till about 10.30pm but not many. But what's wrong with that anyway? I used to play out all the time when I was a kid'.

As well as the Scottish Office research finding that local people felt that the issue of antisocial under-10-year-olds was not an issue, and that the question of irresponsible parents letting their young children stay out late only applied to 'one or two' people, it also found that there was no evidence of wider dangers to children in the Hillhouse area. The summary of the research findings noted that:

> Due to the small number of children who were the victims of crime or road traffic accidents in the 6 month period prior to and during the period covered by the CSI, it was not possible to assess the impact of the initiative on such incidents (McGallagly et al. 1998: 3).

In other words, the statistical impact of the curfew on the safety of children was found to be impossible to assess due to the limited safety issues that existed. Where comparisons were made with Hillhouse and a control area by the Scottish Office research, with reference to crime victimisation rates it was found that the CSI 'had little impact in terms of reducing child victimisation' (McGallagly et al.1998: 26). Finally, with reference to the 229 curfew interventions made by the police between October 1997 and April 1998, this research found that '20 [or 9%] were directly related to child safety issues' (McGallagly et al.1998: 17).[34]

Despite the claims made by the local authority and, especially, by the police, that the CSI was being introduced to protect under-10-year-olds from the irresponsible parents who allowed their children to wander the streets at night, the extent of this problem, the level of dangers present, and the impact the curfew had on the safety of children, were all questionable.

FEAR FOR CHILDREN

Following the first six months of the initiative the number of interventions by the police to deal with young people who were out on the streets 'after dark' without good reason were published by the police. Two hundred and twenty nine young people had been taken home in the Hillhouse area during this time period. However in the Scottish Office research carried out to assess the impact of the Child Safety Initiative it was noted that of the 229 police interventions, only three 'special circumstances' were highlighted relating to poor parental supervision (McGallagly et al. 1998:18).[35]

However, in general terms concerns about child safety were shared by parents in Hillhouse, and the promotion of child safety was supported. In the Scottish Office research it was found that 'despite reservations' about the focus on under-10-year-olds, 'there was a general consensus that the police were right to address the safety of young children' (McGallagly et al. 1998: 60). In discussion with three focus groups, it was also noted that, 'All three groups commended the HCSI for its concern with the safety of young children and showed considerable interest in this aspect of the Initiative' (McGallagly et al. 1998: 63). In other words, despite there being little concern by adults about the reality of the problem of young children wandering the streets late at night, and also despite their being little evidence within the Scottish Office research that young children were practically 'at risk', there was a more generalised acceptance that safety was an important issue for children, that children were indeed more generally 'at risk', and that action taken to promote this could only be a good thing.

Put more starkly, there was little evidence of children being 'at risk' on the streets, and local people recognised this. However there was a wider recognition of the problem of 'child safety' that engaged local adults in Hillhouse and led to them supporting this aspect of the initiative. Rather than there being agreement between the authorities and the public about the practical dangers children faced, the agreement was about the *fear* felt for children and the acceptance that 'child safety' was an absolute. *In this respect the CSI was an engagement with, and promotion of, the culture of fear, rather than a practical initiative to resolve an objective problem.*

As discussed previously, child safety was here not only an unquestioned issue but was also understood as an unquestionably good thing. But rather than engage with fears related to specific issues, the engagement between the authorities and the targeted areas was with a more generalised sense of fear.

Discussing the successes of the initiative with a group of parents, the Scottish Office research noted that one of the positive factors had been that 'this parents' focus group considered that the HCSI had been effective in making parents more aware of the dangers for children out late at night'. *Here the success of the curfew was its ability not only to relate to people's fears, but to enhance them.* Parents were now also believed to be regulating their children more strictly because of these fears (McGallagly et al.1998: 78). For the local authority and police, the greater regulation of these children's time was seen as a positive move to make them safer—despite the reality of limited evidence of any dangers faced by the children.

Ironically, one of the findings in the *Scared of the Kids* research was that the main reason children gave for having to be home earlier since the curfew was introduced was that their parents were worried about them coming into contact with the police. This does not necessarily contradict the idea that many parents supported the initiative, but rather suggests that as well as raising awareness about 'child safety' issues in general, the practicalities of the curfew also led to an unintended fear about police involvement in their child's life. The elevation of fear regarding the police was not something explored by the Scottish Office research.

Having found little evidence of harm towards the children of Hillhouse, the Scottish Office research noted that 'over a third of those children asked felt unsafe when walking alone in their local area after dark'. This 'provides some justification for the present Initiative' (McGallagly et al. 1998:

49). Here again the basis for the initiative was established not through real problems faced by these children, but in the fears they had about going out in the dark.

During the 1990s numerous research projects had highlighted that children, rather than wandering the streets at night, were in fact having their free time increasingly regulated by parents. This research found that the time children were allowed out was decreasing, as was the distance they were allowed to travel; children could play in fewer places and could travel less far from home than previous generations; there was a growth of children whose parents would define them as 'indoor kids' as opposed to 'outdoor kids'; and that children were engaged in more supervised as opposed to unsupervised activities. This research also suggests that a major reason nationally for this high level of parental supervision is fear for their children's safety. In Hillhouse a number of these trends were also identified (Waiton 2001: 59–76).

In this respect, the curfew was simply reinforcing an existing high level of parental supervision. The curfew was reinforcing the idea that a 'safe parent' was a good parent, while targeting those parents who did not share these safety concerns as problematic and a danger to their children and the community. Issues regarding child safety and of what has been termed *Paranoid Parenting* (Furedi 2001b) were institutionalised by the CSI, and a cultural framework was promoted by the authorities that encouraged an exaggerated sense of fear regarding the lives of children.

ADULT FEARS

In Hillhouse there was evidence of a level of fear of crime. However, the notion that this community was being undermined by fear due to young people's criminal behaviour is questionable. The Citizens' Jury that had been set up to look at the issue of community safety, for example, when asked to isolate what it saw as the main problem to solve in the area, named graffiti as the key problem. Graffiti can have a negative physical and psychological impact on communities—however, compared with the image that was portrayed of Hillhouse, of children running wild and young people making people's lives hell, this concern about graffiti raises questions about the extent of the problem with young people in the area. (South Lanarkshire Council 1997a).

The Scottish Office research also found, when interviewing adults from Hillhouse, that the main perceived problem of crime and disorder for the area was caused not by young people under the age of 16, but by 'a small number of "older" young people who tended to be heavy drinkers or drug users and who were, for the most part, unemployed' (McGallagly et al 1998). If this was indeed the main age group committing crimes and being antisocial in the area, then clearly the basis of the curfew and the representation of the problem of 'antisocial youth' was again more problematic than it may first have appeared.

Measuring the fear of crime in the area of Hillhouse, the Scottish Office research concluded that fear was an issue in Hillhouse, but that in certain cases the curfew had done little to resolve this problem. For example, while discovering that 65% of those surveyed had often or sometimes felt unsafe either in their homes or on the street, after six months of the curfew, 'this proportion had only reduced slightly to 60%' (McGallagly et al. 1998: xi). Also,

> Anxiety about groups or gangs of youths or young people remained strong, with three quarters of respondents saying that they found the presence of groups of young people on the streets frightening, both before the initiative began and after the first six months (McGallagly et al. 1998: xi).

This research also found that 'more people were likely to avoid an area after the CSI began (86%) than before (77%)' (McGallagly et al. 1998: xi). But despite this, it was also found that 44% of those surveyed said they felt safer on the streets since the initiative was introduced—partly because of the lower number of young people on the streets.

One question that was not covered by this Scottish Office research was: What is it that the adults are afraid of? They are concerned about 'gangs of young people', but is this because these young people attack them, attack their house, or simply that they make them feel nervous? Also, if the fear expressed by this research related to a serious problem with young people, why were these problems not mentioned by the Citizens' Jury or identified as a problem of crime in the Scottish Office research?

CONCLUSION

Looked at individually, a number of the 'safety' issues being addressed in Hillhouse could be seen as something the police had always been involved in. For example the Children and Young Persons (Scotland) Act 1937 (s.12), 'provides that it is an offence on the part of a parent to neglect his child', and part of the legal justification for the curfew had been with reference to, 'the general duty of the police to protect life and property' (Springham 1998). However, the centrality of the issue of safety was qualitatively different.

Safety was an organising principle in its own right with regard to the community as a whole, and was understood to be central to the well-being of the community. Indeed it was the issue of safety and fear that was understood to be at the heart of what was undermining, and equally what could recreate a sense of community. All aspects of the interactions between individuals within Hillhouse were therefore interpreted within the prism of safety—with even the previously described 'delinquent' or 'deviant' activities of young people being described as 'unsafe'.

As David Garland has noted with regard to the legal system in the UK in the past, 'the British political establishment pursued an ideal of solidarity' (Garland 1996: 406). In terms of rebuilding a sense of community within the curfew-targeted areas, there was an attempt to rebuild this 'solidarity' through the issue of safety. This was not, after all, simply a police initiative, or part of the day-to-day policing of an area, but was a political initiative involving the local Labour council with the backing of the New Labour government. It was in essence a development of the politics of fear.

The basis for the justification of the curfew was in relation to the 'at risk child', the 'fearful adult', and the 'pressurised youth'—each individual within these groups being understood as somewhat isolated and in need of protection. The participation, partnership and community involvement promoted during the Child Safety Initiative were therefore an engagement not with a collective public, but rather with atomised insecure individuals and their feelings of fear.[36] In this respect the authority of the curfew came not from the authorities themselves but from their ability to act as advocates for the vulnerable public.

Standing as advocates of the vulnerable community rather than as political representatives, the local politicians (and indeed the police themselves) were prone to feeling pressured by alternative 'victim' voices. The youth voice in particular, which was mobilised by the children's charities opposing the curfew, carried with it much weight as young people—by their very nature of being 'children' and understood as being a 'vulnerable group'— could be represented as powerless potential victims. Like the council's attempt to advocate on behalf of the public with reference to their vulnerability, the children's charities opposing the curfew did likewise. To counter these claims, the local authority attempted to prove that young people were on their side and that the curfew was in fact defending their right to be safe from harm.

Coupled with the idea of vulnerability, it was this attitude to safety and of people feeling safe that was of key significance for this initiative and, as we will see, central to the issue of antisocial behaviour. Despite the authoritarian nature of the initiative, to dismiss the 'caring' role of the police and simply see a clamp down on youth would be to miss what was new and arguably more significant about this initiative and what it represented.

Safety was key to both the police and politicians' justification of the Child Safety Initiative. Where previously upholding the law and ensuring public order was the framework for police action, now the objective for policing had become safety and the feeling of safety. As Garland notes, in contemporary society, 'community safety' has become 'the chief consideration and law-enforcement becomes a means to this end, rather than an end in itself' (Garland 2002: 171). Reflecting aspects of Wilson and Kelling's 'broken windows' approach to disorder, Elizabeth Burney notes that:

The role of community policing in checking incivilities thereby reducing fear and increasing public self-confidence, is the core message—one which finds resonance twenty years later in Britain in the method known as 'reassurance policing' (Burney 2005: 25).

Reassurance, building confidence and helping the community to feel safe—where all aspects of the more therapeutic management of the people in Hillhouse: Reassurance that was needed—not, it is worth reminding ourselves, because of a serious problem of crime in the area, but because of the understood problem of antisocial youth.

The theme of safety was both a police matter and a political issue, and unlike past historical periods, was here not a means to a wider political end but the end in itself. The chief aim of the new forms of policing being to 'assuage popular outrage, reassure the public, and restore the "credibility" of the system, all of which are political rather than penological concerns', as Garland argues (Garland 2002: 173).

The need for safety promoted by the Labour government was not a mere aside, an appendage to a broader political programme and purpose. Lacking any wider political framework and dynamic, safety was engaged with as the thing in itself. *Safety was the basis of community.*

Through specific community and child safety initiatives, safety was becoming an organising framework for local authority intervention into communities around 1997, and the development of initiatives and practices like the vetting of youth workers and the emergence of CCTV and security around schools was emerging at this time and normalising the basis of safety as a framework for organising everyday life. Structural changes at the time had also helped to develop a more fragmented society, with the decline of solidarity and collective organisations accompanying changes in the family. This process of individuation helped to strengthen the sense of insecurity across society a sense of insecurity that was understood and acted upon purely in relation to 'safety' based issues.

Despite police statements explaining that criminal and antisocial behaviour was not especially high within the targeted areas, by relating to the broader sense of fear in these areas through the discourse of risk and safety there appeared at the same time to be a necessary exaggeration of the social problems being addressed. Instances of nuisance behaviour, helped in part by the language of 'antisocial behaviour' and the 'fear of crime', gave a more problematic and ever-present significance to occasional events.

Despite the aim of the CSI being in part to develop a sense of community, the justificatory rhetoric of the authorities related more directly to the fragmented and vulnerable individual, than to any sense of commonality—except, that is, with the 'common' issue of individual safety and the desire to feel safe. In the process of engaging with people in this way, rather than individuals re-engaging with one another, the connecting framework implicitly being established was between the authorities and the individuated public.

It is at this level that the meaning of responsibilisation should be understood—less as a promotion of individual autonomous action, than as an encouragement of caution and an expectation of reliance upon third party intervention to help manage all the relationships between people.

Despite the promotion of the CSI as a community-led initiative with community participation community action was at no stage promoted in terms of individual activity to resolve issues of antisocial behaviour or even child safety. In essence, the initiative in this respect not only engaged with a general sense of fear and desire for safety, but encouraged all on the estate to stop *acting* themselves to help ensure safety was maintained. Within an 'at risk' framework, where all independent interactions were understood to be potentially dangerous, rather than encouraging self-activity in the construction of the community, the aim of the CSI was to encourage 'self limitation'.

For some critics of the Hamilton Child Safety Initiative—or what they and most commentators described as a curfew—this initiative was another example of a moral panic about 'youth'. Unlike past youth 'panics' however, this one was not legitimised within a Conservative political or moral framework where 'moral barricades' as Cohen described them were created, but was legitimised through the new conservative issue of safety.

In Hamilton the moral barricades were replaced by a safety fence.

3 The Politics of Vulnerability

> The Third Way connected with the electorate, not on the basis of their
> collective purpose, but instead playing upon their individuation and the
> anxieties that arose from it. The voters were no longer represented in
> the polity as the collective subject of the democratic process. Instead
> they were recognised by the state as the isolated and persecuted victims
> of events beyond their control
>
> (Heartfield 2002: 199).

INTRODUCTION

Safety may have always been an issue in everyday life, but it was not a political issue, or a basis for policing, until the 1990s. Likewise the issues associated with antisocial behaviour had little political significance in the 1980s
and began to emerge under the Conservative premiership of John Major.
Tony Blair subsequently made antisocial behaviour into a major political issue, legislating for youth curfews and Antisocial Behaviour Orders
(ASBOs), and within local authorities community safety was established as
a core framework directing the operation of local services. But why? Had
neighbours suddenly come from 'hell' and young people become little terrorists in the space of one generation, or was there some other explanation
for the rise of this 'social problem'?

As social constructionists recognise, for social issues to become 'social
problems' they must be *made*, or constructed. Here an attempt is made to
examine the changing discourse around crime and behaviour through the
1990s, and in particular the changing way in which crime was addressed
and indeed used as a political issue.

In this chapter the focus is not upon the issue of antisocial behaviour
itself so much as the political climate within which the problem emerged. In
general, despite possible changes of behaviour on the streets of Britain, the
argument here is that if antisocial behaviour had not existed, they would
have had to make it up. And as it happens many things were 'made up'—or
constructed as social problems—things that never had been previously, from

'dangerous dogs' to 'neighbours from hell'. Now politics got involved in the day to day running of everyday life—a development that lay the foundations for the politics of antisocial behaviour.

In *Policing the Crisis* (Hall et al. 1978), a book exploring the serious political tensions of the early 1970s, the point is made that,

> Above all (and besides facilitating the routinisation of repression), the law-and-order campaign of 1970 had the overwhelming single consequence of legitimating the recourse to law, to [constraint] and statutory power, as the *main*, indeed the only, effective means left of defending hegemony in conditions of severe crisis' (1978: 278).

For Hall the loss of hegemony of the elite in society resulted in the increasing use of law, order and policing, to maintain order. Discussing the militarisation of the police force at the time, the conflict between the trade unions, student activists, and left-wing demonstrators, and the emerging issue of 'mugging', *Policing the Crisis* documents well the growing use of forms of social control to defeat the 'enemy within'. Crime in general also became more significant as a political issue at this time, however, and in comparison to what emerged in the 1990s, there remained within this policing of the crisis a political battle between left and right, a battle of hegemony—an attempt to 'restore authority to government under the 'theme of national unity' against 'extremists' and the 'possibility of the deadly "student-worker" alliance' (Hall et al. 978: 279). By 1993 this battle was over, and the left—at least in those promoting socialism—had lost. In terms of the fight with the 'enemy within', there was no longer a need for any policing of a crisis, and yet now not only crime, but wider issues of behaviour became increasingly problematised in society. As the 1990s progressed and New Labour emerged as a genuine threat to the Conservative Party and then took office, any radical opposition within politics to the politicisation of crime and disorder disappeared. Now the 'recourse to law' quantitatively increased and was qualitatively transformed as disorder became a problem not of trade unionists, demonstrators or alien muggers—but an endemic problem within everyday life.

A number of the developments that led to the issue of youth antisocial behaviour becoming significant emerged around 1993—something that has been attributed in part to the death of James Bulger. These included the vitriol around the problem of crime, a concern with the collapse of communities, and the cry that 'something must be done'—especially related to young people—who were now portrayed by the prime minister as part of a 'yob culture'.

In 1993 the two-year-old James Bulger was killed by two 10-year-old boys, leading to what has been seen by some as one of the most intense moral panics of the decade, with the killers of James being condemned as evil 'freaks of nature'. The debate that followed did not relate simply to this event but to an understood 'crisis in childhood' and a juvenile crime wave. Stories about child criminals increasingly began to appear, and the Home Secretary attacked the state agencies for going 'soft' in their dealings with criminal youth. Within days of James' death John Major called for a 'crusade against crime' and argued that there needed to be a 'change from being forgiving of crime to being considerate to the victim' (Scraton 1997: 168).

Understandably perhaps, the heightened profile and political rhetoric regarding juvenile crime were seen as being related to the Bulger killing. However, Bulger's death may have helped nudge politicians in a certain direction—but it was a direction they were already travelling. Big though the Bulger story was—it had nothing on the key development influencing politics in Britain and indeed the world at that time, which was the collapse of communism and socialism. This ironically resulted not in a vibrant rise of right-wing politics—but in effect its collapse.

This is the backdrop to the chapter—a collapse of politics of both left and right that created a disorientation amongst the political elite, indeed a profound sense of confusion and loss of direction and purpose. Written shortly after the Bulger killing, the conservative *Daily Telegraph* described this mood in this way:

> A mental state of pessimistic fatalism has the country in its grip. The sense of national despondency is not purely political and economic . . . but spans almost the entire range of human experience. . . . The sense that things have rarely been as bad and can only get worse is now a major influence holding back recovery (Scraton 1997: 49).

As noted in the preface of this book, the Bulger killing was also understood as a symbol of what was wrong with British society for many politicians—including the then Labour leader Tony Blair. The mental state of pessimistic fatalism appeared to be overwhelming not only conservatives but also the now 'New' Labour Party.

THE NEO-LIBERAL FALLACY

The 'law and order' initiatives developed by the Labour government from 1997 reflected, for many, the neo-liberal political framework that grew out of Thatcherism in the UK. Likewise, the increasing policing of society and the imprisonment of a growing number of people—especially in the UK and the US in the 1990s—was, and is, understood to reflect a continuing form of right-wing authoritarian populism. The ideology of Thatcherism, of moral values, law and order, and individual responsibility are thus seen to have survived through the premiership of the Conservative leader John Major and then with the creation and election of New Labour—the new party of law and order.[1]

The predominance of a 'market society' (Feeley 2003: 117) and more individually based relationships (Beck and Beck-Gernsheim 2002) are understood to have helped create a *Culture of Control* (Garland 2002): This culture was predicated upon 'neo-liberal' and 'neo-conservative' policies— 'of market discipline and moral discipline' (Garland 2002: 197). However, while this understanding of the neo-liberal nature of society appears to be relevant in understanding the 'victory' of the market over ideas of socialism in the last few decades, that this has been accompanied by the dynamic *politics* of the right is questionable. Rather than the culture of control reflecting the authoritarian politics of the right, here it is argued that it is the elite's loss of political imagination, as Furedi puts it (Furedi 2005), and the collapse of moral purpose, as described by Christopher Lasch (Lasch 1977: 187), which explains the growth of antisocial behaviour as a political issue. It is in other words the emergence of politics without a meaning or purpose—a micro-politics—rather than any energetic neo-liberalism—that explains the rise of the culture of control.

This is a politics that reacts to events rather than forming them: politics in a panic.

By 1997, crime as a political issue had changed significantly compared to the use of and rhetoric around law and policing a decade earlier. Within politics the discussion about order, particularly in the early and mid 1980s, related in large part to the contestation between the government and the 'enemy within'—the violent trade unionists, IRA terrorists or black rioters. For much of the 'Thatcher decade', crime was associated with the question of *public order*, of groups in society deemed to be a threat to the 'British way of life'. Otherwise, the broader question of crime was addressed within an aggressive promotion of order, authority and the rule of law.

When Labour eventually came to power, the labour movement that had historically made the Labour Party 'the party of the working class' was no longer of significance—and there was no longer an 'enemy within', or if there was this was now understood not to be militant miners or black rioters, but children and rowdy youngsters, who were 'making life hell' for adults on estates. Where Margaret Thatcher had attempted to rally the Conservatives and indeed the nation around her defence of British values of law and order, New Labour's approach to order maintenance focused far more upon the more individualised sense of insecurity—upon the 'fear of crime'—and in defence of not *public order* so much as private peace and a 'quiet life'. This was not however a defence of the Englishman's home as his castle—of neo-liberal man, the assertive, aggressive individualist—but rather a defence of the anxious and chronically vulnerable individual.

In his book *The Unfinished Revolution*, Labour Party moderniser Philip Gould self-consciously recognised that individual fears had emerged due to broad social changes, but nonetheless believed that New Labour must reconnect with voters with policies that are 'tough on crime' (Gould 1999). Engaging with the fear of the fragmented public was in part a conscious strategy adopted by the Labour leadership in the run-up to the 1997 election.

THATCHER'S LEGACY

The Conservative Party throughout the 1970s and 1980s helped to fan the flames of fear with regard to the 'problem' of crime. Many social and political issues were discussed within the context of a problem of 'law and order'. In the 1970 the Conservative government was the first to identify itself specifically as the party of law and order (Pitts 1988). The initially 'refrained' promotion of crime as a political issue reached a 'crescendo' in the 1979 Conservative election campaign, and the ideas developed in the 1970 manifesto, connecting public order to the peculiar 'age of demonstrations and disruption', were forcefully pursued. Crime was now systematically associated with industrial disputes and the issue of law breaking became fused with the question of 'order-defiance' (Downes and Morgan 1997: 288–89). Margaret Thatcher's 'use' of crime was part of a political confrontation—her aim being to defeat the militant 'enemy within' and enforce law and order as she understood it. *Safety* as such was of little political significance at this time.

Describing the Tory approach to crime, Phipps noted:

> Firstly, it became conflated with a number of other issues whose connection was continually reinforced in the public mind—permissiveness, youth cultures, demonstrations, public disorders, black immigration, student unrest, and trade union militancy (Hall et al. 1978). Secondly, crime—by now a metaphorical term invoking the decline of social stability and decent values—was presented as only one aspect of a bitter harvest for which Labour's brand of social democracy and welfarism was responsible (Phipps 1988: 179).

Crime was directly connected to the question of public order and to the wider issue of political order and control. The *typical* criminals, within this politicised framework, were 'outsiders', the violent trade union member or the young black mugger. Traditional British values and individual freedoms were contrasted to the collectivist, promiscuous values of the enemy within (Milne 1995: 26). Even thieves were understood to be part of the 'something for nothing society'. Here the 'criminal', either the burglar or the trade union member, was to some degree understood to be an immoral actor or a political enemy, and the damage being done was not centrally to the victim of crime or the safety of the community, but to the economy and to the moral values and political order of society. Social control and public order were promoted within both a political and moral framework.[2]

For this chapter, Thatcher is understood at one level to be *the last politician*—in the sense that her government had a sense of purpose and engaged in a political battle and attempted to challenge the politics and beliefs of the adult population. In the context of the fight against the 'enemy within', many policies—especially in relation to crime—were carried out within this politicised framework. This contrasts, as we will see, with the growing use of law and order in the 1990s, where the direct regulation of 'behaviour' replaced any wider sense of the role of politics.

At the same time, with reference to what was to come within the new micro-politics of crime, the politics of Thatcherism and the belief in the capacity of the free individual both held back to some degree the rise of the 'victim' within law and order policies, and also limited the more paternalistic, or 'Nanny State', forms of regulation of everyday life that emerged in the 1990s. The responsibility for cutting crime was seen as not simply that of the government or police, but also that of the public, who, it was argued, should take action to defend themselves (Conservative Manifesto 1987). This, after all, was a government that promoted the idea of the strong individual, arguing that people should get 'on their bike' to find work.

However, this is to be too one-sided, as many of the trends that came to flourish in the nineties, regarding safety and the regulation of daily life, were being established in the 1980s—with for example the development of the issue of child safety and child abuse, an issue Margaret Thatcher endorsed herself, helping to promote the 'celebrity' campaign for Childline, a 24-hour help line for children.[3]

As the public sector was reorganised around the market it also developed a more legalistic rather than a political relationship with the public at the level of the individual. The internal coherence of organisations and the mechanism for relating to this more fragmented public led to charters and complaints procedures becoming institutionalised. The first charter, for example, was launched in 1982; dubbed the Council Tenants Charter, it popularised the sale of council houses to individuals.

Also, a more therapeutic approach to crime was developing—in part due to its individualistic nature. Victim Support Schemes grew and were being well funded by the government as another strand to the focus on law and order (Maquire and Pointing 1988). However, notwithstanding this financial support, victims of crime were often used politically, 'paraded' by Conservative politicians and by sections of the media as a 'symbol of disorder', not as the central focus for law and order policy or rhetoric itself (Phipps 1988: 180).[4]

Under Margaret Thatcher, authoritarian measures were developed to back up the battle against the 'enemy within', but otherwise the policing and regulation of people's daily lives was of little political significance. Antisocial behaviour was of no importance at this time nor was the term 'community safety'. The 'class struggle'—the confrontation with the unions—in particular with the miners between 1984 and 1985, and the political battle with Labourism and welfarism, of which the politicisation of crime was a part, appears to have given a certain coherence and political purpose to the conservative political elite. In the 1990s however, John Major could find little to replace this sense of purpose and the growing preoccupation with crime and order as a thing in itself emerged. The drive towards imprisonment, CCTV cameras, and an ever wider range of new laws to regulate society, came not with the politicisation of crime, but with the loss of any cohering sense of political purpose. Law, order and the control of behaviour rather than morals or politics increasingly became the new way to regulate society more directly.

The focus on the individual took a less political form at this time and a more fragmented and legalistic framework became established in many organisations and institutions. New charters and complaints procedures for individuals developed and the language of compensation grew. People living in an increasingly individuated society began to advance their claims for 'recognition' and sought protection from employers, from professional and commercial exchanges and from misfortune from one another.

LIBERTY AND LAGER LOUTS

The idea of 'restoring people to independence and self reliance', as Thatcher put it, meant that despite the attacks on the rights of pickets or demonstrators, the notion of the 'rights' and 'freedoms' of 'law abiding citizens' continued to influence Tory policies (Thatcher 1995: 7). Demonstrators and militants were criminalised and their freedoms curtailed within the discourse of 'public order', but wider law and order policies continued to be influenced and somewhat curtailed by a certain libertarianism within the ranks of the Conservative Party.[5]

Compared with the more victim centred policies developed in the 1990s, this notion of the rights bearing, 'self reliant' individual limited to some extent the policing and regulation of everyday life, as demonstrated within the debate about 'lager louts' in the late 1980s.

Following stories of drink fuelled fights in 1988 in 'once tranquil small towns', concern was raised within the press and by the police about the spread of 'spontaneous' violence and disorder something that was understood to no longer be simply an inner city issue (Measham and Brain 2005: 262). Problems emblematic of these 'problem areas' were now seen to be expanding across the nation—the disease of disorder was spreading and the government called upon to 'do something'. One suggestion was that the cost of alcohol be increased, something that could potentially limit the problem—but that would clearly affect 'innocent' drinkers. Observing the conflicting interests of individual safety and personal freedom, the *Times* noted at the time that, 'Last week, Douglas Hurd, the [Conservative] home secretary, tried to strike a balance between the demands of the anti-drink lobby and the traditional Tory regard for individual freedom', saying:

Few Englishmen are likely to welcome additional restrictions. They will ask why the actions of a hooligan minority should make it more diffi-cult or more expensive for them to enjoy a pint after a day's work or a glass of wine with a family meal. But ministers must also contend with the clear relationship between stupid drinking and crime or disorder (*Times* 26 June 1988).

However, the tension between the idea of the free individual and the developing shift towards a concern with regulating the activities of everyday behaviour was already changing and the focus of crime concern shifting from the (increasingly less significant) 'enemy within' onto other non-political expressions of public disorder. The invention of the term 'lager lout' reflected this change in 1988, as the *Guardian* noted, 'The police preoccupation a few years ago with the inner-city riots and violent unrest has given way to a con-cern about hooliganism in semi-rural towns and resorts' (*Guardian*, 6 April 1988). Noticeably however, it was not the Conservatives who first devel-oped initiatives based on these new 'panics', but Labour local authorities: The Labour led Coventry City Council, for example, being the first to intro-duce a ban on drinking in the street—something that the government were being pushed to do at a national level but refused. A major reason for this by-law it was argued, was not simply because of crime itself, but because the activities of these young people was 'causing distress' amongst the public (*Guardian* 6 October 1988). The 'vulnerable public' for the Labour council took priority over the 'individual freedoms of Englishmen'.

MAJOR REGULATION

Law and order in the 1980s arguably helped to develop what Heartfield describes as a 'police state' (2002: 165). The growing numbers of police-men and women, at a time when public spending on services was being squeezed elsewhere, related not simply to crime but to an increasing concern with public and political order. The Home Office admitted that the police had a 'privileged existence', and had received 52 per cent more funding in the decade following the Conservative election victory in 1979—recruiting 13,000 new officers (*Independent* 8 October 1988). Kenneth Newman, the chief constable of the Metropolitan Police Force, was quite clear about the role of the police at this time, arguing that 'It would be better if we stopped talking about crime prevention and lifting the whole thing to a higher level of generality represented by the words "social control"' (*Financial Times* 23 March 1983). Similarly, during the miners' strike the police in house journal was up front in explaining the role of the police.

Police authority, like the authority of the state from which it is derived, is *coercive*. . . . Where resource to force is necessary, as it inevitably is during mass public disorder, the underlining and defining character of state power—the monopoly of legitimate force—becomes apparent (*Police* September 1984).

Radical critics of the police had noted the political use of policing and the inflation of problems like the mugging 'panic' in the 1970s (Hall et al. 1978). Questions were raised at the time about the way crime and the exaggeration of violent crime in particular was being used as a device to both elevate certain social problems to the detriment of others and to justify increasing numbers and the increasing militarisation of the police.

However, despite the increased significance of law and order in politics at this time, the drive to control society directly and to regulate the behaviour of individuals more systematically did not develop until the 1990s. John Major's premiership, from 1990 to 1997, saw an acceleration of new laws, forms of policing and a greater use of prisons than any time since the Second World War. This was not, however, simply a continuation of Margaret Thatcher's political authoritarianism, but was a qualitatively different shift towards a more technical and 'apolitical' attempt to regulate society.

Margaret Thatcher had politicised crime in the 1980s and developed a more authoritarian society. New laws were developed against 'illegal immigrants' (British Nationality Act 1981); powers were developed against enemies of the state through the Prevention of Terrorism Acts (1984 and 1989), and demonstrators, pickets and marchers were regulated more directly via the Public Order Act of 1986. The fight against crime more generally was also incorporated into Thatcherism through the promotion of contrasting good honest 'British values' of hard work and enterprise. However, more broadly in society, outside of these 'high risk groups', crime and the general everyday antisocial behaviour of individuals was of far less importance—at least in terms of political rhetoric and legal sanction—than it was to become in the 1990s.[6] The idea of rights was also shifting now towards a focus upon the more fragmented notion of consumer and 'victims' rights. Problems that may have been voiced with reference to inequality now developed as part of a campaign for mistreated victims and institutions began to develop policies and practise accordingly.

Under John Major the individuated society became increasingly organised around crime and safety, not as a means to a wider political end, but as the end itself.

Politically, the Conservative Party lacked the coherence of the 1980s and appeared to almost miss the old enemy against which they had developed much of the rhetoric around the issue of crime and disorder. Indeed the old enemy had gone not only at home, but also abroad, with the collapse of the Berlin Wall and the disintegration of the Communist Bloc. The question of what the Conservatives stood for, and what political and moral principles they should fight for was less clear. At one level the government attempted to engage people as individual consumers through their Citizens Charter.

However within the political arena they continued to re-run the battles of the 1980s—an approach that looked increasingly out of date. In 1992 for example, during the general election campaign John Major endeavoured to portray Labour as a socialist party, despite the fact that the Labour manifesto—for the first time in its history—made no mention of socialism. The Conservatives won this election, with a significantly reduced majority, much to the surprise of most commentators. The pollsters themselves had predicted a Labour victory and afterwards explained that many Conservative voters appeared to be 'shy' about voting for John Major. Rather than the Tories carrying the nation with their policies it appeared more to be the case that votes had been cast largely because the electorate could see that There Was No Alternative. The lack of political dynamic at this time was subsequently represented in the way law and forms of regulation—rather than moral and political argument—increasingly became the more managerial way in which government carried out its business.

In 1993 the then Home Secretary Michael Howard 'broke the policy of a century by declaring that "Prison works"' (Dunbar and Langdon 1998: 115). Prison numbers, which had increased between 1951 and 1991 by only 11,000, began to increase significantly and within a decade a further 25,000 people had been imprisoned (*Guardian* 14 October 2005). Similarly, the number of children under the age of 18 in the prison system has more than doubled since 1993.[7] Howard argued that the criminal justice system needed to be transformed from a system concerned with the criminal to one based on the protection of the public. Now the Criminal Justice System itself became the means through which society and the behaviour of the individual would be changed. As Dunbar and Langdon note:

> Both penal policy and relations between government and judiciary had been changed far more within the lifetime of the Major administration than had happened at any of the changes of government since the end of the Second World War, at least (Dunbar and Langdon 1998: 2).

Rather than using law and order to crusade and battle the 'enemy within', John Major in 1993 simply promoted a 'crusade against crime' (Dunbar and Langdon 1998: 115). Now a new enemy was discovered and the focus was placed upon a different section of the working class, the 'underclass' and teenage criminals—joy riders and persistent young offenders. Subsequently, laws were introduced that created, 'a new generation of child prisoners', returning the British Criminal Justice System, 'not . . . to the 1970s but to a period preceding the Children Act 1908' (Goldson 1997: 30). The focus on young people intensified and Home Secretary Michael Howard explained that self-centred hoodlums would no longer be able to hide from the law simply because of their age. The reach of 'law and order' it seemed had not gone far enough into society and communities, and now needed to stretch down even further to punish children. Goldson notes how despite the 'most consistent, vitriolic and vindictive affront to justice and welfare', under Margaret Thatcher, the criminal justice approach to young people developed under principles that resulted in, 'diversion, decriminalisation and decarceration in policy and practice with children in trouble'.

Contrasting Thatcher's promotion of moral values and belief in individualism with the approach of John Major, Hugo Young observed that the, 'Victorian values, to which she pledged herself, were essentially an economic rule-book for individualists, reminding them that thrift and self-help were the necessary accompaniments to both individual and national prosperity'. Rarely, Young notes, did Thatcher, 'posit a social order handed down from above'. However, as Young remarked in relation to Major's promotion of 'family values',

> It is a disciplinary slogan, voiced in ministerial rhetoric which excoriates parents for their slack attitudes, and single parents for even existing. Far from there being no such thing as society, the component members of society need to be told to brace up and take their social responsibilities for what goes on around them, whether through ill-trained children, negligent pastors, unwatchful neighbours or other agents of a failed community. The manual to be issued today from the Department for Education, laying down modes of behaviour, clothing and discipline in schools, marks another stride towards a society upon which Major's ministers, more and more desperate to achieve social control, are trying to impose standards which they, at the centre, define (*Guardian* 4 January 1994).

The increasing use of law to enforce moral behaviour, and of prison to lock more people up, indicated, not the rise of the moral right, but rather its demise. Now more than ever, law and order became the, 'only effective deterrent in a society that no longer [knew] the difference between right and wrong' (Lasch 1977: 187). The 'individual' that had been promoted in the 1980s and the freedom of this individual were now seen less as a positive alternative to the collectivism of Labour, than as a potential problem. With a declining sense of the potential of the individual and a growing concern with order in society freedom itself began to become more problematic in the government's eyes and the meaning of freedom shifted onto issues of protection.

The policing and regulation of public space around this time became more systematic, with for example the massif expansion of CCTV cameras across the UK from 1994 to 1997, largely due to new central government funding of £45 million (*Guardian* 2 April 2006). In Scotland policing was being geared up to 'prevent' crime and violence as part of an attempt to protect the public. In 1993 for example Strathclyde police launched Operation Blade—a campaign that resulted in tens of thousands of young men being searched for knives. This was accompanied by a successful proposal and adoption of the Carrying of Knives (Scotland) Act 1993, which toughened the laws on knife carrying with a maximum penalty of 2 years' imprisonment. Glasgow itself launched its own Citywatch CCTV scheme in 1994, and in 1996 the city enforced a ban on drinking in the street.

The accelerated, more direct, and technical, dynamic to regulate society was emerging at this time and accelerated further in 1993 in part due to the failed 'back to basics' campaign—a campaign associated with 'good old British' and indeed 'English' values of the past. With a declining political and economic coherence and dynamic the Conservatives under John Major became increasingly focused on problem groups in society and moralising about the behaviour of these groups grew. However, the use of traditional morality by the political elite was becoming increasingly problematic at this time both as a political tool and even in terms of cohering the Conservatives themselves. Despite the decline of the old enemy within, and indeed arguably because of it—rather than crime and disorder becoming less significant within politics—it became more important. Now the problem of crime and behaviour appeared to be spreading, like the problem of the 'lager louts' a few years earlier, into an increasing variety of 'cultures of crime'.

In October 1993 as part of the 'back to basics' theme, John Major projected an image of 1950s England as a model for society but even within the right-wing press this idea was seen as quaint but silly. As one *Times* columnist noted, 'Apart from Michael Howard's initiatives on crime, there was little hint of what government could do, short of exhortation, to take society back to older values' (*Times* 9 October 1993).

THE UNDERCLASS

In 1989 communism was 'defeated' and the political landscape that had existed for much of the 20th century was transformed. In Britain, the victory over socialism was also enhanced with the virtual elimination of the trade union movement from the political scene. However, within only a few years any sense of jubilation at this historic transformation in politics had all but disappeared and a growing feeling of unease, indeed of decay began to set in. Rather than revitalising the institutions of Western nations, the loss of the 'red menace' appeared to undermine the sureness and purpose of them. As Susan Buck-Morss notes in her book *The Passing of Mass Utopia in East and West*, 'It is striking how timid the "free world" has become since the end of the Cold War. Everyone is for democracy, but no one trusts its institutions' (Buck-Morss 2000: 256). The market had triumphed, but there were few who felt triumphant.

A new problem 'class' emerged in Britain at this time—the so-called underclass—a new enemy, but more problematically for the government one that had grown during the Conservative years in office. Initially in the mid-eighties the few articles discussing the 'underclass' did so with sympathy for this impoverished group, and framed the discussion in economic terms—their concerns relating to unemployment and the inadequate jobs available for sections of the working class. The debate turned, in the late eighties and then more significantly around 1993, into a moral concern about single parents and criminality—the *Times and Sunday Times* having over 150 articles that discussed this problem in 1994. The discussion about this dependant 'class' allowed for a rerun of the fight against welfarism—but the enemy was no longer the organised working class, but the 'feckless poor' and their children.

Discussing the underclass debate in America, the criminologist Jonathan Simon argued that, with reference to the notion of 'sovereign relationships' where people within a moral relationship, show up as subjects of praise and blame, 'The state's efforts to punish members of the underclass who commit crimes is one of the last traces of a commitment to a shared community with them' (Simon 1987). Simon had little sympathy for the underclass theorists, but observed that by promoting an absolute moral outlook this debate had a universal aspect—a promotion of a common standard to which all should aspire. However, despite this, the British debate about the 'underclass' in the 1990s, and the discussion about the growing problem of crime and 'yobs' contained more than a hint of despair, rather than any great belief in the possibility of reconnecting with this 'underclass'. In 1994 for example, one columnist in the *Times* argued that

> A whole society is under threat and the young are being dragged into a cycle of abuse and despair that will further expand the ranks of the underclass. Apart from the material costs and the shattered lives, this places an intolerable burden on our prisons and court system. All right-thinking people agree that if the plague is not defeated we shall all suffer (*Times* 12 June 1994).

In reality, the idea of a 'shared community' was dying out under John Major's Conservative government—indeed the individually focused 'rights' and 'charters' promoted by the Conservatives through the 1980s and the defeat of the labour movement had helped to create a more asocial climate—something the narrow promotion of economic individualism simply reinforced. Having undermined the post-war collectivist welfare framework that had laid the foundations for the operation of the state and the relationship between state institutions and the public, a sense of confusion about what the new political and 'moral' order should be emerged. This concern about the state of society and its moral purpose was reflected at the time in the publication of conservatives books concerned with *The Demoralization of Western Society* (Himmelfarb 1995), and of a *Loss of Virtue: Moral Confusion and Social Disorder* (Anderson 1992).

The political dynamic that had been largely based upon a challenge to the labour movement and a promotion of economic individualism had by the early 1990s declined as a coherent framework around which the Conservatives could project themselves and engage the public. Those on the right now began to moralise about behaviour in society—and in particular about the behaviour of the 'underclass' and those 'yobs' and 'persistent young offenders' associated with them. However without a wider political, economic or social solution to these problems this moralising was largely empty of moral substance or belief. Lacking any coherence or belief in their own moral pronouncements or the capacity to carry the public the government increasingly sought to use laws, surveillance and regulations to enforce social order directly.

The debate around the 'underclass' was polarised to the extent that liberal thinkers were repelled by the moral condemnation of the poor, however there was nevertheless a certain acceptance, even with some on the 'left', that this new 'class' existed and were a growing problem for society. As early as 1988 for example, Tony Blair argued that

> It remains to be seen whether, with poverty and plenty growing side by side, 'the vessel of state is driven between the Scylla and Charybdis of anarchy and despotism' as Shelley predicted 150 years ago. It may take the poll tax to turn despair into revolt. Or it may never happen. What is certain is that we are now in the process of creating an underclass of humanity in modern Britain that is becoming dangerously adrift from the rest of society (*Times* 1 March 1988).

By 1994 the sense that this 'underclass' had now become established led the liberal John McVicar (the American Charles Murray's adversary in the underclass debate) to argue that

> It is grotesquely irresponsible for him [Murray] to write off a whole swath of people who—while they do constitute a *parasitic and predatory cancer*—are themselves the victims of high unemployment, the increasing disparity in wealth and income and, as the sociologist David Downes once put it, 'the Faustian experiments in social engineering of the Conservative administrations since 1979' (*Sunday Times* 4 September 1994; my italics).

Illustrating the degree to which some 'radical' commentators accepted the extent of the problem of this growing 'cancer' within the working class, the former *Marxism Today* editor Martin Jacques, argued that it was a problem that engulfed 30 per cent of the British population (Cullen 1996: 175).

The difference between the moral conservatives and many liberals and left wingers was in the acceptance or rejection of traditional morality—not in the acceptance of the growing problem of a disordered 'class'. Many on the left, as Cullen noted were no longer promoting a structural analysis or solution to these problems, as they had done previously, but rather, they too, had become, 'obsessed with the moral behaviour of a marginal layer of those living in the poorest districts of British society'. In effect, Cullen explained, 'the term "poor" no longer represents a group of people who are suffering the effects of unemployment or low incomes but simply those who behave in irresponsible and criminal ways' (Cullen 1996: 175).

The debate about the underclass was to some extent a re-run of the 19th century concern with what was then called the residuum, however a major difference was that in the 1880s when this original debate started there was a growing confidence in a political and social solution to this problem. This contrasted with the discussion about the underclass:

> The discussion of the 'underclass' today is strikingly reminiscent of the preoccupation of the late Victorian reformers with the 'residuum'; a section of the poor marked by the depraved and criminal behaviour of its members, deemed to be responsible for their own poverty. But whereas the late-nineteenth century reformers came to regard programmes of state intervention as the solution to the problem of poverty, today's commentators regard the welfare state as the source, and despair of any practical solution (Cullen 1996: 174).

Statistically crime was high at this time, however, there was also a more profound sense of doom which influenced the understanding of crime and disorder. For the right, welfarism was demoralising society, while for the 'left' it was more that Thatcherism had destroyed communities and created a fragmented and greedy society. Whatever the perceived causes however, there was a more general belief amongst the political elite that there was a seriously dangerous 'underclass' growing, and that crime was becoming more ingrained within the culture of society itself.

THE END OF 'CULTURE'

In September 1994 John Major argued for a 'national anti-yob culture', calling for respect to be instilled in children—and also for local authorities to stamp out excessive public drinking. At the time there was a growing discussion about the problem of alien 'cultures'. A 'crime culture', a 'knife culture' and a 'gun culture' were just a few of the key new 'cultures' that were discussed. The image of these dangerous cultures—gave crime and violence a new more permanent and ingrained dimension—something that was understood to be both a challenge to the wider culture of society, but that was also part of that 'greedy' culture. Young people in particular were seen as being part of these 'cultures'—a problem that captured the imagination of conservative but also some radical thinkers. Andrew Calcutt in his *Critique of the Cultures of Crime*, notes for example that while the conservative Theodore Dalrymple talked about the, 'lost children of the video nasty age', and the Sunday Times discussed the, 'savage generation', radicals like Beatrix Campbell warned of the danger of delinquent lads being, 'surrounded by macho propaganda ... soaked in globally transmitted images and ideologies of butch and brutal solutions to life's difficulties' (Calcutt 1996: 29). Youth crime was increasingly being understand and represented through this discussion as a more profound problem for society. Crime was not so much an event or something that was committed, but rather a way of life, something that went to the very heart of what young people, and particularly young men were.

Regardless of the myth and reality of the problem of youth behaviour at the time the extent to which they were understood as 'cultures' gives a sense not only of the perceived problems, but also the sense of impotence and perhaps desperation being expressed by thinkers and politicians. The declining coherence of politics itself was arguably leading to both a profound sense of loss—of 'growing disorder'—and also a sense of distance from young people. Young people it seems were becoming the new enemy within—beyond the reach of society—indeed beyond reason. As Graef notes, at this point in time, the enemy of the 'miners of the mid 1980s [was] replaced by the minors of the mid 1990s' (Graef 1995 quoted in Scraton 1997: 134).

In the mid-1990s the Conservative government was in disarray and the election of a Labour government seemed increasingly inevitable. The issue of crime was if anything more important now and the fear of crime was high—but despite the tough Conservative approach to the problem they were unable to engage the electorate around their policies. There were clearly many reasons for this—and people do not simply vote for a government around the issue of crime—there were significant economic problems and conflict over the issue of Europe for example. However, as we will, see 'New Labour', as the Labour Party was now known, had itself made law and order a central issue.

From the 1980s on, the Conservative party had used moral rhetoric and developed law and order as both a tool with which to beat the left, but also as a way to promote an alternative, a new vision for Britain. Much of the moral rhetoric of the Thatcher government did not result in a coherent policy on the family (Durham 1991: 142): however, traditional institutions like the family and the nation were central to the rhetoric of 1980s Conservatives. By the early 1990s, however, the defeat of the labour movement had created a far more fragmented society, while the cohering basis of the nation and the family was in decline. At this point in time, the law and order policies of the Conservatives changed under John Major and a more systematic and diffuse form of regulation emerged. Major continued to frame much of his crime 'crusade' within the political rhetoric of the past: however, moral pontificating about single parents, and law and order initiatives targeted at ravers and the underclass based on a watered down form of 'class war', could no longer cohere the conservative elite, or engage significant sections of the public as it once had. It was New Labour who were able to engage more systematically with the fragmented and 'vulnerable' public outside of the old moral and political framework of the 1980s, and were able to become the new party of law and order.

NEW PARTY OF LAW AND ORDER

With the decline of the labour movement and the welfare state as a framework for government to organise society and engage with the public, a new basis for policy development and public legitimacy was sought. The collective public of the past was now far more fragmented—and policies increasingly developed to relate to people as individuals, or as consumers of services. However, the loss of collective purpose in politics, of both left and right, resulted not in the dynamic entrepreneurial individual but in a more insecure and uncertain subject. Having jettisoned its relationship with 'old' Labour and without the libertarian outlook of sections of the right, the new Labour leadership was able to reengage more systematically with this individual through their sense of fear and anxiety. This relationship was less political, less a relationship between active individuals and their political representatives than a new form of advocacy and protection of the newly conceptualised *vulnerable public*.

The 1997 General Election brought the first Labour government to power since 1979. It was also the first time the Labour Party made crime a major issue within its manifesto (Downes and Morgan 1997). In the Labour Party document *Tackling the Causes of Crime: Labour's Proposals to Prevent Crime and Criminality*, the extent of the problem of crime and the importance of overcoming the fear of it were explained thus: 'Tackling the *epidemic* of crime and disorder will be a top priority for Labour in government' (Labour 1996: 4)—and—'Securing people's physical security, freeing them from the fear of crime and disorder *is the greatest liberty government can guarantee*'(Labour 1996: 6; my italics).

Before the 1997 election—at least within Labour Party manifestos—crime had been either ignored or associated with wider 'social' issues. As the *Guardian* noted, comparing former Labour Party leader Neil Kinnock with Tony Blair:

> There are areas where Neil Kinnock's manifesto barely ventured. In 1992, crime, for instance, rated five paragraphs and mainly concentrated on improving street lighting. Now law and order rates two pages with the now familiar 'zero tolerance' strategies and child curfews fighting for room next to pledges to early legislation for a post-Dunblane ban on all hand guns. Such policies seemed unthinkable five years ago. However, in this case, Blair's 'radicalism'—with its social authoritarian

tinge—may play better with the centre rather than the Left (*Guardian* 4 April 1997).

The shift in New Labour began in earnest in 1993 when Tony Blair made his first major speech attacking 'crime and the causes of crime'. Here both crime and 'chronic' forms of disruptive behaviour were targeted and subsequently a 'zero tolerance' approach to antisocial behaviour was proclaimed and the Labour leadership moved to distance itself from the notion of crime and delinquency being directly associated with inequality. A 'Quiet Life' from nuisance neighbours and aggressive beggars was proposed, and the idea of curfews for young children aired. When the Conservative government announced a version of the US policy of 'three strikes and you're out', and Jack Straw, Labour's Shadow Home Secretary accepted this policy, a clear 'break with past Labour policy' was established (Downes and Morgan 1997: 100–106).

In Labour's *Partners against Crime*, produced in 1993, the shift in their approach to law and order issues was clarified. Serious acts of violence that 'hit the headlines', as well as daily burglaries, car crime, abuse and petty vandalism, helped to 'make life hell', it was argued, especially for the poor and the vulnerable. Crime was now understood by the emerging Labour leadership as not a transitory occurrence but as an *endemic* part of life that both undermined communities and individuals sense of well being (Labour Party 1993). One problem identified by the *Partners against Crime* paper was that of eroding confidence in the criminal justice system. The government, it argued, had been 'thoughtless, insensitive' and 'cruel' in their treatment of victims of crime and the solution to this insensitivity is to make 'the whole of the criminal justice system become more victim focused' (Labour Party 1993: 22).

By incorporating the fear of crime and also more petty forms of disruptive behaviour in the discussion of crime, New Labour understood there to be a 'chronic' 'epidemic' of crime and disorder. The logic of this approach meant that the entire population became conceptualised as potential 'victims of crime'.

Focused on the public as potential victims of crime, the concern was with the 'damage' done to individuals—the 'fear' and 'misery' caused by a 'life of hell'. Rather than the moral, political or economic concerns about crime, here a central focus became the individual and their personal well being—something that could disrupt communities and society itself. According to this outlook, the greatest liberty Labour could bring to the public was to free people from the fear of crime and disorder. By being thoughtful, sensitive and caring, the victims of crime would thus regain a trust in the criminal justice system and indeed in the Labour Party itself.

In this respect, New Labour had not simply moved away from 'Old' Labour's understanding of crime, but had also moved on from the

Conservative understanding of the problem. An example of this change can be seen within the debate about aggressive beggars.

'AGGRESSIVE' BEGGING

The concern about victims of crime has developed particularly from the 1980s, however the centrality of victimhood to Labour Party campaigning only emerged in the mid-1990s and was expressed explicitly by Shadow Home Secretary Jack Straw when he launched an attack on aggressive begging, winos, addicts and squeegee merchants in 1995 (*Guardian* 5 September 1995).

The question of street begging had been raised a year earlier by Prime Minister John Major during a European Election. Major, whose, 'personal rating [had] plummeted to record lows following the [economic] debacle of Black Wednesday', successfully attempted to raise his profile and support by attacking street beggars as an eyesore (*Times* 3 June 1994).

The Chancellor Kenneth Clarke supported the prime minister's attack on beggars differentiating between alcoholics and mentally ill people and those, 'beggars in designer jeans', who received benefits and, 'think it is perfectly acceptable to add to their income by begging'. For Clarke then the problem was the act of begging by people who wanted 'something for nothing'. The focus of concern was not the beggars behaviour to the public, but his 'scrounging' and fraudulent relationship with the state and therefore with society (*Times* 3 June 1994).

Tory supporters were reported to be singing the praises of the prime minister for his attack on beggars, 'Why should I be paying taxes to support them?' and, 'Half the beggars make themselves homeless', being two examples of the response to government's attack on beggaring (*Times* 3 June 1994). Tony Blair, who was soon to become the new Labour leader, in contrast ridiculed Mr Major's concern about begging, saying, 'There is a bloke living in his street who is dishevelled and aggressive and keeps taking money off people— Kenneth Clark [the Conservative Chancellor]' (*Times* 3 June 1994).

In a media search of 'aggressive begging', the first mention given to this problem in British newspaper was in 1988 with reference to a law in Seattle outlawing this behaviour (*Times* 18 September 1988). The *Guardian* first mentioned aggressive begging in June 1991, this time with reference to a move by the mayor of Atlanta to similarly outlaw begging. It was not until May of 1994 that the issue of 'aggressive begging' became a national political issue and thus a recognised if contested social problem. Major's attack on begging was seen as a European election stunt to gain popular appeal from the right and came at the same time as an anti-begging campaign in the right-wing Daily Express. The issue of begging itself was attacked by the prime minister, including aggressive begging with the *typical* beggar being defined within a framework of welfare scrounging. Labour's Jack Straw at this time acted as a key opposition to Major, who he described as, 'climbing into the gutter alongside the unfortunate beggars' (*Times* 29 May 1994). Major was also attacked by the Bishop of Salisbury and other Labour shadow ministers for blaming the poor for their own plight.

However a year later to the surprise of many traditional left and liberal supporters of Labour the shadow home secretary Jack Straw, using American labels, attacked, 'aggressive begging of winos, addicts and squeegee merchants' (*Guardian* 5 September 1995). Seen as a shift to the right following his visit to New York where Straw met Mayor Rudy Giuliani, various homeless charities and liberal groups and newspapers condemned his 'uncaring' remarks.

Straw's attack on aggressive begging was more sustained than John Major's had been and was presented not as a one off piece of electioneering but as a central element of New Labour's law and order policy. For the first time in the history of British politics Labour were seen and described as putting the Tories on the defensive over crime. Indeed, now it was the turn of the Conservative government to call foul and demand that crime—according to the official statistics—was actually falling.

The attack by the shadow home secretary was linked to John Major's, 'understand a little less—condemn a little more' outlook, developed by the Conservative Party, but the framework for this attack was different. Whereas John Major and his chancellor Kenneth Clarke had attacked the *illegal* problem of begging itself as part of a problem of welfare cheats, Jack Straw was not concerned with the act of begging so much as the *aggressive behaviour* that came with it. Where Clarke had removed 'alcoholics and mentally ill people' from his condemnation of scrounging beggars, for Straw all beggars who acted aggressively were condemned. In practice the alcoholics and mentally ill beggars were perhaps even more likely than the 'scroungers' to be the aggressive problem identified by Straw.

Two years after this initial attack on aggressive begging an initiative in Winchester was launched to clear the streets of aggressive beggars. Wanted posters were put up in off licences to stop the sale of alcohol to the worst culprits, while begging boxes were displayed by banks and shops for anyone that wanted to give to the beggars. Begging was 'legalised' and indeed carried out by the authorities at the same time as the intimidating behaviour of the beggars was criminalised (*Guardian* 14 June 1997).

By the time the election year of 1997 came around the soon to be prime minister, Tony Blair, had elaborated on the *typical* and problematic beggar. This was not a man quietly scrounging money off the public, but the often drunken 'in your face' lout who would, 'push people against a wall and demand money effectively with menace' (*Guardian* 8 January 1997). No figures for the rise in bullying beggars were given but using personal anecdotal evidence Tony Blair noted that he himself sometimes felt frightened when he dropped his children off at King's Cross—a notorious venue for 'winos', prostitutes and 'aggressive beggars'.

In this new offensive against street disorder New Labour redefined begging not as an offence against the laws of society or a political or social problem of welfare cheats but specifically as an offence against the public sense of well-being. Rather than the criminal act of begging being defined as the problem or the scrounging of money by those already receiving benefits, the problem was relocated onto the non-criminal attitude and behaviour of the beggars and the assumed reaction of the public.

Jack Straw believed that the Tories had failed to understand the significance of street disorder as a cause of the fear of crime, the 'loutish behaviour and incivility' that made the streets, 'uncomfortable, especially for women and black and Asian people' (*Guardian* 9 September 1995). For Straw the non-criminal acts involved in 'street disorder' as much as the violent criminal act of 'mugging' contributed to the fear of crime which then sent neighbourhoods into a spiral of decline (*Guardian* 6 September 1995). The public were presented as being *victimised* by the aggressiveness of the beggars and were described by Jack Straw and Labour leader Tony Blair as being 'intimidated', 'harassed' and 'bullied' by the 'incivility' and 'loutish' behaviour of beggars. Straw, using a well worn feminist slogan, demanded that we—'reclaim the streets'—streets that had been 'brutalised' by beggars and graffiti vandals. Except here the streets were not being reclaimed by people acting themselves—rather they were being made safe by the government and the police.

In this respect the shift in Labour policy was less of an authoritarian move towards 'public order' where a problematic and unlawful group are identified and punished. Rather Straw's concern was with a *disordered public*. It was the intimidation of the public that was of concern. It was not so much a move to defend the law and order of society itself so much as an attempt to advocate on behalf of the victims of this form of harassment. It was therefore not the illegal act of begging that was problematised but the previously non-criminal attitude and 'aggressiveness' of the beggar that was made criminal. The offence was not an illegal one against the state, but a form of bad behaviour against the emotional well-being of the individual. Also, whereas the Conservatives had attempted to give the issue a political basis by discussing the problem of welfare cheats, Labour's defence of the public sense of well-being lacked any wider political content. In this respect, despite the problematic nature of the Conservative approach, the legal and political framework within which this was carried out contained a social element to it—the beggar being held to account by society, by law and by politics. Labour's approach was *asocial* and was predicated upon an engagement with the vulnerable individual. The standard of behaviour was not set so much by society so much as by the feelings of the individual—for whom the Labour Party would now advocate.

Interestingly, in an ICM opinion poll of nearly 1500 people, 41% of those questioned said they did indeed find beggars 'offensive' but 51% said they did not. The difference in response between Conservative and Labour voters was minimal. Straw argued that he was acting in the public interest because of the number of complaints Labour MPs and councillors received about this matter (*Guardian* 23 April 1997). The need for a zero tolerance approach to antisocial behaviour was called for. The term zero tolerance being used for one of the first times by politicians since the zero tolerance, anti-domestic violence campaign was launched in Edinburgh in 1992. But instead of defending 'disempowered' women in the private sphere it was now the disempowered individual in the public realm that was central. Many shocked Labour supporters and groups came out against this 'right-wing' campaign and demanded to know what Labour intended to do not just about crime but about the 'causes' of crime. Both Jack Straw and Tony Blair remained unrepentant but noted that they would provide support and housing for the homeless but once this was done there could be no excuse for aggressive begging.

More problematically for Blair and Straw, the issue of beggars as not the perpetrators of violence but the victims of it was raised by a number of charities. The St Margo's Trust questioned whether treating the *vulnerable* in this way would help (*Guardian* 6 September 1995). Crisis argued that, 'Our research indicates that homeless people beg as a last resort and it is a humiliating experience. Crisis would not condone violence but homeless people are more likely to be on the receiving end than be the aggressors' (*Guardian* 11 October 1995).

By advocating on behalf of the *real victims*, the homeless charities put the Labour leadership on the defensive in a way that those arguing for welfare support rather than punishment had been unable to do. Eventually Tony Blair gave an interview to the homeless magazine *The Big Issue*, where he defended his views about aggressive beggars. Here he reiterated his concerns about intimidating behaviour but pointed out that this was not a policy of simply clearing beggars off the street, saying, 'I . . . wouldn't say it's satisfactory to have people arrested for begging. That's a 19th century approach'. He pointed out that he was aware that beggars were often victims themselves of aggressive behaviour which he equally condemned. Blair's approach was to 'make the streets safe' for everyone—'What is needed is not abuse of people who have become homeless, often through great misfortune, but measures to get them out of their situation' (*Guardian* 8 January 1997). In this way Blair extended his policy of defending victims of aggressive and abusive behaviour to include not only the general public but also beggars who were treated badly by the public.

The following day, in a letter to the *Guardian*, John Wadham the Director of Liberty questioned the move by the Labour leader to see social problems as resolvable by 'more laws, more criminal offences and more prosecutions'. However, Wadham also conceded that, 'none of us wants to be harassed as we walk down streets covered in graffiti'. Wadham, was uncomfortable with the overt criminalisation of the homeless as he saw it but had to some degree accept the terms of the debate and the 'social problem' identified by Jack Straw and Tony Blair—that of aggressive beggars harassing the public.

Before 1994 aggressive begging was not a recognised social problem within the press or one being campaigned around by politicians—indeed the term itself at a public level did not even exist. By the time of the election year—1997—the notion of aggressive beggars harassing the public was established. The image portrayed by Blair and Straw was of a victimised public being hounded by these abusive beggars—welfare scrounging was not an issue—indeed the question of begging that had been understood within Labour ranks for decades as an issue of inequality reflecting the need for social change was transformed into one of policing the behaviour of these beggars. The problem of begging according to New Labour was less to do with the welfare of the beggar, but with the well-being of the public. The policing of these beggars was not based on a concern with public order as such but with the damage being done to individual members of the public by the 'abusive' beggars. Despite concerns by various homeless charities, the idea of protecting a vulnerable public was hard to attack. Indeed the counter argument to Labour was that the homeless were even more vulnerable and more likely to be victimised than to be victimisers, however if the problem for homeless people was also that of the antisocial behaviour of others, then the need to resolve this problem—whether of public or homeless antisocial behaviour was accepted. As Jack Straw pointed out his concern was with the 'liberty of victims' whoever they may be (*Guardian* 6 September 1995).

The politicisation and problematisation of aggressive begging was dependant upon an outlook that understood the problem of crime as one of incivility that undermined the feeling of security of the public, and with this a focus on the victims of this behaviour was central. The legitimation gained by the Labour approach was here based not on a political battle between those for or against welfarism, or in defence of society's laws, but on a more therapeutically oriented relationship with individuals (Nolan 1998). The connection between the individual and the state was now more direct and based less on the collective will of the people represented in the laws of society than in the protection of the atomised individual's emotional well-being.

NEW LABOUR AND COMMUNITY SAFETY

The example of the 'aggressive beggar' is useful in that it indicates the attempt by New Labour to change their relationship with the public and develop a form of *advocacy* to engage, what they understood to be a fundamentally vulnerable individual. The approach adopted by the Labour party and the justificatory framework that was being developed was now more therapeutic than political—safety, and particularly the feeling of safety, being the goal.

The use of 'safety' as a political goal developed through the 1990s within both the Conservative and Labour Party, and began to be a more significant basis for developing a relationship between the government, local authorities and individuals. The relationship with the public was transformed in this period from a political one to a more technical and managerial form of protection. A key example of this new relationship was the increasing centrality of ideas associated with 'safety'—like Community Safety, a concept that became one of the new organising principles for local authorities.

Safety in respect to community development emerged as an economic issue under Margaret Thatcher's government, and related to regeneration initiatives developed with the promotion of 'Safer Cities' in the late 1980s and early 1990s. While moving the idea of safety more centrally into the workings of local authorities, safer cities remained, to a degree, an attempt to improve the economic regeneration of an area through safety improvements, and also an attempt to involve businesses in the development of crime prevention initiatives (Cummings 1997). In a sense Safer Cities was more about an internal organisation of local authorities and the development of interagency co-operation than a relationship with the public. But from an initial attempt in the late 1980s to use safety initiatives to improve business confidence and increase entrepreneurialism (Gilling 1999), as the 1990s progressed, the issue of safety became a more central focus for local authorities in their attempt to reengage with the public and develop services for them. Here the re-creation of communities and the relationship between the political elite and state institutions developed more systematically in relation to 'safety' as an end in itself. Emerging during the final years of the Conservative government, the significance of community safety initiatives increased significantly under New Labour from 1997. Where Thatcher had understood the creation of 'safer cities' as a means to developing the economic basis of communities, increasingly 'community safety' was the end point of the new therapeutically conceptualised community.

The development of policies around the idea of 'community safety' had little existence in the public realm until 1987, when it was radical and dejected Labour supporters—criminologists and feminists—who helped develop this idea. In this year the term became more commonly used in the press with reference to the policing and community safety units set up in Labour-controlled London boroughs. Here, the relationship between Labour councils and the public was more explicitly developed within a framework of safety, and helped move these local authorities away from a welfare model to one based more on the protection of individuals and 'victimised groups'.[8]

As the nature of politics changed and the public, particularly the working class, became more disaggregated, the relationship between the state and the individual increasingly became organised around safety issues. This development also emerged within the workplace at this time and helped to transform the relationship between the public and many public sector workers. Reflecting the more insecure and fragmented climate of the 1990s, this relationship developed around the sentiment of vulnerability. Professions that were renowned for their 'caring' approach to a public of which they once felt part were increasingly encouraged to monitor the behaviour of their 'clients' and 'customers', and to protect their members from antisocial behaviour.

Trade unions, for example, transformed their role in this period, from one of collective bargaining to agencies involved in protecting the security of their members. At the Trades Union Congress annual meeting in 1996, Frank Chapman of the electronics union the AEEU explained that, 'Our members want zero tolerance of criminal, offensive and loutish behaviour'.[9] At the same conference, Tony Rouse of the Civil and Public Services Association said that his staff, 'go to work daily knowing they may be seriously assaulted', while Bernadette Hillon of the shop-workers' union USDAW explained how 350,000 sales staff suffered violence at work in 1995—partly because of people 'losing it' when they bought lottery tickets (*Guardian* 11 September 1996).

Despite a lack of figures to compare the level of victimisation by the public with past experiences, the notion that antisocial behaviour was on the rise became commonplace and public sector workers were increasingly encouraged to institutionalise measures to evaluate the extent of the victimisation of their workers—victimisation and violence being redefined as not only acts of physical, but also verbal, 'assault' (Waiton 2001: 40). Local Authorities, and Labour Authorities in particular, also began to develop the notion of 'community safety' as a priority category around which to develop services, and 'multi-agency' initiatives were recommended by the Audit Commission in 1996 which suggested a statutory duty be imposed on local authorities to establish youth offending teams from representatives of social services, health and education authorities as well as the traditional law enforcement agencies (Waiton 2001: 31).[10]

By the 1997 general election, the 'politics of left and right' had little meaning. *Now politics was increasingly about the managing of public services and the management of public insecurities and behaviour.*[11] Indeed, with the end of welfarism and 'Old' Labour, the promotion of concerns connected to antisocial behaviour were developed in the 1990s most fervently by sections of the labour movement.

Community safety was 'pioneered initially as a social democratic and 'welfarist' antidote to the retributive drift in national criminal justice policy'. It was a term and framework that attempted to 'tackle certain risks and sources of vulnerability' especially by local government—and particularly Labour local authorities, and as such it developed the notion of a new collective or communal approach around the issue of safety (Squires 1997). This new approach was seen by some on the left as being 'ostensibly positive, progressive and, even democratic' (Squires 1997) but as Gilling notes, 'On another level, however, it is possible to discern a subtle but highly important manipulation of community safety into a more coercive or intolerant form' (Gilling 1997).

Prior to the 1990s, the Labour Party, the labour movement and Labour local authorities had often acted as a barrier to the politicisation of crime as a social problem. With the transformation of Labour politics, not only was this barrier removed, but also New Labour organisations become the most vociferous advocates of community safety. In the 1990s, unions and local authorities, in unison with Labour politicians, developed a relationship with the public based not on a wider social, political or moral framework but focused upon the vulnerable individual and his or her sense of security and well-being. The relationship with a 'victimised' public was also being developed by the Conservative government, although with one foot still in the past, there remained a tendency for the Tories to prioritise the targeting of deviant 'groups' within a more class-based political, and traditional moralistic, framework. For example with the Criminal Justice Act of 1994, the Conservatives targeted particular deviant groups like squatters, new age travellers and ravers—an Act that received significant opposition from the liberal press.

Unlike the Conservatives who continued to use the traditional moral and confrontational rhetoric of the 1980s in their condemnation of yobs and criminals, New Labour adopted the more 'amoral' form of moralising that relied not upon political and traditional values but upon an individuated sense of fear and insecurity. New Labour's *cosmopolitan authoritarianism* was far more appropriate for the more 'liquid' relationships of the time (Bauman 2000a). *Relating to the public as vulnerable individuals, Tony Blair was able to tap into the culture of fear and use 'safety' as a modern day slogan—a therapeutic promise of a quiet life for all.*

Labour were also more able than the 'uncaring' Conservatives, to stand up for 'victimised groups', for women, blacks and gays and to promote a 'caring' concern for the vulnerable but within the context of being 'tough on crime'.

Community safety was also an idea being developed by the Home Office in the late eighties and early 1990s—for example with the publication of the Morgan Report in 1991—an issue around which a certain crisis of legitimacy within the police and criminal justice system could be overcome. 'Community safety', as Gilling notes manifested itself as another 'ideology of partnership: a sense of togetherness and unity of purpose'. It was also able to overlap with the 'preventionist consensus' over crime, especially 'over minor crimes and disorder'. Something that connected the zero tolerance approach with community safety (Gilling 1997).

In the 1990s, 'vulnerability' became an increasingly important framework through which society and individuals were understood. The Conservative Party's association with moral and political pronouncements about 'muggers', 'scroungers', the 'gay plague' and so on added to its hard-nosed, 'get on your bike' image, and meant that its capacity to relate to the more universalising sense of victimhood was limited. New Labour, however, having unshackled themselves from the 'old' labour movement were able to relate to individuals—but individuals not as political subjects—but as isolated and diminished subjects—as victims.

CONSTRUCTING VICTIMS

The changing emphasis within the Labour Party in the late 1980s towards issues of crime and antisocial behaviour was influenced in part by the work of left realist and feminist criminologists who had an active role within Labour local authorities. Through the work of writers like Jock Young, crime was made into a 'working-class issue', due largely to the transformation in how large sections of the working class were understood: namely, as 'victims' rather than active citizens.

Social changes and political defeats of the labour movement had a profound impact upon subsequent developments within local and national government alike during this period. However, the role of claimsmakers on the left was also significant in turning crime into a 'radical issue'.

The increasing centrality of victims to not only the criminal justice system but more broadly to political and social problem formation has been noted by various sociologists (Best 1999; Garland 2002), and within criminology itself the victim had become increasingly important as an area of study (Maquire and Pointing 1988; Rock 1990). The rise of victim-oriented research in criminology developed with the growing concern with the fear of crime—a fear that was initially identified by conservative thinkers but increasingly became a social problem focused upon by feminists, and then left realists. This development ran in tandem with a growing pessimism within radical circles about the dynamic potential of the working class, or of the welfare state to transform society, and resulted in a radical reorientation around the problems of crime, harassment and forms of antisocial behaviour. Whilst being a product of a declining labour movement and the result of the failure of welfarism, the ideas of these radicals also helped to elevate the concern about crime and they acted as key claimsmakers of victims of crime.

The first significant identification of and support for 'victims' emerged in the US in the form of a conservative reaction in the 1960s to criminal justice processes that were understood to be more concerned with the rights of criminals than with *victims' rights* (Best 1999: 98). Reflecting a more distant and pessimistic belief in the state policies of the time, this defence of the victim also signified a sense of alienation from social institutions and political processes. By the 1970s this pessimism towards welfarism, and the rehabilitative approach within the American criminal justice system, was becoming more pronounced—and there was a growing sense that, in terms of state responses to crime and punishment, 'nothing works' (Feeley 2003: 119).[12] This pessimism was also emerging within the UK, and the vision and optimism of the expansive politics of the welfare state began to unravel (Garland 1985). By the 1980s numerous Home Office reports were arguing that the government could not resolve the current crisis within the criminal justice system.

The claim for the rights of victims represented a certain shift within social thought about the relationship of the individual with society. Where previously the criminal justice system was understood as a representation of the laws of all within society in relation to the criminal, by focusing upon the victim of crime, the priority was given to the individual who had been 'damaged' by the criminal and also who felt estranged from the existing justice system.

The battle to centre the victim within criminal justice developed in the 1980s but remained contested; and Ashworth's view that it was questionable, 'whether the particular victim's interests should count for more than those of any other member of the community', remained the established opinion (Cretney et al. 1994: 16). However, as the former director of the Howard League, Martin Wright, noted in the *Guardian*, times were changing. This was reflected, for example, in the draft Declaration on the Rights of Victims being discussed for the first time at the United Nations Congress on the Prevention of Crime and the Treatment of Offenders (*Guardian* 28 August 1985). A similar trend was also becoming apparent within popular culture, with the emergence of programmes like *Crimewatch* on the television. Producer Peter Chafer explained why the programme was such a success.

> Ten of fifteen years ago I don't think it would have worked because . . . then we were concerned as a society about what it was we were doing to people to make them criminal. . . . In the past three or four years we've suddenly said to ourselves, 'To hell with the criminal, what about the poor bloody victim?' (Schlesinger and Tumber 1993: 22).

Concerns for the 'poor bloody victim' emerged alongside the growing concern with the fear of crime—both 'victimhood' and fear reflecting an increasing sense of distance and loss of connection between the individual and social processes. *The estrangement felt by the public from 'their' society and their sense of powerlessness was, through the prism of victimhood, increasingly institutionalised.*

In the UK the idea that the fear of crime was a direct consequence of crime itself remained highly contested in the seventies and eighties and both radical and Home Office criminologists challenged this idea. Sparks, Glenn and Dodd in 1977 argued that 'feelings of crime or insecurity appear to have many sources, and to be strongly influenced by beliefs, attitudes and experiences which have nothing whatever to do with crime', and that, 'we need to be very cautious about interpreting literally expressions of uneasiness about other aspects of experience, or about the state of the world in general' (in Jones 1987: 192–98). Similarly Smith noted in 1984: 'In sum, fear is frequently generated quite independently of either the mass media, or people's direct experiences of crime' (Smith 1984: 293). Indeed, as van Dijk notes, in the initial discussion about the fear of crime in Britain, fear itself was seen as a problem which undermined communities—not in terms of the level of anxiety it created, but in the exaggerated response by those living in fear, where, 'Those who [took] special measures to protect their households against crime were said to exhibit a 'fortress mentality'' (van Dijk 1994: 122). In this respect it was those people who feared crime 'too much' who were seen as being antisocial and helping to undermine communities, rather than criminals or antisocial youth.

The idea and significance given to the fear of crime remains contested within criminology and the reality of this specific fear has been challenged and arguably been shown to be exaggerated (Farrall et al. 1997; Farrall and Gadd 2004). However the emergence of the concern with the fear of crime as a problem in its own right has grown within politics and in the policies developed by governments from the early 1990s. This development was assisted most systematically within criminology by sections of the feminist 'movement' and by left realist thinkers, particularly with the growth of 'victim surveys'.

THE RADICAL CONSTRUCTION OF VICTIMHOOD

Throughout the 1980s and 1990s research had been carried out to identify victims of crime. Within strands of feminist thought, this research attempted to challenge the idea that fear of crime was to some extent irrational,[13] by illustrating the extent to which women and other 'vulnerable groups'[14] developed a sense of fear due to their experiences of 'minor' everyday harassment. Indeed, in the UK, the prioritisation and representation of the victim emerged most fervently within the feminist writing of the 1970s and 1980s with the 'discovery' of violence and abuse against women and children (Jenkins 1992: 231). Rather than associating the fear of crime within wider social and political developments, this research largely analysed the direct experience of 'victims' within their local communities and in so doing focused concern upon the interpersonal relationships between people. Junger for example attempted to prove that the 'experiences of sexual harassment, which usually are not serious but could occur relatively often, can lead women to be fearful and restrict themselves to their homes' (Junger 1987: 358). Other research has 'discovered' teenagers and elderly women to be 'victims of harassment', with the 'experience of crime' being the core concern addressed (Hartless et al. 1995; Pain 1995). Despite often contradictory evidence of the significance and even the extent of the victimisation under study, this research had an underlying and in-built acceptance of the vulnerability of those people being studied. For example Hartless and colleagues note with 'surprise' that, of the young women who said they had experienced sexual harassment of some kind, 'only 8% . . . said they had been "very scared"' (1995: 119). Surprise at any level of robustness and at the ability of 'vulnerable' individuals to cope with unpleasant experiences was coupled with a trend to interpret any evidence of fear as a product of harassment. Pain, in her analysis of fear amongst elderly women, raises the question of why older men fear crime more than young men. Despite the myriad possible reasons including physical frailty, social isolation or a sense of powerlessness and estrangement from society which could be the cause, Pain speculates that perhaps it is due to their *vulnerability to harassment*, 'especially in very old age, to abuse from carers inside or outside the immediate family' (Pain 1995: 595).

Whatever the myth or reality of the experience of harassment by these 'vulnerable groups', there was an implicit and sometimes explicit assumption within this work that communities are being undermined by crime and more particularly by everyday forms of harassment. This problematic behaviour, it was assumed, would have a long term and cumulatively damaging impact upon the individual and subsequently on communities as a whole. Here we see a complete turnaround from the argument put in the 1970s by radicals who questioned and even denounced the 'fear of crime' as a reactionary sentiment. Rather than questioning the nature of this fear and its origins, in some strands of feminist criminology there was a tendency to accept the problem of fear and to then discover the cause of this fear within the realm of abusive personal relationships. Whereas previously radicals had attempted to challenge the official statistics on crime and deny the 'social problem' of crime, increasingly this feminist criminology reversed this approach and attempted to prove that crime, harassment, and what would later by called 'antisocial behaviour' was even more of a problem than was officially accepted. Being a 'victim' of crime and antisocial behaviour was no longer simply a passing event, but became something that defined the lives and identity of 'vulnerable groups', and these 'radicals' became promoters and claimsmakers of these problems. The concern raised here was specifically developed with particular reference to less serious or non-criminal offences, and was also bound up with the centrality of the fear of crime as a significant factor to be taken into account within the criminal justice system. Regardless of the intentions of the researchers themselves, one logical outcome of this process was to help problematise and ultimately criminalise everyday behaviour and interactions—to help develop the 'politics of behaviour'—and thus to support the trend towards the 'policing' of relationships.

In the 1980s feminist and left realist concerns about the impact of crime on individuals and society drew closer to the official criminological approach at the time—especially with the common use of victim statistics.

'Establishment' criminology had however undergone its own transformation during this period moving from a positivist belief in society's capacity to overcome the problem of crime to an 'administrative criminology' (Young 1988a: 174). This administrative criminology, associated with Wilson's (1975) approach to crime, was a more pragmatic method of dealing with the effects of it. Despite the political nature of much of the feminist and particularly the left realist approach to crime, the common bond that had brought them and the official criminologist closer to one another was a diminished belief in social possibilities to resolve the problem of crime. With a greater pessimism about society and a greater sense of distance from social change and outcomes, radical and conservative thinkers became more preoccupied with the plight of the victim. The public, or at least substantial sections of it were now increasingly conceptualised as being what Stanko described as 'universally vulnerable' (Pain 1995: 596).

FEMINISTS AND LEFT REALISTS AS CLAIMSMAKERS

The significance of crime and behaviour for New Labour was assisted by the work of feminist and new realist thinkers of the left in the 1980s, who helped to formulate an understanding of the public as vulnerable. This vulnerability was understood to be the product of antisocial behaviour within the day-to-day relationships of significant sections of society. Rather than a right-wing authoritarian issue, here the fight against crime and antisocial behaviour was reposed as a means to recreate community.

In Philip Jenkins' analysis (*Intimate Enemies: Moral Panics in Contemporary Great Britain*) of the emergence of panics around child abuse in the UK, he notes the significance of feminist as claimsmakers:

> From the mid-1970s on, there evolved in Britain a strong feminist movement, which had had an enormous impact on many aspects of society and politics. . . . Feminist ideas soon prevailed in radical and left-wing journals . . . and were commonly expressed in liberal newspapers like the *Guardian* . . . [and] by the mid-1980s, fifty local authorities had women's committees (Jenkins 1992: 35–36).

By the late 1970s, many of the feminist activists had already broken with the 'radical' outlook within criminology and were equally critical of socialist ideas on the left, turning away from issues of social equality and focusing more upon problems that emerged in the relationships between men and women. Indeed as one author noted, by the 1980s the women's movement as a radical drive for equality had fragmented into individualistic concerns and a separatist celebration of 'womanhood'. Where many early socialist and liberal feminists rejected the idea of difference between men and women, a number of feminists in the 1980s appeared to celebrate women as caring rather than violent—illustrated by the peace camp at Greenham Common, which excluded men because of their 'violent tendency' (Marshall: 1982: 48). This more disparate form of feminism did, however, as Jenkins notes, make a substantial impact upon politics in the UK—as did the left realists, led by Jock Young, who, like these feminists, had become disillusioned with the idealist beliefs of the radical left.

In the editor's introduction to *Confronting Crime* in the mid 1980s, Matthews and Young pointed out that, 'if the women's movement has indicated the way forward in terms of the creation of a radical victimology, it is now time to extend its theoretical and political potential' (Matthews and Young 1986: 3). Crime for these left realists needed to be taken seriously and victims needed to be placed at the centre of concern for criminologists and the state. The role for socialists was now to engage with, 'problems as people experience them' and to tackle the problem of crime—a problem that can destroy communities. Crime, was clearly a reality for many in Britain at the time, and especially for those living in poor urban areas, although the extent to which it was central to their lives in the way it was understood is open to doubt. However, for left realists, crime and antisocial behaviour became a prism through which problems in these working-class areas were understood. As Matthews and Young argued—expressing sentiments that were later to be echoed by the likes of New Labour's David Blunkett:

> Crime is of importance because unchecked it divides the working class community and is materially and morally the basis of disorganisation: the loss of political control. It is also a potential unifier—a realistic issue, *amongst others*, for recreating community (Matthews and Young 1986: 29).

By engaging with the immediate experiences of a disaggregated community and understanding crime as a major cause and solution to this loss of community, Young, along with other realists and feminists, attempted to turn crime reduction into a working-class issue and in the process became significant 'anti-crime' claimsmakers on the left.

In the 1980s both feminist and left realist thinkers had a significant influence in the left-wing Labour-run inner-city councils—carrying out victim surveys, and sitting on a number of council boards particularly within the Greater London Council. Developing out of the radical framework of the early 1970s, a number of feminist and realist criminologists became disillusioned with the fight for political and social change and, rather than challenging the issue of crime as an elite concern or method of social control, increasingly identified crime as a major issue, particularly for the poor, women and blacks who were now understood as being 'victims of crime'. Carried out within a critical feminist and 'socialist' framework that was often 'anti-police', these radicals focused their concerns on the most deprived and fragmented communities, discovering that crime was not a myth, as past radicals had argued, but a reality. Indeed crime was seen as a 'working-class problem' and issue to be addressed (Jones et al. 1986).

The identification of harassed victims of antisocial behaviour rose proportionately with the declining belief—particularly of the left realists—in the possibility of radical social change. *As the active potential of the organised working class to 'do' something about Conservative attacks on the welfare state declined, Jock Young and others uncovered the vulnerable, 'done-to', poor.*

Discussing the shift in Labour councils from radicalism to realism Young noted that:

> The recent history of radical criminology in Britain has involved a rising influence of feminist and anti-racist ideas and an encasement of left wing Labour administrations in the majority of the inner city Town Halls. An initial ultra-leftism has been tempered and often transformed by a prevalent realism in the wake of the third consecutive defeat of the Labour Party on the national level and severe defeats with regards to 'rate capping' in terms of local politics. The need to encompass issues, which had a widespread support amongst the electorate, rather than indulge in marginal or 'gesture' politics included the attempt to recapture the issue of law and order from the right (Young 1988a: 172).

It was sections of the left who, with the support of their victim surveys, both discovered and advocated on behalf of women, blacks and the poor as *victims* of crime, the problem of fragmented communities being located within the prism of crime, antisocial behaviour and the fear of crime. Indeed crime and the fear of it became so central to Young's understanding of the conditions of the working class that, when finding that young men's fear of crime was low, despite them being the main victims of crime, he argued that in a sense they had a false consciousness. Rather than trying to allay women's fears about the slim chance of serious crime happening to them, Young questioned whether it 'would not be more advisable to attempt to raise the fear of crime of young men rather than to lower that of other parts of the public?' (Young 1988b: 172).

Based upon a critique of the romantic notions of radical criminologists, but within a climate of political defeat and working-class fragmentation, Young increasingly related to large sections of the working class as victims, on whose behalf he advocated. While often carrying out more accurate research of crime, the tendency was for Young and his co-authors both to exaggerate the significance of crime and to generalise an understanding of the public as fundamentally vulnerable—within the narrow parameters of crime and antisocial behaviour. In the demoralised and poverty stricken inner-city areas of London, like Islington, where crime rates were five times the national average, the equally demoralised realists concluded that it was the problem of crime that 'shaped their lives' (Jones et al. 1986: 201). While correctly noting that crime was not a fantasy for the people of Islington, these realists noted that a third of the women of the area avoided going out after dark, concluding that this represented a 'virtual curfew of the female population' (1986: 201). This misrepresentation of one third of women being transformed into the entire female population reflected not simply an exaggeration, but a newly developing conceptualisation of the public more generally as vulnerable—something which was to become more central to the Labour Party's understanding of social problems in the 1990s and would help to transform the relationship between citizen and state.

CONCLUSION

As Squires notes, for left realists universal victimisation is a characteristic of citizenship. Young felt that through this understanding communities could be reactivated, as he states,

> [R]ealisms emphasis on risk leads to a mode of self-government, through an act of self assertion. Through such self-assertion ironically, a sense of community is fostered and a mode of belonging endorsed as natural and convenient (Squires 1997).

With fear of crime understood to undermine community, the left realists radicalised crime and as Gilling notes, 'In such a context, fear is as much a welfare need as poverty' (Gillinig 1997). The outcome of this approach was however to help to stimulate a culture of fear rather than any wider sense of community.

Discovering victims of crime was by no means a uniform development, and differences of opinion and prioritisation existed amongst those advocating on behalf of differing 'vulnerable groups'. Indeed identifying victims of crime was not a solely radical pursuit. For administrative criminologists and some conservative thinkers the victim was becoming more central to the approach to crime and criminal justice in the eighties. Claims on behalf of victims were becoming more systematic and politicised by the late 1980s, and had to some degree already been institutionalised with, for example, the introduction of the Victims' Charter by the Conservative Government in 1990.

Vulnerability, a category given to specific 'groups' that classified them as in need of protection by their very nature of being black, women, or poor, increasingly became a term used for ever more groups in society and ultimately to the population as a whole. Claimsmaking on behalf of 'victims' similarly developed in this period and carried with it moral weight that united radicals and conservatives and became a framework of relating to society that was difficult to challenge. Soon almost all claims for groups in society began to take this form of protecting victims and the vulnerable: the aggressive beggar preyed upon the vulnerable public, while the vulnerable beggar was a victim of aggressive members of the public; and the antisocial youth made life hell for vulnerable communities, while alternatively aggressive policing victimised these young people.

Before 1970, social problems associated with victims of crime and the fear of crime had little or no academic, public or political presence in British society. However, by 1990, *victims* and the *fear of crime* were becoming increasingly important concepts informing how the problem of crime was understood—and more generally how social problems within communities and society were addressed. On the left this development emerged as belief in social possibilities declined, and within certain radical circles the previously understood creative capacity of the working class, and indeed of humanity in general, was replaced with a concern with its destructive potential. Within the criminal justice system there was also, post welfare state, a need to develop a new framework of operation that both gave it internal and public legitimacy. Where some practical measures to provide victim support had become institutionalised in the criminal justice system in the 1980s (van Dijk 1988: 120), the centrality of the individuated victim within politics was held back by the remaining political contestation between the Tories and the 'Old' labour movement. For the victim and the 'vulnerable public' to become central to politics and indeed to the state's relationship with the people, as Maguire and Pointing (1988) noted, 'fairly major reforms of the relationships between State and citizen' would need to occur. As we have seen with the example of the aggressive beggar, this transformation did indeed take place and was fundamentally dependent upon a change in the nature of subjectivity within politics and the consequent transformation in the understanding of the electorate from active individuals or a collective agent to a more passive and diminished vulnerable public.

This transformation in the relationship between political thinkers and the public was influenced by sections of the left, but also within conservative thought with the relative failure of the Conservative government to create a vibrant economic and moral culture founded on the entrepreneurial individual. Margaret Thatcher's ideal of restoring people to independence and self reliance, as Heartfield notes, failed even in terms of 'rolling back the state' (2002: 156). State subsidies replaced nationalised industries; 'dependency' on the state increased in the form of unemployment benefits expanding the number of those reliant upon the state more than any other post-war government; regulation of industry in the form of organisations such as Ofwat increased; and from 1985 to 1994 the number of quangos increased exponentially, rising to 5521 by 1994. Rather than the rise of the *free* market, what emerged was an alternatively regulated society, and despite the defeat of collective working-class institutions, 'flowing individualism' did not emerge (Heartfield 2002: 158–60).[15]

The political victory of the Conservatives over the labour movement had so successfully demobilised mass opposition that as Heartfield argues, 'the elites had almost succeeded in dismantling the connections between people and government'. In the UK and indeed across Europe there was at this time a significant decline in popular organisations of the left, of trade union membership and votes for social democratic parties. But soon after, 'as if in tandem, the parties of the right suffered a similar collapse in membership, vote and support'—party allegiances collapsed and even in the United States there emerged 'third parties' and individuals, like Ross Perot, who took votes off the major political parties (Heartfield 2003: 273)

Within this context, the UK government began to engage not with a *public* for their political loyalties, but with a now more fragmented electorate. Where the fear of crime had been seen within government circles as somewhat irrational and exaggerated in the 1980s, in the early 1990s, lacking a wider political project, it was this individuated fear that became the basis of government policy and practise.[16]

As we have seen with the example of the aggressive beggar, the Conservative Party, in part, continued to understand and organise its policies in relation to the imagined problem of welfare dependency, but its rhetoric sounded increasingly hollow and its capacity to cohere even conservative thinkers was becoming increasingly problematic (Calcutt 1996).

By 1994 Labour were well ahead in the opinion polls helped by their transformation into the new party of law and order illustrated in their support of the Conservative government's Criminal Justice and Public Order Bill. Prime Minister John Major continually attempted to paint Labour as the 'villain's friend', but to no avail, and the Conservative Party's disarray continued the following year, illustrated by the leadership challenge to John Major and by the then inevitable Labour landslide victory in the 1997 general election.

The issue of antisocial behaviour was at this time becoming a significant social problem. This development was not however the result of a dynamic right-wing politics. Similarly the rising prison numbers did not reflect the growing influence of the moral right in society—but rather its decline. People were being locked up, monitored by CCTV, targeted for their antisocial behaviour not as part of a vibrant neo-liberal political agenda—but because of the loss of one. *Antisocial behaviour emerged not as a political issue, but rather as a replacement for a political relationship with the public.* Rather than a political agenda engaging the active energy of the electorate towards a 'public' goal, the issue of antisocial behaviour engaged individuals as insecure, passive and vulnerable—their 'right to a quiet life' being advocated on their behalf by the micro-managers of the new political elite.

The Conservative instinct (at least in theory) to limit state activity was changing in this period and being 'tough' increasingly related to direct forms of regulation and protection of the public, rather than to the political battle of the previous decade. Crime panics developed apace in the 1990s under John Major, while at the same time the Labour Party itself became the 'new party of law and order', competing with the Conservatives to look 'tough'.

'Panics' around crime were not new, as Cook observes—indeed the 1970s and 1980s were decades when 'mugging' and 'hooligans' were big news. In this respect one could make the case that little had changed in British political life (Cook 2000: 207). However, this would be to miss the profound changes not only in politics, but in the politics of crime that emerged in the 1990s. Cook herself notes that one of the changes between the 1990s and the previous decades, was the collapse of the labour movement. But this was no side issue—it was a change that transformed the nature of crime policies in the 1990s.

Ultimately, while the concern with the 'victim of crime' had been growing since the 1970s, it was only with the collapse of the contesting ideologies of Britain's two major political parties that the victim took centre stage. Labour's ability to engage with the idea of victimhood—often framed with reference to 'vulnerable groups'—was coupled with their condemnation of the greedy individual of the 1980s, and helped to develop both a more authoritarian and more 'caring' therapeutic approach to crime and anti-social behaviour. In adopting the individually focused concerns expressed through the underclass debate, crime was accepted by Labour as being more of a behavioural than a structural question. However, this focus on behaviour was to emerge with a more 'inclusive' language, outside of the traditional moralising of conservatives. Individual rights were defended—but these rights were redefined as rights of protection from others and from fear. Right-wing authoritarianism and attacks on the poor and 'vulnerable' were now replaced with the defence of the poor and vulnerable as victims of crime. Tapping into the culture of fear and promoting the new 'morality' of safety, Labour were successful in presenting themselves as the new party of law and order who could tackle the more widespread 'epidemic' of crime and disorder and in so doing protect the *vulnerable public*.

By the time of the 1997 general election, as the *Guardian* law correspondent noted, all parties' proposals on law and order were about, 'public reassurance rather than crime-fighting' (*Guardian* 16 April 1997). Within six months the Hamilton curfew had been implemented. Before this election the ailing Conservative Party had continued in vain to use the crime card as its own and attempt to label Labour as soft on crime. Where the previous Labour shadow home secretary Roy Hattersley, in the late 1980s, had made civil liberties the key test of the government's criminal justice legislation, Tony Blair argued that 'reducing crime had to be the first test and civil liberties the second' (*Guardian* 30 January 1996). Labour had been transformed as a political party that was now even more able than the Conservatives to play the crime card and in effect transform what liberty meant, from freedom of action to freedom from the action of others.

All the building blocks for the politics of antisocial behaviour were now in place and with Labour's election the laws, initiatives and political rhetoric about this 'social problem' developed a momentum that would soon make antisocial behaviour one of the core issues of the twenty first century. By

2006 the logic of micro-politics had resulted in over 3000 new criminal offences being created by the Labour governments—'one for every day it [had] been in office'—this contrasted with 500 new laws developed by the Conservatives in the nine years before Labour came to power. This 'frenzied approach to law making' emerged at the same time as police chiefs were considering 'asking ministers for a set of new measures to allow them to impose "instant justice" for antisocial behaviour'. The rate at which offences have been created has also accelerated with each Labour government, 'In 1998, Labour's first full year in power, 160 new offences passed into legislation, rising to 346 in 2000 and 527 in 2005'. The Liberal Democrat MP Nick Clegg who uncovered these figures argued that,

> Nothing can justify the step change in the number of criminal offences invented by this Government. This provides a devastating insight into the real legacy of nine years of New Labour government—a frenzied approach to law-making, thousands of new offences, an illiberal belief in heavy-handed regulation, an obsession with controlling the minutiae of everyday life (*Independent* 16 August 2006).

Whatever the problem of crime and antisocial behaviour it was not the nature of these problems themselves that led to them becoming social problems in the form they now take. Despite the insecurities felt by the more fragmented public and the relatively high statistical crime rate, there remains a tendency for politicians to exaggerate still further the problem of antisocial behaviour and fear within neighbourhoods that are understood to be 'terrorised' by antisocial youth.

As Cummings argues in relation to former Labour home secretary David Blunkett's belief that reducing antisocial behaviour will create a rise in civil republicanism:

> A crucial point missed by most commentators is that the fear of crime is an expression of atomisation rather than a cause of it. And except in a few extreme cases, it is a nagging sense of unease rather than crippling fear that people feel, even in rough areas. People generally get on with their lives, while worrying that they are vulnerable to unspecified threats. The politics of antisocial behaviour gives shape to these threats by focusing people's unease on clear targets, typically young loiterers. This institutionalises atomisation rather than overcoming it by officially endorsing a fearful attitude and undermining people's confidence in their ability to negotiate problems without official support (O'Malley and Waiton 2005: 7).

4 Diminished Subjectivity

Now for the first time—outside of the extremes of conservative think-ing—a misanthropic strain emerged that questioned whether MAN was indeed the central figure of the human story, and whether he deserved to be

(Heartfield 2002: 21).

INTRODUCTION

In the previous chapter the focus was largely upon changes in politics that developed in the 1990s—changes that suggest this was a new period of authoritarianism, one predicated upon the development of micro-politics and the growing regulation of everyday life and behaviour. Here this argu-ment is examined more theoretically. If the representation of the changes in politics thus far are correct to any extent, then perhaps a more profound problem is being raised—the very nature of human subjectivity in contem-porary modernity.

The question of modern (or post-modern) day subjectivity has been addressed by a number of scholars in recent decades, for this chapter the work of Frank Furedi, James Heartfield and equally that of Christopher Lasch are seen as being most useful in addressing this question. For all three this issue is understood within a social, political and cultural framework of *low expectations*; for the American Christopher Lasch writing in the 1970s what had emerged was a *Culture of Narcissism*; following this, more recently Furedi has identified a growing *Culture of Fear* and a *Therapy Cul-ture*—something that he and Heartfield discuss with reference to the idea of 'diminished subjectivity'.

The scope of the concept—diminished subjectivity—is vast in its impli-cations for how society is understood today, here it is used to interpret the changing form of the politics of crime, the developments within the criminal justice system over recent years, something that has been influenced by the more limited outlook of those on both the left and the right, and ultimately the rise of the politics of (antisocial) behaviour.

In brief, the concept refers to a loss of faith in humanity—a loss of belief in society and the individual subject—something that has encouraged a more limited view of both social possibilities and individual capacity: The individual himself becomes seen as both more degraded or evil and at the same time more passive and vulnerable.

Across the political spectrum the declining confidence or belief in the human potential to *make* history or to even direct social change in a meaningful way has resulted in a situation where, as Furedi notes, risks have become the 'active agents and people—at risk [the] passive agents in society' (Furedi 1997: 64).[1] This development has perhaps influenced and been influenced by, most acutely, 'radicals' who having lost a belief in social progress have themselves become prone to *panic* and to develop solutions to social problems not based on a sense of positive transformation but on the need to *conserve* and to *regulate* increasing areas of life, including industry, the environment and also relationships between people (Durodie 2002; Cohen 2002: xxiii). This outlook of 'damage limitation' has come to inform the practices of society's institutions and influence the way individuals understand themselves.

The failed social, economic and political experiments of left, and also the right, by the early 1990s had led to what Feeley and Simon describe as a, 'decline in social will' (Feeley and Simon 1992: 469). Despite the triumph of the market, it was not the 'market individual' or promethean man that stepped forward, but rather the victim and the vulnerable public. This does not mean that this development marks the, 'death of the subject', but rather, as Heartfield argues, 'the human subject persists, but in denial of its own subjectivity'. The notion of diminished subjectivity in this respect is not a description of individuals as such, but is a cultural phenomenon that informs institutional practices: practices that have increasingly developed to regulate the public who are themselves constructed as diminished subjects.

The image of the individual and to some extent the self-image that individuals take on board today is one prone to a sense of vulnerability, and is best expressed in the concept of the *victim*. The victim, as Best argues, is often portrayed as blameless and powerless (Best 1999: 100), and whereas past moral weight was given to saints in the Renaissance period, or heroes in the nineteenth century, the iconic individual carrying moral weight in late twentieth and early twenty first century society is that of the victim (Best 1998: 138). This transformation in the understanding of humanity reflects both a more passive sense of human capabilities and also a more negative sense of what humanity represents. It has also helped to form the framework within which individuals have increasingly come to understand themselves.

As Heartfield notes in *The 'Death of the Subject' Explained*, 'The free willing human Subject is the cornerstone of contemporary society. Every aspect of our civilisation takes the free Subject as its basic assumption' (2002: 5). From work contracts between individuals, marriage contracts, contracts for mortgages with banks or in the act of voting, the 'free willing Subject' is central. However, as we have noted thus far and will go on to examine further, the nature of this subjectivity has diminished and undermined the very meaning of 'rights' and 'responsibility' that once lay at the heart of the Subject. At its most extreme or undiluted form it could be argued that rather than the Subject being the cornerstone of society—it is seen as the new enemy of it—an aggressive abuser of today's diminished subject.

DIMINISHED LEFT

The trend to identify and understand the public in terms of its vulnerability was something that informed the turn towards crime as a significant social problem by radicals in the 1980s. For the new realists, both a more passive and more negative understanding of individuals and in particular the working class was represented. The issue of crime and antisocial behaviour was not a major focus of concern for these criminologists until their own subjective understanding of social and political possibilities had declined.

Part of the reason for the left realists' orientation towards an understanding of the working class as victims was that the more active and dynamic sections of the working class were understood to be part of the problem. In a sense what developed was the problematisation of subjectivity itself—in the form of the problematisation of the aspirations of the *active man*. One caricature of this *man* was the 'Essex Man'—the upwardly mobile, greedy, selfish Thatcherite, who was blamed for the consecutive Tory election victories by many of those on the left, a caricature that was explained in theory within the notion of Thatcherism and hegemony.[2] The greed and selfishness of the Essex man was for left realist Jock Young the same greed and selfishness that resulted in crime and antisocial behaviour on estates. For Young, crime was a product of capitalist values played out on the streets, of 'individualism, competition, a desire for material goods and often machismo'. Values that in more optimistic times would have been understood as largely aspirant—something socialists could tap into when the market failed to deliver—were now reconceptualised as criminal and anti-communal (Lea and Young 1984).

The understanding of the greedy working-class Tory voter was developed most systematically by Stuart Hall, within his analysis of Thatcherism. The use of Gramsci's theory of hegemony 'offered a way of theorising the political crisis of the Left and understanding how the Right had come to dominate' (Finlayson 2003: 117). Fundamentally, Hall did this by undermining the idea of political consciousness and of the fluidity of subjectivity by identifying an ideology—'Thatcherism'[3]—which developed not simply as an idea that people agreed with but rather as something that got under their skin and 'inserted itself into people's experience and common sense, redefining their identity and sense of interests' (Finlayson 2003:117). While correctly criticising economic determinism in traditional Marxism, this approach did not simply elevate the significance of ideology so much as to transform ideology and subjectivity into a *thing*. Now the ideas of the working class were understood to develop in relation to a more statically conceptualised *culture*. As Malik notes in relation to the concept of culture in race, culture had increasingly become understood in the latter half of the twentieth century as a more fixed conceptualisation of what we *are*, as 'static and immutable', related to unconscious tradition rather than with 'conscious activity', not the 'conscious creation of humanity but the unconscious product of human activity which [stands] above and beyond society' (Malik 1996: 154–62).

Ironically, within criminology, the static 'cultures' of deviants was something that was first theorised by radical rather than conservative thinkers, as Calcutt has observed with reference to British criminologists in the late 1960s (Calcutt 1996). Although these 'cultural' differences—these deviant *subcultures*—were originally analyzed with a positive gloss, by the 1990s the conservative notion of '*cultures* of crime', or what today has become a concern with 'gun culture' or a 'knife culture', took on a more overtly negative and authoritarian dynamic.

In the 1980s realists like Lea and Young coupled their pessimism about social change with a discovery of a 'culture' of selfishness and greed amongst the working class. Describing the problem as they saw it in 1984, Lea and Young argued that crime, rather than being in opposition to capitalist values, was an expression of them. By this the left realists were not referring to Marx's understanding of alienation and the inequalities produced under capitalism, but rather to the *values* of the working class themselves and in particular to the, 'antisocial egoism which permeates the totality of behaviour and values within capitalism' (Lea and Young 1984: 55). In a sense subjectivity was one-sidedly understood to have been objectified by the market, and through the ideology of Thatcherism.

Past theories connecting capitalist values to criminal activity often took on a more optimistic note. American author Daniel Bell, discussing how the gangster was understood in the US in the 1950s, noted that 'He was a man with a gun, acquiring by personal merit what was denied him by complex ordering of stratified society', a man who was taking a 'queer ladder of social mobility' (Bell 1962: 129). Similarly on the left, deviant behaviour was often seen as understandable given the limitations of capitalist society. Here subjective action, even if deviant, was to a certain degree seen as acceptable or understandable and even positive.

Deviant groups and the 'rituals' of youth 'subcultures' were also, mistakenly, at this time elevated in importance as sites of 'resistance'—another example perhaps of the more limited expectations of what resistance and indeed politics were coming to mean for some on the left (Hall and Jefferson 1976).[4]

By the early eighties, the realist criminologists had already begun to see subjective intent as something implanted by the capitalist system that was a problem (of greed and selfishness) rather than a potential solution to social problems. Meritocracy and aspirations of individuals, without a belief in social progress, became problematised and understood more negatively to represent a 'dog eat dog' mentality. Young men who felt able to 'take care of themselves' in public, for example, were, more generally and regardless of whether they had committed criminal acts or not, seen as being 'macho' and potentially violent; they were also understood to be in denial of a more real understanding of themselves as potential *victims* of crime (Young 1998a).

With the understanding of people as victims a more diminished subject was discovered and engaged with through the 1990s. At the same time, the idea of the greedy Thatcherite individual was also predicated upon a more static and immutable sense of subjectivity. Rather than being able to politically challenge the outlook of this 'selfish man', the call was to police him, and to regulate his excesses. The democratisation of the police force—and the involvement of the working class in the policing of the selfish members of the community—was one way the left realists felt the fear of crime could be overcome and the greedy criminal dealt with (Jones et al. 1986).

The reaction by many on the left to events in the 1980s was in response to real changes and to the genuine decline of collectivism and to political defeats of the labour movement. However, the left realists reacted by seeing people as *too* active and dynamic (and as greedy individuals) when in fact they were less so—being reduced to mere individuals rather than actors as part of society itself. 'Thatcherite' individualism was interpreted as a powerful new culture rather than as a reflection of the diminished collective agent, and consequently realists ended up advocating a culture of restraint in its place.

THE DANGERS OF FREEDOM

Interestingly, the notion that key sections of the working class were becoming more greedy and selfish has been questioned in research looking at the rise and fall of Essex Man. Questioning the structural explanations for the Tory voting worker, including the collapse of manufacturing jobs, the growth in home ownership and *the shift from a collectivist to individualist perspective*, Hayes and Hudson noted that

> We were sceptical of the idea of an autonomous correlation between changes in working class social structure and changes in working class political behaviour. We chose to look at the social and political attitudes of the skilled working class to see if in fact these changes had eroded a sense of working class identity in the light of a clear falling off in the vote for Labour. We found that Basildon's C2's did not conform in any way to the academic stereotype of what they were supposed to be. The key point to highlight here is the neglect of the essentially *aspirant* nature of the skilled working class (Hayes and Hudson 2001: 14; my italics).

The support for the Conservatives was here found to be less connected to structural changes or to an acceptance of Thatcherite 'ideological convictions' than to a negative experience of Labour's welfarism, connected with poverty and an individual, pragmatic aspiration for self-improvement. Rather than the working class having been transformed by a hegemonic Thatcherism, the authors stated that 'the results of the Basildon survey reveal that conservative policies are not capable of enthusing anybody. If anything, it is the lack of popular attachment to the Conservative programme that needs to be explained' (2001: 65).

Ideas of the free individual subject were associated with free market theorists in the 1980s. However, as Heartfield argues, the problems of the eighties, at a time of TINA,[5] became associated not with the failures of the market, but as a problem of freedom itself.

> The communitarians criticised subjective freedom because they took on face value the claims of the Thatcher and Reagan governments to represent individual freedom. Their response was ultimately a conservative response to the socially corrosive effects of market policies. But because the argument that there was no alternative to the market had been won, the culprit identified for the problems of the eighties was the selfish individual (Heartfield 2002: 154).

Within realist and feminist criminology the problematisation was often of the active subject itself. Freedom, without a positive belief in social change, was increasingly seen as being problematic and indeed dangerous. Aspiration became greed, self-reliance became machismo, and active subjective engagement with others increasingly became understood within the Foucauldian framework of power and its abuse.[6] The emergence of the 'radical' concern about crime as a 'real' issue—while relating to some genuine problems in society and a significant rise in 'recorded crimes'—was influenced by the more pessimistic sense of social and political possibilities. Now issues of abuse, harassment and violence (issues that were not new to communities) became more central to how some on the left understood and interpreted individuals and society. The Foucauldian understanding of society, with its problematisation of subjectivity (Heartfield 2002: 20) and its pessimism about human action, also became more influential at this time; an understanding, as Stone explained, within which we find 'a denial of the Enlightenment as an advance in human understanding and sensibility', with a 'recurrent emphasis on control, domination, and punishment as the only mediating qualities possible in personal relations' (in Harpham 1999: 68).

Within the social sciences risk theorists like Ulrich Beck in the early 1990s also developed a sociology of pessimism which understands human knowledge as more one-sidedly destructive rather than creative and a positive development (Beck 1992). Within certain strands of criminology there was a similar framework of understanding, except rather than relating to global problems, the problem became the free individual and the action of individuals was increasingly understood to be damaging. Instead of being subjective actors, through the prism of the victim and notions of vulnerability, the public increasingly became understood as being subjected *to* hardships by selfish, abusive villains. Replicating their own disengagement with positive subjective (or political) action, this trend to conceptualise subjective activity in a negative or diminished light became a foundation stone upon which the politics of New Labour was established: a politics, or more accurately a 'process', without a subject (Heartfield 2002:174).

VICTIM POLITICS

The coupling of political disorientation with an understanding of the public as being victimised by antisocial behaviour led to an increasing attempt in the 1990s by the political elite, and particularly New Labour, to re-engage the disconnected public through its fear of crime around the new 'moral' absolute of safety. The rights campaigned for by the Labour leadership were not classical rights and freedoms of the individual, but the right to be protected—the right to a 'quiet life'. Community Safety emerged, particularly after Labour's election in 1997, as a key organising principle for local authorities, and community 'participation' developed around this safety agenda, predicated on an engagement with a more passive and fearful public and the need to regulate behaviour.

Within the framework of TINA, the economic and political contestation of left and right was lost and social policy developments increasingly took on an individual and managerial orientation. Social problems were now largely understood with reference to the minutiae of everyday life, rather than to grand social visions based on political or moral principles and beliefs. Without the economic and political framework of the past, the fragmented public was engaged with at the level of the individual—and more particularly as emotionally constituted individuals. Expressing how you felt and engaging with the feelings of the public increasingly became the basis of political rhetoric and the justification for social policy interventions. This engagement with the emotions of the public was framed with certain emotions in mind and with an understanding of an 'emotional deficit' within communities. *Therapeutic man was understood not as a vibrant and strong character, but as a more fragile individual who needed protection and support.*

A more therapeutic relationship with the public was developed by New Labour—a relationship predicated upon a sensitivity to how the 'vulnerable public' felt. Engaging with 'victims of crime' and the fear of crime, a challenge was made to the 'thoughtless, insensitive' and 'cruel' treatment of these victims by the criminal justice system (Labour Party 1993: 22). 'Freeing people from the fear of crime' was now the 'greatest liberty government [could] guarantee' (Labour Party 1996: 6). Subsequently, the management of the emotions—the anxieties and fears—of individuals was now more central to the concerns about crime and disorder in society.

Within this cultural and political framework, a trend developed for 'victim' groups to emerge, groups in which individuals found meaning through their experience of crime. Mothers' campaigns, for example, developed in the nineties, supported by the unquestioned moral weight that victimhood provides. Following the model of the Mothers Against Drunk Driving campaign, that was launched in America in 1980, a variety of 'Mothers Against' groups formed in Britain. Beginning with Mothers Against Murder and Aggression in 1993 there emerged mothers' campaigns against drugs, violence, guns, knives, crime and telecommunication masts. These 'victim' groups were often generated by the personal loss of a child or loved one—they related to safety issues—and campaigned for new laws and regulations to raise awareness and make others safe. Promoting the dangers of crime for example, Ms Shakespeare of Mothers Against Crime explained in 2004 that 'Nobody is safe' (*Birmingham Evening Mail* 11 March 2004).

'Awareness' campaigns gave out, and indeed continue to give out, the message that you need to be more aware (or fearful) than you are, and attracted significant media interest and political support. The cultural validation given to campaigns of this sort acted as a further spur to the spiral of crime 'panics'. The new and growing 'moral' position of the victim in society made these campaigns newsworthy, while the therapeutic engagement with the public made grieving mothers—and indeed 'victims of crime' more generally—an important group in society. Speaking 'from the heart', the emotions of a mother who has lost a child, within a therapeutic culture, were not only very difficult to challenge, but were often actively courted by the political elite, who attempt to regain legitimacy by displaying their emotional awareness.

By the late 1990s local politicians and councillors from both the Conservative and the Labour Party were working with and expressing their support for groups like Mothers Against Drugs and Mothers Against Violence and Aggression. Part of this support being given by, for example, Labour councillor Gaille McCann (*Scotland on Sunday* 25 October 1998), and Conservative MSP Bill Aitken was in opposition to the uncaring criminal justice system that was said to be 'out of touch' with these victims' groups 'feelings' (*Daily Mail* 27 January 2000).

Into the third term of the longest serving Labour government of all time, the political debate programme *Question Time* involved a telling encounter between the late Robin Cook MP and Baroness Shirley Williams.[7] Following the news that violent crime had substantially increased, Labour's Robin Cook attempted to put the new statistics into perspective:—If we used the same statistical method for compiling figures on violent crime as we did in 1997 we would find that violent crime has actually fallen, he argued. Baroness Williams of the Liberal Democrats in response, attacked Cook for his insensitivity to the victims of violent crime, putting him on the defensive.

Despite Robin Cook's initial attempt to introduce an element of objectivity and perspective into the discussion about 'soaring violent crime'—following William's attack he backed down and pointed out that he accepted that indeed if you were a victim of violent crime—then the figures were irrelevant. The 'victim' had won again—or at least the now all powerful victim advocate—this time in the form of Shirley Williams.

This example is illustrative not only of the iconic position of the victim today, but also of the way even when politicians attempt to challenge the doomsayers they often lack the moral or political will or energy to see off the victim advocate whose power is often overwhelming.

ANTI 'SOCIAL' THERAPEUTICS

As James Nolan has noted with reference to state legitimation, by the end of the twentieth century the therapeutic ethos had become central to the justification of the state.

Describing this therapeutic development within the criminal justice system and the changing relationship between the state and the criminal, Nolan notes:

> Where once the self was to be brought into conformity with the standards of externally derived authorities and social institutions, it now is compelled to look within. . . . In other words, the contemporary cultural condition is such that externally derived points of moral reference are not available to individuals as they once were. Instead, cultural standards for judgement, guideposts for actions, understandings of oneself, and the tools for navigating through social life are likely to be rooted in the self (Nolan 1998: 3).

The problem of crime and disorder in this respect related less to the laws of society and the upholding of these laws by the state as an expression of the 'general will', than to the protection of the emotional well-being of the individual. Consequently, policing of society has become increasingly founded more on the fears of individuals than in carrying out the will of the *public*, and a more directly therapeutic relationship has developed between the authorities and the individual.

Furedi also notes that adults and children are encouraged to think of themselves today as vulnerable or as victims, continually being invited, 'to make sense of their troubles through the medium of therapeutics'.

> Take the example of crime. The belief that the impact of crime has a major influence on people's emotional life is a relatively recent one. Back in the 1970s, crime surveys tended to suggest that the impact of most crime on the victim was superficial and of relatively short duration. . . .

But during the past 25 years, criminologists have adopted a radically different interpretation of the effects of victimisation (Furedi 2004: 112).

For Furedi, a dialectical relationship has been established where therapeutic cultural and institutional practices firstly leads to the understanding of the harm done to victims of crime being exaggerated, and also helps orient the public towards a therapeutic understanding of themselves and their troubles. Consequently, 'social' values—the externally derived points of moral reference—and indeed the political and communal connections with others—are undermined further. Therapeutics while appearing to offer individual liberation and choice—of 'self-realisation', identifies the cause and solution to social problems with reference to the self thus disconnecting the public from society and indeed individuals from one another and exaggerating further the sense of personal vulnerability.

Within criminal justice the penal approach of the right and the more 'caring' therapeutic approach can be seen in the move away from practices of traditional rehabilitation to increasingly locking people up and/or developing more self-referential therapeutic practices, exemplified most clearly in the drugs courts in the US that are being developed in the UK, and also in the growth of restorative justice practices.

James Nolan's critical approach to therapeutics is founded upon a sense that it too is profoundly asocial. Examining the, 'emergence of a therapeutic culture with the universal discrediting of rehabilitative practices', Nolan notes that the rehabilitative ideal is 'dedicated to the achievement of social purposes', in that it intends to 'bring the offenders' behaviour and attitudes into harmony with certain values socially defined and validated'. Here the judgement about right and wrong was seen to be based upon social norms, not individual judgements. In contrast, the therapeutic ethos is more centrally disposed to 'assign ultimate moral priority to the self, over and against society' (Nolan 2001: 179).

> Whereas the emphasis of rehabilitative or adaptational therapy was to bring the individual into harmony with society, [today's] therapies of liberation see society as oppressive and as contributing to a person's illness. Society, as it were, is the cause of a person's sickness (Nolan 2001: 180).

This estrangement from social norms and outcomes is also reflected in the punitive approach to crime developed in the 1990s, in that it is similarly distanced from the idea of rehabilitation and reforming the criminal into an upstanding citizen, and it more negatively attempts simply to keep criminals off the streets. The pessimism about social change that developed out of the 1970s' rejection of welfarism here takes on a more detached view of the criminal. Where the tabloids shout for more prisons, the more 'liberal' therapeutic approach attempts to heal the criminal by relating them to their inner selves and by raising their self-esteem, or by giving emotional support to victims. In neither approach does the 'social' have a place at the table.

The therapeutic concern with the victim of crime has run in parallel with the conservative promotion of this victim—reflecting a move away from a social engagement with law and order and towards a more individually oriented concern for victims of crime. But as Nolan has pointed out, 'The therapeutic emphasis on the victimised and emotive concerns of the self are tendentiously anticommunal', and at a time of a growing concern with the need to rebuild communities, he asks, 'How . . . can such an orientation effectively provide the basis for a new form of civil solidarity?' (Nolan 1998: 301).

DIMINISHED SOCIAL DIMINISHED INDIVIDUAL

In the UK, like the USA, a therapeutic relationship with the public has developed at the same time as a more punitive approach to criminal justice emerged. Both of these developments can be understood as a more alienated engagement between the individual and the state—an engagement predicated upon a diminished sense of the social and also of the 'moral individual'.

Right realism—an outlook that developed in the USA in the 1970s and influenced the rise of 'administrative criminology' in the UK—was based on a critique of sociological positivism and radical criminology, fundamentally arguing that there was no point in attempting to work out the cause of crime when all that was needed was a set of measures to control it. What resulted in a number of technical or practical approaches to crime reduction was however, in the broader sense, an expression, like the left realists, of pessimism about social change and development—a limiting of expectations of both understanding crime—but more importantly of engaging with and changing the public and society more generally. The exasperation of American conservatives in the seventies—was expressed both in the growth of penal policies at the time, and in popular culture

In films like *Dirty Harry*, *Death Wish* and *Taxi Driver* a sense of frustration about crime is mixed with a demand—or more accurately a scream— that 'something must be done'. The vigilantism of Harry Callahan, Paul Kersey and Travis Bickel expresses well both the sense of urban decay and violence that was understood by some to have taken over American cities and also the exasperation and disconnection felt towards the establishment and indeed the public. Ultimately, across this genre of seventies films there is little sense of hope but rather of hopelessness, of inevitable defeat and decay: The scum on the streets were winning—and were being helped by the liberal institutions in American society.

The promotion of vigilantism and the right realist reaction against 'liberal excuses' for the causes of crime was based upon an estrangement from the 'social' and from society's institutions—from politics and ultimately from the 'public' itself.

Right realists while connecting with victims of crime and more generally with a sense of alienation amongst an increasingly anxious public, addressed crime not through politics and social ideals but through a rejection of this wider engagement with society. We need, argued James Q. Wilson 'a more sober view of man', foolish aspirations needed to be abandoned 'and utopian things forgotten'. Individual victims, rather than social changes, Wilson argued, should be the focus for public policy and policing alike. We may only reduce robbery by 20 percent—he stated, something that 'would still leave us with the highest robbery rate of almost any Western nation', but this, 'small gain for society [was] a large one for the would be victim' (Wilson 1985: 250).

Only a decade earlier the optimism of the sixties and of the Western World had been encapsulated in Neil Armstrong's statement that landing on the Moon was 'One small step for man, one giant leap for mankind'. For Wilson there was no connection between man and mankind—small gains would now be measured in the benefits offered to the isolated individual. For a conservative social theorist from the most powerful nation—that had embodied the aspirant character of the 'free world'—Wilson's outlook sounds very uninspiring—indeed highly pessimistic—but it was widely endorsed and Wilson himself became the advisor on crime to Ronald Reagan.

In rejecting any attempt to find the causes of crime however, Wilson was not only diminishing the potential of society to resolve this social problem, but was at the same time degrading the idea of the individual subject: Firstly in his focus on individuals as 'victims' of crime—but also and perhaps more significantly in his assessment that in general we needed a more 'sober view of man'.

Wilson was a key influence on what Jock Young defined as 'administrative criminology' which assumes that criminals are rational actors who weigh up the costs and benefits of crime. But this idea of the rational actor had little in common with the enlightenment belief in rationality—indeed the opposite. Rather than viewing mankind in general as rational or potentially rational and capable of addressing all social and scientific problems, administrative criminology was founded upon the loss of belief in finding wider causes. Consequently the 'man' they addressed was a rather shallow one dimensional man, with the idea behind rational choice theory reducing him to a crude bean counter—a potential criminal if the price was right: The belief in 'rational choice' theory expressed more a belief in the greedy nature of the individual than a passionate belief in rationality and in humanity.

The use of prison to deal with criminals and crime took off in the U.S.A. at this time—and latterly in the U.K., following Home Secretary Michael Howard's 'Prison Works' speech in 1993. Howard's speech at the Conservative Party Conference was used to promote the 27 new ways that more people would be put in prison: Where increased prison numbers had for much of the twentieth century been seen as a sign of failure for society, for Howard the question was no longer about society as such—but the protection of the public. 'We shall no longer judge the success of our system of justice by a fall in our prison population,' Howard stated (Dunbar and Langdon 1998).

A more pessimistic climate emerged from the 1970s—a period where 'nothing' seemed to work. Now pragmatism and an 'administrative' approach replaced both social ideals and a belief in the Rational subject, and the purpose of prison changed to address inmates with a more 'sober' vision of who and what they were. The decline in belief in social solutions and a more degraded view of the individual meant that prison became less a place for the 'moral individual' to pay his debt to society and to overcome his own sense of shame—aka Dostoevsky's Raskolnikov—than a mechanism to clear the streets of criminals. Rather than an expectation that prison would both punish and reform, the underlying outlook was to simply lock wicked people up and 'throw away the key'.

If the 'prison works' approach reflected a more asocial outlook and a diminished view of the individual subject, a similar sentiment was embodied within the therapeutic culture and practices that were also developing at this time—and that have come to prominence in both Britain and America in the 1990s.

In the US, Nolan has observed the emergence of the therapeutic state in the huge rise of 'emotional damages' claims in the late 1970s and 1980s; the rise of psychologists as expert witnesses; the development of therapeutic drugs courts and the expansion of therapy in prisons. In the UK, Furedi notes that the 'application of the treatment model is deeply entrenched within the British criminal justice system', with this treatment extending its reach with more offenders being 'forced to attend courses in anger management, drugs and alcohol addiction or sex therapy' (Furedi 2004: 64) As well as a number of these specific forms of therapy, the more all encompassing reorientation of the criminal justice system around the victim has been grounded in an engagement with the emotional well being of individuals' experience of crime and indeed their experience of the justice system itself.

Rather than therapism being seen as a more caring option within the criminal justice system, it is seen as highly problematic by writers like Nolan and Furedi. Methods of therapy are often understood to be more progressive—compared to a penal approach that is seen as authoritarian and right wing, however, in essence they both represent a more asocial approach to the issue of crime—an approach that became most pronounced in the UK in the 1990s.

THE VENEER OF POLITICS

Examining C. Wright Mills' conception of the *public* as opposed to a *mass*, we are able to identify a distinction between an autonomous public that has a separate life from social institutions, where, 'virtually as many people express opinions as receive them', and perhaps most importantly can 'find an outlet in effective action against, if necessary, prevailing systems and agents of authority'. This contrasts with a mass, where 'far fewer people express opinions than receive them', and where 'the community of publics becomes an abstracted collectivity of individuals who receive impressions from the mass media' (Mills 1968: 355). *Public* opinion for Mills is there-fore predicated upon an *active* ebb and flow of opinion where anyone can speak and, most significantly, *does*. Action by democratic institutions thus emerges from this 'general will' of the people. Rather than the public and the democratic institutions *reacting* to society they collectively create it.

Today, it appears that Mills' notion of a *mass* society is more prevalent.[8] However, this development has a dialectical component and can be seen in relation to politics and democratic institutions themselves. Logically, the transformation of a *public* into a *mass*, with the implied interconnection between the public and society's institutions, necessarily means that this transformation could not occur unless there was an equally profound trans-formation in politics itself. If in the late twentieth century icon of the victim we see a more powerless, socially alienated individual—within the political elite, a similar development must have occurred.

In Alan Finlayson's *Making Sense of New Labour*, the emergence of New Labour is understood to represent a move away from politics and towards a form of social engagement based more on *sociology*. What Finlayson means by this is that the government has become distant from the 'energy of soci-ety'—politics—and has become more of a technocratic manager of a process that it believes to be beyond its control. Whereas political developments are predicated upon an ideology or philosophy and a movement from the pres-ent to the future, politics under new Labour is more about a sociological examination of the *facts* of society and a subsequent development of policies according to these facts. Having lost an engagement with the idea of politi-cal agency, New Labour increasingly responds to social facts, which they believe create certain types of *behaviours* (Finlayson 2003).

For Heartfield, the Third Way represents a 'process without a subject' (Heartfield: 2002: 174). Illustrated in Fairclough's examination of the lan-guage of New Labour, we find government documents are increasingly expressed with, 'passive sentences without agents' (Fairclough 2000: 24). Similarly Fairclough notes how change is discussed by Labour ministers as a noun rather than a verb, and the absence of 'responsible agents further contributes to constructing change as inevitable' (Fairclough 2000: 26).

Citing the examples of 'globalisation' and 'modernisation', both Fin-layson (2003) and Heartfield (2002) suggest that these concepts, rather than reflecting profound economic and social changes, are rather expres-sions of the political elites' sense of the rudderless nature of society: a sense expressed by New Labour in that they are 'not the authors of their own destiny' (Heartfield 2002: 180).

The *search* for a big idea, which has troubled political leaders in the West for the last decade, gives an indication of the dislocation of the political elite from social processes. Where ideas previously emerged from society and the conflicting tensions and movements within it, today the new political elite believes think tanks and policy officers can invent them. Dislocated from a *public*, acting more as sociologists than as political parties, and attempting to engage with a society that feels beyond their control, the political elites' own sense of anxiety and alienation has developed into a propensity to engage individuals through their personal insecurities. The elites' own sense of diminished subjectivity helps them to both understand themselves and the public through the prism of the *victim*.

As well as the political elite reacting to society through their own sense of anxiety, being dislocated from the *public* and from a social will, they are inclined to search for points of contacted with the electorate. Participation subsequently becomes an aim in itself and has, through the 1990s and into the twenty-first century, become increasingly developed at a *micro*, or local level—the community (Gilling 1999; N. Rose 1996; Flint 2002). As Alice Miles has pointed out, with reference to the move to regional governments and the rise of Antisocial Behaviour Orders (ASBOs), 'Our rulers are in denial about the big issues and are seeking refuge in little things' (*Times* 3 November 2004).

While politicising 'little things', the role of governance has also developed, increasingly incorporating institutions, both voluntary and state-run, in the management of initiatives that attempt to regulate society more systematically and often engage with the public through issues of community safety (N. Rose 1996). Many of these institutions, for example trade unions, as discussed earlier, or housing associations and departments have also been transformed and subsequently developed a relationship with their *consumers* or *clients* based on the protection and regulation of their behaviour and that of their neighbours (Cummings 1997; Flint 2002).

Finally, and in relation to the changed operation of politics, organisations like the police have become more directly involved in the participatory concerns of the state. With antisocial behaviour—noise, graffiti, vandalism and so on—being understood to 'undermine community spirit', the police themselves have, according to one Chief Constable, become 'formidable agents of change' (Dennis 1997: 116). With fear of crime and antisocial behaviour being understood as the key to what makes or undermines a community, the police have come to understand their role less in terms of enforcing law and order, and more in relation to how people feel—Stratchlyde police chief John Orr, for example, argued that the 'feel safe factor is the primary measure' against which the police should be judged (Dennis 1997: 121).

That the police in Britain can today understand themselves as having a role in rebuilding communities by their own actions gives a sense of the declining significance of politics and the *public*, it also reflects an increasingly technical approach to community building, and the growing centrality of safety to individual, public and political life.

THE WEASEL WORD—COMMUNITY

A noticeable development in the discussions about crime in the 1990s was the increased use of the idea of 'community'. In terms of a framework for discussing issues of crime the idea of community stepped in, where previously ideas of nation and class had been. Discussion about Britishness and British law and order, or of understanding crime from a 'working-class perspective' declined and interest and concern about 'the community' rose.

At an abstract level what this discussion about community represented was the decline of subjectivity. Community is in a certain respect a space without a subject, an imagined place and entity with little or no political or social existence. Historically the issues and identities that could tap into the energy of the public—that could engage their subjectivity—related to nation and class. This discussion of community on the other hand was not generated by public passions so much as the decline of these previous passions and political loyalties. Discussing community had the advantage of avoiding politics—while maintaining a collective sense, a warm space where people felt part of something—without actually being part of something. At the same time, the idea of community was able to avoid—indeed sidestepped—the issue of individual rights. By promoting this subjectless space, individuals and their freedom could be pushed aside for the more important interest of the 'community', or as Heartfield puts it, 'the "community" is a lifeless abstraction, invoked only as the restraining limitation upon the individual subject' (Heartfield 2002: 55).

Lacking a collective subjective engagement with the public through issues of nation or class—and with a diminished sense of the individual subject—the 'community' was the perfect site for micro-politics: It consequently became a framework of intervention that was no longer predicated upon the understanding of individuals as active subjects. Sovereign rights and individual rights had at their core an active component; now in comparison the 'right' of people in the community was the right to be protected. This new 'collective' was promoted and engaged with not as a community of interest—an active entity in its own right—but rather as a collection of insecure individuals, who needed and demanded to be made safe.

THE POLITICS OF FEAR

The retreat into 'community', the concern about 'little things' and the elevation of private *troubles* into social problems, were all part of the micropolitics of the 1990s—as was the issue of safety. All of these issues have become more pronounced and significant with each newly elected Labour government.

Safety as a new 'moral' absolute under New Labour has developed apace, and the attempt to regulate social processes that appear to be beyond their control has led to more laws and more new crimes being created than by any other administration.[9] Relating to a more fragmented public there is simultaneously an attempt to reconnect with people through their fears. Safety has consequently become the organising principle of the politics of fear. As Heartfield notes, whereas the Third Way in the UK and US has failed to connect people to a social vision, this does not mean that they have made no connection: 'If they have failed to appeal to a collective vision of the future, both the Democrats and New Labour have managed to relate to a more atomised electorate, by playing upon its fears' (Heartfield 2002: 195).

New Labour's campaign advisor Philip Gould, in his 1994 document, 'Fighting the Fear Factor', argued that the public were insecure and anxious and more inclined to fear that things may get worse rather than better. Given these circumstances Gould believed that the right had used fear as a way of gaining support. Despite Gould noting that much of this anxiety had developed because of social changes, and despite his concern with the reactionary use of fear, his proposals were for Labour to connect, 'with the populist instincts of voters through policies that are tough on crime'. In Gould's book *The Unfinished Revolution* he explains: 'Progressive parties have learned to ... connect directly with the insecurities of working families', and that this is necessary because, 'in an increasingly fast-changing world, insecurity is likely to grow, and with it the basis for fear campaigning' (Heartfield 2002: 195).

New Labour developed their own form of fear campaigning, and did so more systematically than the Conservatives by relating not to the *public* with politics, but to the *mass* of individuals through their fears and anxieties.

CONCLUSION

The rise of the victim voice within public and political life is remarkable and has over two decades transformed the way the public is understood in the UK—and to some extent how individuals understand themselves. From a focus upon certain groups in society, today the label of victim and of vulnerability can be attached to almost any individual, as the diminishing of the subject becomes a universalising cultural phenomenon. The meaning we give to terms and categories of people has similarly changed. The term 'working class' for example is more likely to invite images of poverty and helplessness than of collectivity and strength. Indeed as the image of the victim has gained status the attempt to represent interests through the language of vulnerability has grown—to gain social recognition it appears one must illustrate and promote your powerlessness. *As the public world has shrunk the world of the vulnerable individual has expanded and become central to policy and practise in state agencies and local government.* Consequently, *public* issues that were significant for much of the twentieth century—like unemployment—have literally become invisible in the political and public imagination—or they are represented as another example of victimhood. At the same time, the more fragmented and therapeutic framework within which social problems are formed today is illustrated for example in the way that the number of work days lost from strike action has been replaced by the loss of between '5 and 6 million working days [that cost the U.K.] more than £5 billion a year' from the 'epidemic' of work stress (Wainwright and Calnan 2002: 1).

The diminished subject has many facets, it is the powerless victim—it is also the asocial individual. Indeed the disconnection of the individual from society helps to explain today's *culture of fear*—an anxious culture embedded within what could be described as *The Lonely Crowd* (Riesman 1961). As Nolan has observed, despite the positive and sometimes radical image of therapy within modern society, its very essence is its self-referential nature—an inward turn that is less the product of vibrant individualism than of a collapsing public realm that previously gave meaning to people's lives. Again the issue of unemployment is of note in this respect—in that the benefits of work are increasingly understood not in terms of work itself, of production, activity or a contribution made to society, but in terms of its impact upon ones self esteem and 'happiness'. Value it seems can only be given to something if it refers to the inner self. Ironically, the political and cultural framework today institutionalises this asocial and self-referential approach—reinforcing both the insecure and asocial nature of society.

Today's political elites are themselves lonely—as Finlayson argues—they act as sociologists rather than politicians—observing the facts of society, facts that they themselves have little relationship to or influence over. For the elite and the public, the world is seen through the eyes of the isolated individual—for whom society is always 'out there'. As Heartfield notes,

> To individuals who are isolated, society ceases to be an extension of themselves, and becomes instead a vast impersonal force. The more isolated and helpless the individual feels, the more adamantine in its indifference is society (Heartfield 2002: 56).

This sense of dislocation from society effects not only individuals—but has also become a perspective of both conservatives and radicals—who have lost faith or belief in their own capacity to influence social change. Realism has become the norm—a realism predicated upon the more degraded sense of the subject—as wicked and/or vulnerable.

The framework of diminished subjectivity has likewise degraded the meaning and content of rights. Charles Clarke, Labour's Home Secretary in 2005, gave for example a perfect illustration of how the idea of rights has come to mean the protection of the vulnerable, 'We all have a right to live free from harassment. But with those rights come responsibilities and we all need to play a part in tackling disrespect and unacceptable behaviour', he argued (Jameson 2005:183). The inactive nature of these 'rights' are clearly seen here as something that is given by the state to the individual—with an underlying threat that the protection provided by government is dependant upon your responsible behaviour.

The diminished nature of rights are ideally located within the 'community'—a subjectless space. Discussing the Antisocial Behaviour Act (Scotland) 2004, Kay Tisdall has noted the extent to which this Act extended further the reach of local authorities into regulating the behaviour of parents. It changes the balance between the children, their parents and various arms of the state, she notes, and 'It gives a new role to the "community", although with little attention to how "community" is defined, whom that may include or exclude, and which people and organizations can claim to represent it' (Tisdall 2006) Indeed the arbitrary nature of this form of representation and participation illustrates the largely artificial nature of 'community'.

The diminished sense of rights and freedom has been both promoted by the new political elite—but is also something that reflects the declining aspiration for personal activity and liberty. For example, the decline in libertarianism amongst the British public that had been identified in the mid-1990s continued into the twenty-first century. In the 2007 Social Attitudes Survey (relating to a survey in 2005) it was found that only 15 per cent of Labour voters opposed identity cards compared with 45 per cent in 1990. In less than a generation libertarianism in the UK appears to have all but died out, and as Professor Conor Gearty noted, 'It is as though society is in the process of forgetting why past generations thought those freedoms to be so very important' (*Guardian* 24 January 2007).

The diminished elite have themselves also helped to make 'little things' the basis of politics, issues that may previously have engaged the attention of local councillors and social workers, becoming the basis of national policy and political rhetoric. As the imagination of politicians shrinks, the minutia of everyday life has become more important and understood as more problematic. The diminished subjectivity of the elite has not only limited their vision, but sullied it—greed, selfishness and a myriad violent cultures haunts them as they look at children misbehaving and see yobs and terrorists—the brothers and sisters of James Bulger's killers.

The crisis of belief and the loss of political direction and a *social will* in the 1990s encouraged both a tendency to regulate society more directly and lock more people up, but also to moralise about 'little things'. The minutiae of everyday life, the focus on community, and the engagement with the 'troubles' of the public, became the basis of political action and explains the rise of not only the politics of crime but more specifically the politics of antisocial behaviour.[10] Lacking a 'vision thing', the demand that the public learn the difference between right and wrong was no longer founded upon a moral or political basis, but on the more vacuous amoral absolute of safety. The beliefs and behaviour of people were to become judged not in terms of their relationship with society and their 'public' actions, but on the personal interactions that were problematised through the radical language of harassment and abuse—the ultimate act of responsibility being a 'zero toler-ance' approach to personal and public life.

C Wright Mills, discussing the need to help constitute an active *public*, believed that for this to occur the 'troubles' of everyday life needed to be made into 'issues' (Mills 1968). These troubles, Mills felt, could only be fully understood by being situated within society as a whole and transformed into 'issues' that could then be addressed by the *public*. Rather than troubles, it was 'issues' that would then become understood as the *social problems* to address. The 'troubles' of local communities before the 1990s were gener-ally not made into *social problems*. However, with the loss of a political and social will, these troubles have been engaged with more directly and in a sense the political elite, backed up by key institutions including the trade unions, have, rather than making 'issues' out of troubles, made *troubles* the *issue*.

The problems of everyday life, in the form of antisocial behaviour, have under the New Labour governments become the basis of politics and the newly institutionalised framework within which to reengage the atomised individual. Having lost a *social will* and the *energy of society* to redirect social process and structures, a therapeutic culture has developed within which state institutions relate not only to individuals and 'little things', but to the *emotions* associated with them.[11] As Furedi notes

> Unable to change the circumstances that cry out for decisive social pol-icy, the promoters of the politics of behaviour attempt to alter individ-ual lifestyle. As Christopher Lasch argued in his critique of therapeutic politics, the state bureaucracy seeks to transform 'collective grievances into personal problems amenable to therapeutic intervention' (Furedi 2005: 150).

5 From Moral to Amoral Panics

> It is widely acknowledged that this is the age of the moral panic
> (Thompson 1998: 1).

INTRODUCTION

The term 'moral panic', first used by Jock Young (1971) and immortalised by Stanley Cohen (1972), today has almost 300,000 'hits' on the internet referring to it and has become both an established concept within the social sciences as well as a popularly used form of condemnation of irrational anxieties and issues within society. One of the books in a Routledge series of 'Key Ideas', written by Kenneth Thompson in 1998, is dedicated to *Moral Panics*, and it is from this book that the above quote is taken. Ours, it appears, is an age of moral panic. Chas Critcher (co-author of *Policing the Crisis* [Hall et al. 1978], another book famed for its explanation of moral panics), writing in *Moral Panics and the Media*, also believes that 'moral panics are around us all the time' (Critcher 2006: 3). Critcher notes that interest in moral panic analysis, after a lull in the late 1970s, was reawakened in both the United States and the UK by the issues of child abuse and AIDS.

When first addressing the issue of the Hamilton curfew, and subsequently the wider issue of youth antisocial behaviour, the sociological framework used here to understand these developments was that of the moral panic. What appeared to be an exaggerated concern with the issue of youth crime and disorder seemed at first to fit this model—a disproportionate and hostile reaction to a threat in society, a problem that was challenging its values, that was given a stereotypical media image, and which led to the demand for greater social control of both young people and the family. However, the extent to which the construction of the issue of antisocial behaviour can be understood as a traditional moral reaction is questionable. Rather, today's reaction to problems in society has developed with the collapse rather than the enforcement of morals (and more specifically politics) around the new *amoral absolute* of safety. Here this idea is explored further with particular reference to the idea of moral panics—a concept which it is argued has not only lost its meaning—but has at times become part of a new framework of *amoral panics*.

Since the early writings on moral panics much has changed, indeed the term itself has not only become an established sociological concept, but is used so widely that much of the specific features first explored by Cohen are often lost. Almost any reaction to an event, it appears, can be described as a moral panic today—especially when the issues being promoted stem from those seen as being on the right. Other issues, related to health scares like BSE ('mad cow disease'), have been understood through the framework of moral panics. Issues of a generalised state of 'risk' and 'fear' have also been explored within sociology, and again examined with reference to—or at times in opposition to—the idea of moral panics.

Key themes addressed within the sociology of moral panics remain relevant to understanding social anxieties. The question of societies values in a changing world—the demand to overcome what Tony Blair described in the 1990s as a 'moral vacuum'—the media reaction to issues of crime—concerns about the family and of youth—and the, if anything, more significant issue of social control. However, society has changed. The political framework in particular that informed the studies of Cohen—*Folk Devils and Moral Panics* (1972), Hall et al.—*Policing the Crisis* (1978), and also Pearson—*Hooligan: A History of Respectable Fears* (1983) has been transformed. The previously central question of left and right is today at best marginal—if not irrelevant. The existence of an organised working class—of the aspiration for socialism, or the aggressive promotion of 'Victorian values'—has also declined. Indeed today, many of the 'fundamental values' that were seen to lie at the heart of moral panics of the past have been transformed: The promotion of The Family has become replaced by an acceptance of families, Britishness now embodies the idea of multiculturalism and even the Conservative Party rarely campaigns around traditional moral values. At the same time, as Cohen has himself noted, new 'panics', crimes and social problems have emerged in recent years, not through the activities of old moral campaigners, but from a more 'radical' and feminist perspective—with hate crime and stalking for example incorporating issues of race and gender—the significance of safety and the protection of the victim, rather than of traditional moral values being central to these developments.

Whereas panics in the past were often occasional, short-lived, focused on specific groups and activities, and generated by conservatives, today 'panics' come from various sections of society, and cover an ever-wider array of issues, from the MMR vaccine to bird flu, the millennium bug, paedophiles, binge drinkers, sexually transmitted diseases and passive smoking, to name but a few. Whatever the myth and reality of these 'panics', the language of 'epidemics' and 'chaos' used to describe them depicts a society that feels out of control, and expresses a deep sense of pessimism about the future. Rather than panicking being the preserve of reactionary traditionalists, it seems that to one degree or another we are all in a panic about something.

At the same time, the ability of those in authority to use panics to their advantage has also been questioned. Today, many panics are not only promoted by less predictable groups and individuals, but, like the MMR panic (Fitzpatrick 2004), have helped to undermine rather than shore up the authority of the political elite (Ungar 2001).

One interesting aspect of this idea of the 'panic' is its implied understanding of the public as being in a state of 'mass delusion'—as being irrational—or even a 'mob'. At a recent conference on 'Moral Panics: Then and Now,' Stanley Cohen noted that at the time that *Folk Devils and Moral Panics* was written he was challenged about the way this idea portrayed a potentially 'atavistic mob'. In the early 1970s Cohen felt that this aspect of the moral panic thesis was problematic—but noted that today this was no longer a concern.[1] In the promotional notes for this conference held in March 2007, the idea of a moral panic was presented as being a concept that explores 'apparently irrational public anxieties'. This idea is used as short hand to some extent, but compared with the wider focus upon the elites, moral campaigners, and agents of social control, this concern with the 'irrational public' is perhaps illustrative of what the term moral panic has often come to represent.

The idea of 'moral', within the moral panic framework, is also something that was and is used fairly loosely. Within Cohen's work the term was used to describe the form of a conservative reaction to wider and more significant underlying social, economic and political changes. However, the issue of morality is also useful to explore in and of itself, not least of all because within moral claims there are two core elements that have declined today and help to explain the more generalised *amoral panics* of the 21st century; firstly the traditional idea of being moral holds within it a social component—a grand narrative or at least a wider ideal and story about humanity—and secondly in upholding absolute standards, moral campaigners, at least in theory, maintained and promoted an idea of the responsible, moral individual.

NOTHING HAS CHANGED?

Reading much of the literature on moral panics one could be forgiven for thinking that little has changed since the 1970s and 1980s. The old battle between the right who panic and the left who challenge these panics still informs the framework of how the moral panic is often understood. The moral right are still identified as being central to today's panics—with tabloid newspapers in the UK like the *Sun* and conservative papers like the *Daily Mail* being singled out for particular attention in an attempt to expose moral panics.

Academic journal articles also continue to discuss moral panics with reference to events in the 1980s. Andrew Hill, in the *British Journal of*

Sociology for example, wrote an article about 'Acid House and Thatcherism' in 2002. More recently still, in 2005 David Waldron wrote an article about 'Role-Playing Games and the Christian Right'. Usefully Waldron notes that attacks on gamers peaked between 1988 and 1992, before explaining that

> In fact, after 1992 I have been unable to find any letter, articles or editorials on the topic except for several retrospective examinations of the history of gaming between 1997 and 2000 and an article dealing with prejudice against Christians from within the gaming community . . . in 1999 (Waldron 2005).

Useful though these articles are, their publication suggests more than a 'nostalgic' look back at how things used to be—but rather sit comfortably alongside the, if anything, intensified concern about moral panics and the understanding of the significance of 'neo-liberalism' and 'neo-conservatism' for society.

Core moral panic text books, also tend to focus on modern panics as a conservative attempt to 'restore moral certainty' (Critcher 2006: 9). In Thompson's *Moral Panics* he concludes by explaining that

> We have brought together analyses of ideology and discourse to show how in Britain and America, the media have been given prominence to a discursive formation that articulated together a combination of neo-liberal individualism and neo-conservative nostalgia for a moral golden age—an imagined national community unified by common values (Thompson 1998: 141).

Chas Critcher, editor of *Moral Panics and the Media*, focuses on the right-wing, conservative nature of moral panics. After noting the 'panics' about binge drinking, cannabis smokers, gypsies, asylum seekers and terrorists, he argues that moral panics have assumed an increasing political importance in Britain. 'Most of the issues I have just listed', he continues, 'were produced early in 2005 by Conservative newspapers and politicians in an unsuccessful effort to prevent the Labour Party from being elected for a third consecutive term' (Critcher 2006: 3). Critcher's defence of the Labour Party, in opposition to the 'moral conservatives', is however a curious one given Labour's own political engagement with issues like binge drinking, smoking, immigration and terrorism. Indeed, the government having recently banned smoking in public places have stepped up measures against 'binge drinkers' with a £4 million campaign targeting 18–24-year-olds. The TV advert for this campaign with the tag line 'Know your limits' portrays young people falling victim to horrific accidents, rapes and assaults after a night out.

Panics it seems are often only recognised by radical academics, when they come from those on the 'right' or by those wearing a dog collar.

COHEN AND HALL

Stanley Cohen carried out the first major work on moral panics in Britain in 1972.[2] Cohen's analyses of the scare surrounding the Mods and Rockers fights in the early 1960s looked at moral panics in terms of what the Mods and Rockers *represented* in society. Rather than their actions being significant in themselves, Cohen argued that the Mods and Rockers were seen and treated as a symbol of Americanised affluence and youthful hedonism. Developed from an understanding of disaster research, Cohen saw moral panics as an expression of social anxiety, brought to the surface by a particular event or action. For a once 'great nation' such as Britain, this influence of the US upon young people, Cohen argued, was seen as problematic—both in the values they were seen to uphold, or those they were seen to reject, like the ethics of sobriety and hard work (Cohen 1972).

Cohen not only launched the term moral panic, but also was the first to analyse what he saw as the spontaneous collective behaviour involved in these panics, which were short-lived and developed outside of societies' key institutions (Goode and Ben-Yehuda 1994). The media exaggerated the problem (Cohen 1972: 32–33); the police and courts were activated and pushed for more powers to deal with the problem, thus escalating the issue (Cohen 1972: 88–91); politicians denounced the fighting as 'evil' and called for new laws (Cohen 1972: 138); local action groups emerged—a 'germinal social movement' (Cohen 1972: 120)—to demand tougher remedies (Cohen 1972: 125); and the public reacted to all of the above developments. The result: a fully fledged moral panic.

Stuart Hall's examination of the panic surrounding 'muggers' in the 1970s suggested that news about crime was becoming a moral tale reinforcing what is right and wrong (Hall et al. 1978). Hall's analysis adopted and developed elements of Cohen's work on moral panics, analysing key concerns about affluence and changes to the 'traditional' ways of life.[3] Elements of social change and changes in attitudes amongst the young, took on a 'folk devilish' form in the black mugger—a reflection of an alien who has no sense of respect, hard work, morals or family values and who was making the streets into a no-go area. The mugger, Hall and colleagues explained, was a symbol of social decay that was first imagined and then discovered (1978: 161).

Hall et al.'s analysis both looked at structural reasons for the rise of the mugging panic and also adopted Gramsci's concept of hegemony: the birth of the 'law and order society' in the 1970s being an expression of the inability of the state to win the hearts and minds of society, reflected in the more overt use of power to control sections of the population. As Hall explained, 'A crisis of hegemony marks a moment of profound rupture in the political and economic life of a society, an accumulation of contradictions' (1978: 217).

The development of this panic and a more openly coercive state occurred at 'exceptional' moments, triggered in the late 1960s by the 'exhaustion of consent' in society (1978: 219). Here the 'control culture' and the media, followed by the police and courts, reacted more quickly, without much pressure from below, to events in society, creating a 'general panic' about social order (1978: 222).[4]

The media coverage of mugging, Hall believed, reflected firstly a sense of social loss, concern about family breakdown and moral decline; and secondly an image of the decaying inner city as a 'ghetto'. Here, the concern about social decay was mixed with a sense of loss of 'the family' and was expressed in relation to not only youth, but an alien body of youth—black youth.

A key focus within Cohen and Hall's moral panic research was not so much the problem raised by these panics, but the reaction to them. As Stuart Hall explains in *Policing the Crisis*:

> We want to know what the social causes of 'mugging' are. But we argue that this is only half—less than half—of the mugging story. More important is why British society *reacts to mugging*, in the extreme way it does, at that precise historical conjunction—the early 1970's (Hall et al 1978: vii).

Usefully in *Resistance through Rituals* edited by Hall and Tony Jefferson, an attempt is made to chart the changing form of moral panics, from 'Discrete Moral Panics' in the early 1960s where a dramatic event leads to public disquiet, moral entrepreneurship and a response from the 'control culture'; to 'Crusading' around issues like drugs and pornography in the late 1960s, where the moral entrepreneurs are sensitised to certain issues and are almost waiting for a dramatic event to occur to latch onto which again leads to a response from the 'control culture'; and finally the 'Post Law 'n' Order Campaign' of the early 1970s where society is more sensitised to moral concerns and the control culture is already geared up to respond to any 'dramatic event' that occurs (Hall and Jefferson 1976: 76). In essence this mapping out of moral panics depicts the politicisation of moral issues: A development that emerged through the 1970s and 1980s as part of the conservative challenge to the existing welfare framework, the organised working class in the form of the trade unions, a concern about 'alien cultures' and the sense of British decline.

AMERICAN SOCIAL CONSTRUCTIONISTS

As Cohen was developing his work on moral panics in the UK, in the US similar work was being carried out by sociologists looking at the issue of deviance from a 'labelling' perspective (Best 2004). This work took as its starting point a questioning of the accepted, official, objective description of crime and deviant behaviour. Rather than drug-takers and other deviants being simply deviant by nature of their behaviour, it was argued that they were deviant because their behaviour was labelled so by others, especially those in authority. Therefore rather than viewing deviant behaviour as an objective activity or fact, as positivists had done, the labelling of deviant behaviour was investigated.

For constructionists or 'subjectivists', social problems and therefore moral panics are seen as problems that have been identified and collectively defined. These social problems and panics are therefore not objective realities in and of themselves, but rather are constructed (Becker 1991, Best 1993, Jenkins 1992; 1998, and Spector and Kitsuse 2001).[5] Indeed, Cohen himself also believed that 'it is the perception of threat and not its actual existence that is important' (Cohen 1972: 22).

American social constructionist Philip Jenkins argues: 'It is impossible to define a problem in an objective or value-free way, since talking about a "problem" or a "crisis" ipso facto implies that there is a solution, that change of some kind is necessary and desirable' (Jenkins 1998: 4). For Jenkins, the very way a problem is discussed, and solutions developed, implies a certain value-laden view of the problem and of society. However, while maintaining a critical approach to 'objective' social problems, Jenkins and most social problem researchers also attempt to examine the strengths and weaknesses of objective evidence—rather than seeing the objective world as purely a subjective construction.

The approach adopted by American sociologists Philip Jenkins (1992; 1998) and Joel Best (1993; 1999) grew out of Social Problem Theory in the 1970s.[6] This approach, known as contextual constructionism is more flexible methodologically than the strict constructionism of Spector and Kitsuse (2001) as it allows for the usefulness, and examination, of objective 'facts' and statistics, while retaining a critical understanding of them (Best 2001a).

In this way these contextual constructionists are able to explain in more depth why certain social problems or moral panics emerge when they do by examining in more detail the values and rhetoric used by certain groups and situating them within broader patterns of social problem construction.

SOCIAL PROBLEM OR MORAL PANIC?

Social problem theory is raised here because it is a more flexible methodology than that associated with moral panics, in terms of examining social problems. Indeed as Cohen himself notes:

> *Folk Devils and Moral Panics* was informed by the sixties fusion of labelling theory, cultural politics and critical sociology. Today's students

of moral panics do not have to engage with this theoretical mix-up. They can go straight into the literature on social constructionism and claimsmaking. This is a well developed model for studying the contested claims that are made—by victims, interest groups, social movements, professionals and politicians—the construction of new social problem categories (Cohen 2002: xxii).

Goode and Ben-Yehuda, while recognising much overlapping in moral panic theory and social problem theory, also point out that there are 'at least three' basic differences between them. Social problem theory, unlike moral panic theory, need not have a 'folk devil', in that it need not show a discrepancy between the degree of concern and the actual problem. Disproportionality is not necessarily relevant, and while 'moral panics' imply a substantial change in the mood of a group or groups in society towards a particular issue, social problem theory can study any problem regardless of the 'panic' surrounding it (Goode and Ben-Yehuda 1994).

For social problem theory, issues that become institutionalised are in fact perhaps more important to study than those that erupt and then disappear. This is of particular relevance today, with the emergence of a 'risk society' or 'culture of fear' within which anxiety about social problems appear to be a permanent rather than a fleeting phenomenon.

Moral panic theory generally starts from a belief that an issue is being exaggerated, that Mods and Rockers are not such a threat, that mugging is not as widespread as assumed, or that the concern about antisocial behaviour is unjustified and not based on a 'real' increase in this problem. For social problem writers, the myth or reality of a social problem is not necessarily important. Crime may be high but this doesn't explain why it has become a 'social problem' in and of itself. For a social problem to be constructed someone must raise it as a problem and campaign around this issue, and politicians and key social institutions must pick up on this issue and help promote it. Social issues like crime, even when on the increase, need not become 'social problems' around which campaigns are built.

Another difference between moral panic theory and social problem theory is the political nature of moral panic theory. Jenkins has noted that the vast majority of moral panic research has been developed within a left/liberal framework (Jenkins 1992: 145), a framework within which outbursts of traditional conservative morality and issues associated with the new right are challenged.

However, moral panic work is not, argue Goode and Ben-Yehuda, inherently political and ideological. Jenkins (1992: 173) has used moral panic theory to explore the work of 'radical' feminists in the UK and the US who helped to create and promote a moral panic around child abuse. Similarly, Cohen has argued that the methods used in the 1960s and 1970s to explore the crusades against marijuana and homosexuality could equally be used today to examine modern-day moral panics that have been promoted by left/liberal activists around issues concerning industrial pollution, smoking and pornography (Cohen 1988: 260–63).

It is true that moral panic theory could be used to examine panics on the left and the right. However in practice this has rarely materialised. Rather moral panic research has tended to remain within an 'anti–new right' framework. This has been less the case in the US, where there has been more significant work carried out examined radical and feminist panics, for example over the issue of child abuse (Jenkins 1992, 1998). Researchers who focus solely on 'right-wing' panics that often take a traditional moral form, are consequently unable to examine more recent panics that take a non-moral or amoral form.

In general it is still true to argue that 'moral panics'—or at least social anxieties—emerge and are generated at times of social change by conservative elements in society made insecure by this social change. *However, the question for today is what form does this conservative impulse take?*

WHO MAKES MORAL PANICS?

The question of *who* makes moral panics or social problems has been contested over the years and has often been connected to issues and questions of morality and ideology, material interest, and status interest (Goode and Ben-Yehuda 1994: 124–43).

The Marxist approach adopted by Hall (1978) locates the rise of moral panics with the *elite*.[7] Other researchers, especially those from the US, identify *interest groups* as being central to the claimsmaking process.[8] Alternatively, others argue that moral panics emanate from the public themselves, or from the *grassroots* of society (Goode and Ben-Yehuda 1994).

Most studies of moral panics incorporate elements of all three theories, related to the *elite*, *interest groups*, and the *grassroots*. For example, moral panics cannot exist without an element of grassroots support; however, these panics, even if originating within the public, only become defined as social problems when interest groups or elite groups take up the issue. In the end, the study of moral panics must recognise that 'No moral panic is complete without an examination of all societal levels, from elites to the grassroots, and the full spectrum from ideology and the morality at one pole to crass status and material interests at the other' (Goode and Ben-Yehuda 1994: 143).

The question of the 'panic' itself, is however far from clear. What turns a 'concern' into a panic, and how can this be measured. This is especially relevant in relation to understanding the 'irrational public'. The 'moral panic'—at least in terms of its popular usage—does at times contain a sense of an 'atavistic mob'—at its most extreme, conjuring up an image of a torch carrying horde taking to the streets to avenge themselves of the Frankenstein monster within their community. But do the public really panic, and indeed did they really panic about Mods and Rockers or even about muggers? The idea of a 'public panic' is also perhaps even more problematic in today's more fragmented times—times when a collective response to *issues* has been replaced by a more diffuse and individuated anxiety about *troubles*.

The American Philip Jenkins, who has written some of the most insightful books on moral panics has described what a panic is—as a 'wave of irrational public fear', elaborating that the 'word panic, however, implies not only fear but fear that is wildly exaggerated and wrongly directed', something he notes that emerged for example in the 1940s and mid-1980s. However, Jenkins in *Moral Panic* goes on to explain how at these times, 'concern over sexual abuse provides a basis for extravagant claimsmaking by professionals, the media, and assorted interest groups, who argue that the problem is quantitatively and qualitatively far more severe than anyone could reasonably suppose' (Jenkins 1998: 7). This approach replicates his earlier study in *Intimate Enemies: Moral Panics in Contemporary Great Britain*—a book that explores the issue of child abuse and the 'panic' over satanic ritual abuse. In both books what Jenkins is really describing is a panic amongst professionals and the media—a panic that no doubt influenced the public mind set—and added to what Furedi describes as a culture of fear—but does this necessarily indicate that the public itself was in a 'panic'?

The significance of the media has also remained central to moral panic research, the headline stories often within the tabloid press being used as evidence of a panic. However, despite the influence of the media over the public as regards moral panics being seen as important, Hunt believes that 'no theory of moral panic has yet provided a satisfactory explanation of the relationship between the media and public opinion'. Indeed he notes, that the problem with a number of moral panic studies is that they do not separate the media from reality. In other words, just because the media panic about mugging does not mean that this was how the public reacted (Hunt 1997: 645).

Here the point being made is that press cuttings are an unreliable guide to public opinion. Indeed, when looking at Cohen's Mods and Rockers 'panic' it appears that the public were far from panicking.

While Cohen recognises the broad political framework within which the Mods and Rockers moral panic was developed, his theoretical development from labelling theory directs him to focus much of his work on those who label the Mods and Rockers as deviants—particularly the media. But, while Cohen notes that there was a public reaction to the Mods and Rockers violence to some degree, he also notes that the mass media response was more stereotyped than any sample of public opinion. Arguing that 'In this sense the public could be said to be better informed about the phenomenon than the media or the moral entrepreneurs whom the media quoted' (1972: 66).

In a small survey Cohen carried out himself in Brighton, only 6% of those questioned thought there was more violence 'today' than in the past and somewhat surprisingly 70% of the parents he asked said they wouldn't mind if their children went down to the beach with a group of Mods or Rockers. Also 80% of those asked were critical of the media's portrayal of the Mods and Rockers. In this respect, at least in terms of the grassroots theory of moral panics, it is highly debatable to what degree the Mods and Rockers incident could be described as a moral panic—or at least as a 'popular' moral panic.

THE CHANGING FACE OF 'MORAL PANICS'

Both the rise of 'moral panics' within conservative sections of society, and the interpretation of them by radical thinkers as moral panics, emerged at a specific moment in history and reflected a certain clash between the 'left and right'. However, by the early 1990s the conflicting understanding and approach to moral panics was becoming confused. At this time of political change, the left appeared to accept more readily the 'reality' of certain 'panics', while at the same time the right began to question the traditional moralising that had once been the bedrock of these panics. Rather than this development simply reflecting objective changes in society—it reflected more significantly a change in the outlook of both the left and right.

Analysing the 'language' of moral panics Hunt, in his study of broadsheet newspapers, identified a number of developments in the use and understanding of the term 'moral panic'. A term that had previously been used by the left to challenge the exaggerated reactions of conservatives was, by the end of the 1980s, being questioned by liberal and left-wing individuals and newspapers: crime in particular was becoming a social problem newspapers like the *Guardian* began to recognise as being 'real', rather than a 'moral panics' (*Guardian* 28 August 1989). By 1993, Hunt noted, 'A succession of similar articles appeared in both left-wing and right-wing papers throughout 1993, attacking 'progressive criminologists' for dismissing the crime epidemic and crisis in values as "moral panic"' (Hunt 1997: 642).

On the left, the term moral panic was also being used and defended as a way to target other groups—like 'feckless fathers'—who were seen as the real cause of problems in communities. At the same time within the right wing press the moral panic label was being used to challenge the exaggerated claims of the radical panickers around issues of smoking and satanic abuse.

Finally, while there was a trend amongst liberal and left-wing thinkers to accept rather than challenge what would previously have been seen as panics, simultaneously many of those on the right were becoming uncomfortable with the use of morality to attack groups in society. Questioning moralistic reactions by the Conservative government under John Major to the killing of toddler James Bulger by two 10-year-old boys, and also challenging the moral campaign to get 'back to basics', both the *Times* and *Sunday Times* expressed a concern that the government 'was losing sight of reality'. 'The ambivalence about moral panic,' Hunt noted, 'illustrates the writers' doubts about the popular credibility of moral language' (Hunt 1997: 642).

A new 'language' was needed at this point in time: a language that could endorse panics as real, but without the traditional moral framework of previous panics. As part of this linguistic project, Hunt observed, 'the term "moral panic" itself had to be redefined as a form of civic consciousness, an expression of public anxiety rather than a conspiracy of elites and interest groups' (Hunt 1997: 646).

What would previously have been seen by some radicals as a panic was now more readily seen as being 'real'—an objectively legitimate social problem that needed to be addressed. However, at the same time the moral basis for panicking was becoming problematic.

As the editor of the *Independent* noted in February 1993, 'we have lost all sense of direction ... [but] ... we are all becoming moralists now'— moralising (indeed panics) about behaviour was increasing, but this did not represent the growth of morals or 'moral' panics.

LOSS OF MORAL AUTHORITY

A central element to moral panic studies has, as the name suggests, been focused on the *morality* of those panicking and promoting these panics. However, when looking at the construction of social problems in the 1990s, the question of what moral values were being defended is less clear. The 'class war' may have been won, but as American conservatives quickly recognised, the 'culture war' was being lost and traditional conservative values that had been the basis of moral panics up to this point were in decline.

Part of the 'tradition' of moral panics has been the concern about nationhood and national decline. In Pearson's book, *Hooligan*, he explains how crime and violence in Britain has often been portrayed as un-British and a threat to the 'British way of life'. Even the word 'hooligan' developed from an Irish name and has been counterposed to the 'English national character'.[9] The 'Victorian values' espoused by the Conservative Party in the 1980s involved the politicisation of, and moralising about, traditional Britishness. Similar values had been expressed in a more embryonic form, or at least in a less politicised framework, in the early 1960s and laid the basis for the panic over Mods and Rockers and the subsequent work by Cohen.

As well as a concern about nation, the family has also been a core concern within moral panics. Britishness was seen as being under threat from 'muggers' in the 1970s, for example, and here black youth symbolised not only a racial threat but also a threat to the family. As Hunt (1999a) explains, the main anxieties over youth and crime were linked by the mugging panic to a deeper layer of anxieties about parental relations, fragmenting communities and the end of neighbourliness. Many of these concerns can still be seen today when issues to do with youth antisocial behaviour are raised. However key differences exist in the moral language that would be seen as acceptable today. The use of 'racial language', for example, and the traditional defence of Britishness and the British way of life, are more problematic, while even the defence of 'family values' is more difficult than previously.

Critcher notes that, 'all moral panics are ultimately about reconfirming moral values'. This involves the defining, labelling and punishing of unacceptable behaviour to confirm who we are and what we believe in or stand for and where we draw the boundaries around our community (Critcher 2006: 9). But it is far from clear who 'we' are and what 'we' believe in today. As Alan Hunt has observed, 'Today there is no 'natural' system of social order and no possibility of promoting a Durkheimian moral education which could inculcate the rules of morality "elaborated by society"' (Hunt 1999b: 11). This was a problem that the increasingly rudderless conservative elite, faced in the early 1990s.

A significant moment in the declining usefulness of 'moral' panics can be seen in 1993, when John Major's 'Back to Basics' campaign was widely ridiculed.[10] This reflected not the end of moralising, but rather the growing difficulty that even a Conservative Prime Minister had in using traditional morals for political purposes. Following this moral campaign, *The Independent* condemned Major's attack on single mothers, noting: 'Conservative politicians are subjecting them to a vilification that would be illegal if addressed to racial minorities' (Cohen 2002: xxviii).

The loss of faith in the moralising of the elite, even within conservative sections of society, was clearly expressed by Roy Chapman, chairman of the Headmasters' Conference, who in attacking Major's campaign against 'yobs' stated:

> The family no longer provides either the cohesive force or the base line in standard behaviour. The church seems prepared to accept anything except intolerance, while the government seems to operate on the basis of political expediency, rather than on coherent policies, much less principles (Calcutt 1996: 33).

In the US a similar trend was in evidence, as traditional morality was seen to decline as a source for cohering the elites and for gaining public support. As Goode and Ben-Yehuda noted, in 1992 the Republican presidential campaign in the United States was initially and substantially based on 'family values'—with its attendant attacks on homosexuality, abortion, divorce and other presumed Democratic-tolerated vices—'a theme which failed to catch fire with the American voter' (Goode and Ben-Yehuda 1994: 35).

The reason for this 'failed campaign' is partly due to the confusion of moral absolutes—even amongst the elite in society, as American writer Katie Roiphe points out in her book *Last Night in Paradise: Sex and Morals at the Century's End*:

In the fifties, there were curfews on college campuses and social taboos against getting a "bad reputation" or losing your virginity before you got married. But now we have no popularly accepted moral attitude about sexuality that can be passed down from one generation to the next. Is it all right for teenagers to have sex, or isn't it? Is it morally wrong or just physically dangerous? We don't have answers. It's not just that different people have different answers, but that, for the first time in recent memory, we don't have an official answer, an answer that extends from *Oprah* to Hollywood to the editorial pages of the *New York Times* (Roiphe 1997: 163).

Traditional morals, based on conservative notions of the nation and the family, which had been the basis of most moral panics up to this point, were becoming more problematic by the early 1990s. They were problematic not only in terms of their relevance to the public, but even in terms of the cohesion and coherence they generated within the elite itself. *Crucially, this loss of moral certainty or absolutes helped to exaggerate the sense of panic amongst the elite.* However, the decline in the capacity of traditional morality to promote absolute values against perceived threats did not result in the reduction of panics in society. Rather, panics escalated and were increasingly engaged with and even promoted by government—in part because of its own loss of moral (and political) authority. Traditional conservative moralising remained, but was becoming less significant as a basis for anxieties and panics that from this point on were taking a less moral form. Conservatives like the American Gertrude Himmelfarb and Charles Murray became significant moral entrepreneurs at this time, but their moral approach to illegitimacy and marriage no longer had the capacity to carry conservatives, let alone the general public. Despite the intensity of the moral debate in the early 1990s—*moral* panics were no longer de rigueur.

In 1996 the liberal columnist Polly Toynbee perceptively noted:

We live in curiously schizoid times: so much public comment is at variance with most people's private experience. In the real world people are more liberal than ever before. They are less censorious, more open minded about cohabitation, homosexuality, babies born out of wedlock and divorce than at any time in history. Soap operas tell the story well. Within families and among communities of friends and colleagues, we are tolerant as never before (*Independent* 16 November 1996).

In the new 'tolerant' age, old-fashioned moralising made less sense. However, the conservative concern about the dangers of too much individual freedom did not go away but was intensified and replaced by a secular concern about safety. Toynbee herself illustrated this trend well in the above article, when having celebrated the decline of conservative morality put forward her own 'moral' warning, arguing that, 'Freedom brings more diversity, more choice—but the flip side of freedom is more risk, danger and dislocation'. Now, even for liberal thinkers, freedom was becoming associated with risk and danger rather than liberation. The new basis for moralising developed not around traditional morality, but around what Furedi describes as the 'morality of low expectation'—a morality that encouraged the public to 'Know your limits'.

THE CONVERGENCE OF LEFT AND RIGHT

The desire to control, regulate and limit individual behaviour has historically been a preoccupation associated with conservative thinkers and groups. However over the last few decades, social problems that focus upon problematic behaviour and explicitly or implicitly promote the need for more regulations in society have increasingly come from 'radical' individuals. Within a critical understanding of society, but with a focus on individuals' 'abusive' behaviour, this radical approach often portrays the problem as being far more serious and widespread than previous conservatives ever did.

Writing in *The Sunday Times* in 1994, Gertrude Himmelfarb bemoaned the decline in morality associated with *the* family, while perceptively recognising that the new moral—or amoral—absolute of the late twentieth century was developing around the issue of child abuse.

> As deviancy is normalised, so the normal becomes deviant. The kind of family that has been regarded for centuries as natural and moral is now seen as pathological, concealing behind the façade of respectability the new 'original sin', child abuse (*The Sunday Times* 11 September 1994).

The above quote is used by Kenneth Thompson in his study of *Moral Panics* (1998: 92), in which, as we have seen he discusses panics in the 1990s as being the outcome of 'neo-liberal individualism and neo-conservative nostalgia for a moral golden age'. However, while this was true to some degree, the 'panics' being generated by radicals, like that of child abuse (Jenkins 1992, 1998), are not seen by Thompson as a form of panic.

As Fitzpatrick observed in relation to the AIDS panic, the anxiety and fear about AIDS did not erupt through the moral promotion of the idea of a 'gay plague'. Rather, this panic only developed a momentum in society once the moral campaign was overtaken by the new 'secular' campaign for 'safe sex'. Examining the figures of AIDS infections in the UK at the end of 1999, Fitzpatrick notes, that out of the high-risk categories, only 171 people had contracted AIDS through heterosexual sex. Yet, the government campaign on AIDS in 1987, the 'biggest public health campaign in history', had portrayed the disease as one that would become an epidemic transmitted through heterosexual sex if 'safe sex' was not practiced. This campaign Fitzpatrick argues had a profound effect on society and was 'the greatest health related scare of our time' (Fitzpatrick 1998: 13). Fitzpatrick accurately describes how, in the late 1980s and early 1990s, new social problems related to atomised individuals, not through traditional morality but through the new language of risk and safety. Moralising, he argued, no longer needed a 'dog collar' (Fitzpatrick 2001).[11]

For Furedi, the AIDS panic was a key moment in 'moral' panics, one where the traditional moralists merged with a new 'radical' sense of anxiety:

> The high point of the unexpected synthesis between conventional moralizers and proponents of the new etiquette was over the issue of AIDS. . . . Initially, it was the right-wing moralists who sought to take the initiative. . . . In the AIDS literature, this attempt to create an anti-gay moral panic is still presented as the dominant theme around the issue. But in reality, the anti-gay presentation of AIDS soon ran out of steam. Proponents of the new etiquette succeeded in redefining AIDS. It was agreed that AIDS was not just a disease which afflicted gays— 'everyone was at risk' (Furedi 1997: 166).

A concern raised by Furedi (1997) is that whereas radical thinkers continue to challenge old-fashioned moral panics by the right, another panic is often put in its place. Cohen, in his introduction to the third edition of *Folk Devils and Moral Panics*, similarly hints at this problem, noting with reference to comments made by American experts challenging the idea that schools are dangerous places:

> As these stories unfold, experts such as sociologists, psychologists and criminologists are wheeled in to comment, react and supply causal narrative. Their ritual opening move—'putting things in perspective'—is not usually very helpful: 'School Still Safest Place For Children; Many More Dead at Home Than in Classroom'. (Cohen 2002: xiii)

Here, the traditional panic about violence and a need for law and order in public, or within institutions like schools, is replaced by a panic about violence in the home.

From a certain feminist perspective, the concern about a 'violent society' was turned inwards, and became focused on the family. Viewed through the prism of patriarchy, as Victor argues, male dominance in society and its exploitation of women and children has become the essential underlying threat to the moral order of society (Victor 1998). The development of the feminist understanding of crime and violence as an endemic part of women's existence, had by the early 1980s already impacted upon the way some radicals understood crime. Steven Box, for example, in *Power, Crime and Mystification*—a book best known for its promotion of the idea of corporate crime—argued that, 'it is clear that it is no longer a tiny minority of women who are raped and sexually assaulted, but a substantial proportion' (Box 1983: 130).

As radicalism declined in the 1980s, the interest in social problems relating to violence and abuse increased and 'radical' panics emerged.[12] Crime, violence and harassment and abuse that had largely been seen as a problem of the minority were now understood to be ingrained within society.

US sociologist Donna Killingbeck for example, after exposing the 'construction of school violence as a "moral panic", goes on to argue that the problem with this right-wing moral panic is that it misses the many and varied ways that violence occurs within schools that make it almost endemic. The elements of harm in schools can only be understood, she argues, once the following have been recognised:

> (1) the emotional and psychological pain that results from the domination of some over others, (2) the focus on interpersonal relationships that ignore the violence of social processes which produce systematic social injury, such as that perpetuated through institutionalised racism, sexism, and classism, and (3) the symbolic violence of domination, or the subtle form of violence that brings coercion through power exercised in hierarchical relationships (Killingbeck 2001: 10).

Unlike past writing on moral panics that emphasised the disproportionate concern about violence emanating from conservative elites or interest groups, here one concern about violence is simply replaced by another, more radical, Foucauldian concern about the centrality of power and violence to the experience of children in school. Issues like 'racism, sexism and classism' are here challenged within the framework of a concern about violence. Violence becomes *the* issue, and alternative approaches to dealing with and regulating this 'problem' are constructed.

The changing nature of radical thought can be seen in how even classic studies of panics are reinterpreted today. In the youth focused magazine, *Young People Now*, a retrospective review of *Hooligan* was written by Rob Allen, the director of Rethinking Crime and Punishment and a member of the Youth Justice Board. Reiterating Pearson's argument in *Hooligan*, Allen notes that, 'the last 10 years have seen plenty more media moral panics: about persistent young offenders, paedophiles, drugs and street crime'. However he goes on:

> Rereading Hooligan, I took a different message than first time round. It is the continuity of hooliganism makes it more, not less, of a social problem. In policy terms it boils down to whether we take the American route of dealing with the poorest through prison, or a more European approach of building up economic, social and educational responses (*Young People Now* 21–27 January 2004).

Whereas Allen had understood Pearson's work in the early 1980s as a correct challenge to the moral panics surrounding youth crime, by the beginning of the twenty-first century his view had been transformed into an acceptance of the problem of hooliganism. What is interesting in this review is that Allen does not try and argue that things are worse and society has changed, but simply states that his understanding of youth crime has changed. Allen had previously understood *Hooligan* as a book that challenged the anxieties of the elite—now Allen has come to endorse these anxieties.

The question of freedom had always been one that conservatives were uncomfortable with, morality itself often being used by them as a form of control—rather than liberation. However, now, as Toynbee expressed well, freedom was for liberals and some radicals, increasingly understood as bringing with it, 'risk, danger and dislocation'. As the moral right stuttered and the ideas of the left became discredited, left-wing and right-wing campaigners converged more systematically around the core value of the 1990s—safety. The new 'moral' code to direct intimate relationships came from those promoting 'safe sex', while relationships between neighbours were soon to be regulated by local authorities around the idea of 'community safety'.

That the safe sex campaign was a panic was recognised by some liberal commentators but this was of no concern. Mark Lawson for example discussing the campaign believed that, 'the government had lied', but for him it was a 'good lie'. At the same time many conservative thinkers like Charles Sykes, hailed the safe sex campaign for creating a new form of sexual responsibility (Furedi 1997: 167).

Unlike a number of conservative panics that tended to target the immoral minority,[13] the new safety panics generalised a number of problems. Now everyone could die of AIDS, while child abuse was portrayed as being endemic to society. Where the moral right had hoped to restore society to a golden past, the new amoral panics had no idealised vision of society: the aim for individuals was simply to be safe. With many of the new safety campaigns being generated by radical thinkers, opposition to these panics remained limited, and in the case of the AIDS panic, this new amoral approach was adopted by the Conservative government under the leadership of Margaret Thatcher, with the support of almost all radical groups and thinkers. Consequently, the anxieties within society expressed through this and many other panics were increasingly institutionalised and helped to forge the new social and personal 'moral' norm of safety.

The American conservative Gertrude Himmelfarb, from a moral, pro-family perspective, believes that an issue like, 'child abuse is grossly over-reported', but that the issue of crime, is, 'underreported because we have become desensitized to it' (1995: 236). The reality is however that both issues were becoming and having remained significant 'social problems' around which society has become organised. In the US for example, despite the falling rate of homicide since 1993, the coverage of murder on the news has increased by 700%. Killingbeck notes how the media construction of 'crime waves', by raising public outrage, has helped to influence policy on crime and punishment. The 'media crime wave' has been deemed by the Center for Media and Public Affairs as number 10 on the 'Top Ten List of Media Distortions of the 20th Century' (Killingbeck 2001: 6).

Crime and youth crime 'panics', as Killingbeck's work illustrates, have remained issues that radical academics examine and challenge—often within an anti-new right, or anti-moral framework. However, the growth of concern and policies associated with crime, while incorporating traditional moralists, do not generally come within a moral framework—and it is this that 'desensitizes' conservatives like Himmelfarb who correctly observes a fall in moral claims being made about deviant behaviour, but incorrectly believe that this means that there has been a fall in the concern about crime—when in reality the opposite is the truth. Crime has never been so central to the political and popular imagination. Moralising about behaviour has arguably never been greater—but it is the safety agenda that is at the forefront of this development. In reality, the 'problem of crime' and of a wider sense of disorder has resulted in it becoming a 'social problem' of concern for politicians of all persuasions, consequently, more laws, and initiatives, and more forms of surveillance and incarceration have developed than ever before.

INSTITUTIONALISED PANIC

Youth crime and 'antisocial behaviour' have, over the last decade or so, become more established as social problems. Having often been a site for occasional panics by a minority of conservatives, today these concerns about youth are more mainstream and widely accepted as issues to address. Panics about youth and youth crime were central to Cohen and Hall's classic moral panic studies in the past. Likewise Pearson's study of past 'respectable fears' has noted the significance of panics about youth. However, one key difference in the reaction to the fear about youth crime in the late twentieth and early twenty-first centuries compared with these earlier periods is that while previously the political elite generally did not 'over-react' to moral panics, today the elite are often at the centre of promoting 'panics' and issues associated with a loss of order.

Examining past 'moral panics', it is clear that at different times sections of the British political elite, rather than elevating concerns connected to moral and crime panics, actually either challenged them or dampened them down. A sense of purpose within the elite appears to have mitigated against a panic reaction within the establishment itself. For example, Pearson notes how, in the 1840s, liberal members of the British elite saw the panic about crime as a problem not to be overly concerned with, as the development of the rational individual—especially amongst the poor—would, it was believed, result in an end to crime (Pearson 1983: 175).

Similarly, in a different historical and political period, Pearson notes that despite continuing anxieties being expressed about family values, the destruction of community and lawless youth by movements like the 'Scrutiny' group in the 1920s, running alongside these complaints 'and often holding them in check' was a counter-movement, which involved a 'quite different moral emphasis'. Despite there being strong evidence for a sharp rise in crime and violent crime—like a 70% rise in shop raids and a 90% rise in bag snatching between 1925 and 1929, which Pearson believes was almost certainly connected to the availability of the motor car—there was no subsequent 'law and order' campaign.

Indeed, comments from Robert Baden Powell in the 1920s appear almost unbelievable in today's climate of crime panics. As the *Times* reported:

> To him it was rather a promising sign, because he saw in those banditry cases, robbery with violence, and smash and grab, little 'adventures'. There was still some spirit of adventure among those juveniles and if that spirit were seized and turned in the right direction they could make them useful men (1983: 34).

Similarly, in Parliament, reports about motor banditry in the press were ridiculed as gross exaggerations and police memoirs, while recounting no go areas for the police, described much of the 'action' on the street as people having a 'good time'. Other examples of magistrates are cited, where stealing off the back of lorries was dismissed as 'perfectly innocent joyriding' and the 'line between mischief and crime' was said to be 'not easily drawn' (Pearson 1983: 42).

Looking at Cohen's *Folk Devils and Moral Panics* we see that a significant reaction of the government, politicians, educationalists and religious leaders in the 1960s was not to inflame the moral panic but to dampen it down. As Cohen notes:

> At times of moral panic, politicians in office, even though one might expect them on the basis of their personal records to be full of moral indignation, often act to 'calm things down' and minimize the problem. Thus it was with the [Conservative] Home Secretary, Mr Henry Brooke, the only participant in the first debate who expressed an awareness of the exaggerations and distortions (Cohen 2002: 113).

Also, as Goode and Ben-Yehuda note regarding the institutional legacy left by the Mods and Rockers panic:

> Some panics seem to leave relatively little institutional legacy. The furore generated by the Mods and Rockers in England in the late 1960s resulted in no long-term institutional legacy; no laws passed (although some were proposed), and the two germinal social movement organizations

that emerged in its wake quickly evaporated when the excitement died down (Goode and Ben-Yehuda 1994: 168).

As we have seen, from the early 1990s the centrality of crime and crime 'panics' to political life and institutional frameworks has developed apace. Centred upon the safety of *victims*, a raft of legislation has developed with increasing rapidity, not simply in relation to 'panics', but also as part of government programmes and manifestos. New terms like 'binge drinking' have emerged which give a greater sense of young people being out of control: terms that are used and promoted by all political parties. Issues of crime, violence and today even antisocial behaviour are rarely 'put into perspective' or 'dampened down' by government ministers. Rather, the extent of the problem of crime and behaviour is often pushed most vociferously by the government itself.[14] Whether 'binge drinking' has increased or not, the framework within which this panic amongst certain professionals and politicians has taken place is both one of a general sense of disorder in society and a concern about the *safety* of those young people drinking and the *safety* of those they come into contact with. Moral ideas of 'sobriety and hard work' are at best secondary within this debate, and play no part in the government 'awareness' campaign about this issue.[15] The government's 'Know your limits' campaign against 'binge drinking' for example, is neither moral, nor does it appear to be a panic. It potentially raises the fears about young people who drink—but is done so in a more 'caring' way—in an attempt to keep all young people—including those who drink—safe. It is a now, very typical 'tolerant', amoral panic and one that has few opponents.

Today, with safety as a new guiding principle that faces little opposition, government and professional intervention into the everyday lives of the public that incorporate often alarming images of 'risk, danger and dislocation' are simply seen as 'good practise'.

THE MORAL SUBJECT

The moralising of conservatives over the past few decades is correctly understood as an anti 'social' attempt to repose social problems and represent them as problems of individual morality. At the same time the concern about traditional morality has historically, at least in part, been an issue for conservatives who have attempted to limit freedom, challenge the naïve belief in rationality and the humanist values of the enlightenment. However, the new safety-based panics are predicated on a far more asocial and individuated basis, with the 'moral' reference point relating to the self rather than to any wider outlook or set of beliefs. Despite the reactionary nature of conservative moralising, it also embodied a 'communal' sense, as well as an expectation or desire for a robust moral subject. Traditional moral panics upheld a set of values that were felt to be under threat. As such, despite the conservative nature of them, an attempt was being made to reengage individuals with society or with a wider set of beliefs or values often associated with a 'golden age'. The new amoral framework however embodies both a more limited expectation of individuals and a more diminished sense of collective meaning.

Even Margaret Thatcher's famous pronouncements about there being 'no such thing as society' embodied what Hunt describes as a 'social unit'—the family. A family that was a social institution, with a set of values—but that was also made up of 'autonomous parties equally capable of exercising responsibility and capable of cultivating robust virtues and initiative' (Hunt 1999b: 195). Margaret Thatcher may have been against the left-wing understanding of the 'social' but her vision was not of simply robust individuals—but individuals with strong connections to the family and the nation.

Being 'moral', as Himmelfarb herself has noted, was historically not a purely conservative pursuit but something that has guided how a variety of thinkers understood the individual and society. In the nineteenth century for example, the idea of 'virtue' was commonly accepted by critics of much of Victorian life, like Charles Dickens, who challenged those who, 'strayed from the path of virtue by committing those all too common sins of vulgarity, philistinism and intolerance'. Plato, Aristotle, Augustine and Aquinas, she notes had their own 'virtues'—virtues that centrally were 'the standards against which behavior could and should be measured'. For Himmelfarb the idea of virtue was social, with for example 'secular philosophers' of the seventeenth and eighteenth century, who subverted classical virtues, but all of whom 'insisting upon the importance of virtues not only for the good life of individuals but for the well-being of society and the state' (Himmelfarb 1995: 9–13).

Within criminology Bauman's study of *Social uses of Law and Order* similarly notes how Bentham's moral principles were grounded upon a high expectation of the individual, and a belief in 'social' norms. Prisons were to be used not simply to control the individual but to improve him. Prisons were *houses of correction*, the purpose of them being to, 'bring the inmates back from the road to moral perdition', and return them to the fold of 'normal society' and to 'social competence' (Bauman 2000a: 29–30). In contrast Bauman notes that the modern day Pelican Bay prison in California for example has no rehabilitative expectation. With a lack of face to face contact with guards or inmates, living in windowless cells, these prisoners are locked away—not seeing and not seen. These prisons that 'could be mistaken for coffins', may appear to be a high tech version of the Panopticon—but as Bauman notes, there is no expectation of any form of training (or indeed of moral improvement). For Bauman a key reason for this change is the changing nature of work—of the declining need for labour—and more especially of 'disciplined labour', something that Bentham's model prison was geared towards. But more than this: The idea of morally uplifting the individual into the norms of society only makes sense if the idea of the morally responsible individual makes sense—and is the norm—and also if there is a firm set of 'social' values that can bind the individual to society. As Feeley and Simon have argued, today the belief in individual transformation that was guided by a strong sense of collective meaning has all but disappeared—the task for the new penology, they note, is 'managerial not transformative' (in Garland and Sparks 2000: 197). *Where Durkheim saw society's reaction to crime helped to shore up the beliefs of that society—today society's reaction to crime is an expression of a lack of belief.* The belief in the moral individual and the capacity to socialise inmates has diminished and Pelican Bay prison is one expression of this current amoral and indeed asocial climate.

The expectation of the individual to be transformed and indeed to transform himself has significantly declined and to a large extent undermines the basis of traditional moralising. The issue of drug taking—that has excited moral outrage for decades—is today engaged with very differently by institutions and experts. Rather than there being the cultural expectation of individual responsibility regarding drugs there has developed an understanding of the drug taker as a victim. The libertarian—'legalise drugs'—outlook, and the condemnation of drugs by the moralists, both presumed a responsible subject. This idea of the individual has changed and institutions now treat almost all drugs within the medical framework of addiction.[16]

There remains a belief that traditional morality lives, and even that it has become a growing problem. However moral arguments and especially laws based on moral principle are on the margins of society and out with key institutions. In the UK the Christian moral right in the United States is often pointed to as evidence of the rise of moral fundamentalism, however as Furedi has noted—even within the promoters of Christianity—for example with the rise of 'Intelligent Design'—there is in fact a move away from core idea of faith and morality. As he argues, the ideas behind Intelligent Design rather than being an expression of the Christian faith reflect a concession to science by Christians.

> Unable to justify creationism as a matter of faith based on divine revelation, advocates of Intelligent Design are forced to adopt the language of science to legitimate their arguments and the existence of some kind of God. This highlights their theological opportunism and inability to justify religion in its own terms. Of course Intelligent Design isn't science; but its appeal to faith in science exposes the limits of the authority of religious faith today.[17]

In Alan Wolfe's *The Transformation of American Religion* he notes how Christianity is itself become more asocial and losing its wider moral framework: It is becoming 'new age', self-referential and therapeutic:

> Talk of hell, damnation, and even sin has been replaced by a non-judgemental language of understanding and empathy. . . . More Americans than ever proclaim themselves to be born again in Christ, but the lord

to whom they turn rarely gets angry and frequently strengthens self-esteem. . . . far from living in a world elsewhere, the faithful in the United States are remarkably like everyone else (Wolfe 2003: 3).

The religious in America he argues increasingly use the nonjudgemental language of understanding and empathy. They have, 'succumbed to the individualism, and even on occasion the narcissism, of American life'—in essence religion has become like everything else. Religion has become personalised, more tolerant, and there is a 'distrust of leadership that reflects similar crisis of confidence involving business and politics'. Religion Wolfe argues, has neither declined or advanced; it has been transformed: 'Once upon a time, the New Left and the counterculture dispensed with ideas about acting responsibly in favour of living authentically. Now the same idea, and even the same kind of language, has passed over to Christian theologians' (Wolfe 2003: 250–51).

Religion is engaged with and indeed promoted more through the individual self than through a wider system of meaning—a system of meaning that had a firm moral grounding. Today old moral issues are less likely to be addressed through this moral framework—something that was recently demonstrated by the Church of England in their opposition to pornography.

On the 6th February the Church of England's general synod announced that it would be debating a call for tighter controls on pornography. However the reason for their concern was not because of the immorality of pornography—but rather that it was 'exploitative'. Negative and degraded images they argued were 'putting the public at risk' (*Guardian* 6 February 2007). The safety of those people working in the industry—and that of the public in general was how the church now understood this previously moral question.

Rather than an absolute set of moral values having a dynamic in society and laying the basis for norms and panic reactions when these norms are seen to be threatened, the trend today is the opposite. Morals themselves are extraordinary today—by being moral or holding absolute values you are today an 'outsider'. As the language of even Christian preachers moves from absolutes—from universal standards—and towards the therapeutic language of self esteem—or safety—we see, as Nolan describes, the development of laws, political rhetoric and social policy itself being legitimised through therapeutics.

In these amoral times there is little expectation of human transformation, perhaps most clearly expressed in the newly labelled 'paedophile' who has no capacity for moral improvement but must rather be monitored and supervised throughout his life. Recidivism has become the expected norm for anyone entering prison—and these institutions are no longer seen as houses of correction but as mere training grounds for criminals. The moral—or even 'social'—incorporation of prisoners into society is no longer the guiding principle and a more therapeutic relationship has developed. Likewise in society more generally the engagement between those in authority and the public is both less moral and less social. Amoral engagement is more 'tolerant', 'non-judgemental' and 'personalised' engaging with individuals to keep them safe from others and from themselves.

Within this amoral climate the basis for 'panics' has changed. For 'moral' panics to take hold there needs to be norms, collective absolutes, and institutions that people feel part of. Today however, rather than their being powerful absolute, collective beliefs and values that can mobilise the elite and the public to panic, it is more true to argue that the only absolute is that there are no absolutes. And it is this that generates today's panics.

THE NEW 'MORAL' ICON—THE VICTIM

Through the 1990s the language of 'risk' developed, and became a new amoral framework that informed the regulation of everyday life. The understanding of the individual as vulnerable both undermined the idea of the robust moral subject and at the same time opened the door to ever more concerns or panics about behaviour. This weakened or diminished self became far more susceptible to dangers, disease and harm, with new found forms of harassment, abuse and offence growing year on year.

Two significant contributors to the understanding of modern moral panic and social problems are the American social constructionists Joel Best and Philip Jenkins, both of whom have explored the growing centrality of the victim to social problem formation and upon the newly emerging 'moral panics' in late twentieth century society. In *Moral Panic*, Jenkins points out that in the 1980s a whole new branch of the legal profession developed in relation to lawsuits undertaken on behalf of victims (Jenkins 1998: 219). This, rather than being a peculiarity of law, reflected what Jenkins describes as the new child protection movement's emphasis on the experience of the victim:

> For the first time in history, perhaps millions of people, mainly but not exclusively women have constructed their self-identity in terms of the experience of sexual victimization. Networks of survivors became a powerful interest group, protesting any weakening in societies' vigilance against abuse and launching virulent attacks on therapists or writers who dared to speak of 'false memory' (Jenkins 1998: 234).

Rather than victimhood being merely an objective existence or experience, here it is understood as, in part, an identity developed and indeed promoted at a particular time.

Joel Best has traced the historical emergence of 'victimhood' within the US, identifying this understanding of the individual as a central tenant of claimsmaking in the modern period. This is something that has similarly developed in the UK and more generally within Western culture. In *Random*

Violence Best highlights a cultural trend that has influenced the way in which individuals and issues are understood and the subsequent impact that this has had on laws and policy developments. Tracing the emergence of 'victim rights' advocates in conservative claims for 'victims of crime' in the sixties, and within the women's movement who campaigned for laws against various forms of abuse in the seventies, Best points out that the concept of victims often accepted uncritically today is not simply an objective term but has developed over time with the help of victim centred claimsmakers (Best 1999: 94).

A significant development identified by Best is the growing use of and strength gained by those using the 'victim' framework to present their case. Victims of crime, for example, may be labelled as victims by conservative groups campaigning on their behalf, while those attempting to defend the 'underclass' that are blamed for these crimes similarly use the language of victimhood to develop counter-claims. As Lee also notes, the framework within which the 'religious right' now opposes abortion is less in relation to morality and religion itself than with reference to the woman as a victim of post abortion syndrome (Lee 2001).

Discussing the convergence of left and right in their campaigning on behalf of the victim, Best argues that:

> Both the right and the left now portrayed the victim as a sympathetic figure, using victim imagery to promote crackdowns on crime or calls for social reform, respectively. Both conservatives and liberals treated victims as powerless unfortunates, blameless for their circumstances and suffering at the hands of powerful exploiters (Best 1999: 100).

Social problems analysed by various professions within the sciences and therapeutic field expanded at this time and overall, 'a broad range of authorities—including social movement activists, political conservatives and liberals, therapists, scientists, and lawyers—became more likely to talk about victimization in society' (Best 1999: 102). This framework of understanding social problems, the language and the rhetoric, has, Best argues, now become dominant in the development of how new crimes such as stalking are discussed and made into social problems.

One significant aspect of these developments in the US, with reference to the changing form of morality and moral panics, is the extent to which a claim about victimisation 'stakes out the moral high ground' (Best 1999: 109). As Sykes argues, 'the route to moral superiority . . . can be gained most efficiently through being a victim' (Best 1999: 138).

The 'ideology of victimization', Best illustrates, has been taken up within academia—in lectures and education—with teachers looking out for child victims, the law—giving increasing priority to the victim, the mass media— talk shows, and even in religion—where concern for victims is expressed as a moral good (Best 1999: 117).

One consequence of this focus upon victimisation is that 'new crimes' are understood within this framework, more people have become seen as 'victims' and more laws have developed to protect the victimisation of one individual from another. Within this framework of understanding society and social problems, there is, argues Best, a more generalised sense of anxiety that, in relation to crime, has helped create a 'sense that contemporary society is plagued by random violence' (Best 1999: 5).

For Best, the idea of random violence did not represent the real world, as relatively few people faced serious crime and the vast majority of these crimes occurred in particular areas and were often done to particular groups in society. The idea of random violence has developed in the US, Best believes, as a wider expression within society of a sense of risk and fear.

The fact that victims have become so central to claimsmaking and the wider culture suggests that there is a greater sense of powerlessness within certain groups and arguably more generally across society: a sense of powerlessness that encourages a greater sense of anxiety and increases the tendency for 'panics' to erupt.

Thompson has noted that the current period is often understood to be one of an 'age of moral panic'. However, this understanding, which continues to see panics as a product of neo-liberalism and traditional conservatism, is both one-sided and fails to recognise the more significant development of amoral panics. We are indeed living in an era of panics, but these panics are being generated by 'left-wing' and 'right-wing' campaigners around issues of safety and often in defence of *the victim*. Conservatives may continue to campaign on issues like abortion and crime, but they do so less as a promotion of moral values than through a more therapeutically oriented language that engages not with the 'moral majority' but with the fragmented individual.

Social problems and 'panics' that have a bearing on society and are institutionalised are no longer developed in relation to the morally responsible individual. Rather they are developed around the 'demoralised' subject. The victim campaigners, unlike their moral predecessors do not demand that people stand on their own two feet and take responsibility for themselves. As Himmelfarb notes, the new morality shifts 'responsibility from one individual to another'—the victim being helpless and abused by the 'hegemonic' person. The panic is consequently turned against those deemed to have power—or indeed even to represent the moral subject (Himmelfarb 1995: 162). Nor do these new amoral campaigners—the 'New Victorians' as Himmelfarb has labelled them—promote and fight for a set of values and beliefs that they feel can cohere society. Society as such is not their concern, the concern is with the damaged and vulnerable self, a call for recognition, and a demand that 'something be done'.

One form of panic today, somewhat ironically, comes in the form of the anti-moral panic—a panic within which the very idea of having strong moral beliefs and a strong sense of self discipline is both incomprehensible and understood as alien and dangerous. People with beliefs above and beyond themselves are today seen as strange—perhaps as the new 'other'. Panics now develop around a generalised sense of individual, rather than collective, anxiety—and the amoral framework of safety has developed to connect with this individuated sense of insecurity. While collective, value laden absolutes have declined, new safety based 'absolutes' have developed within this climate—with child safety (as we saw in the example of the Hamilton curfew) being the most powerful. This new form of panic not only lacks a 'moral' basis—but is at times distinctly anti-moral—illustrated in the current concern about the iconic moral man—the priest.

The panic about 'paedophile priests', described by Philip Jenkins in *Pedophiles and Priests: Anatomy of a Contemporary Crisis* (1996) is a perfect model for the new secular panics. Here—despite evidence that abuse is rare amongst Catholic priests and indeed rarer than the abuse carried out within other faiths—Jenkins notes how Catholicism itself has been put on trial: Celibacy, he notes has been problematised.

Following the moral panic format we find that the 'exaggerated concern' about paedophile priests created a 'disproportionate and hostile reaction' to a 'threat to the individual' (rather than to society), a 'problem that was challenging its values' (of safety), that was given a 'stereotypical media image' and that led to the 'demand for greater control'. Within a more cynical and 'value light' society the priest is the perfect new folk devil—a strangely self disciplined believer, a man so distant from his *self* and so committed to something beyond himself—something must be afoot. Celibacy—as a denial of your inner self and emotional drives (and addictions), has, in today's amoral therapeutic times, become not only an impossibility—but a perversion.

The values of duty, chastity, sobriety and self discipline that formed the core standards of the past moral campaigners are today felt to be so alien that those who embody them are seen as a threat to the new amoral and diminished norms and expectations of the modern individual.

FROM MORAL PANICS TO A FEAR OF RISK

Where moral panic theories like Cohen's often analyse what were occasional outbursts within an otherwise stable or calm society, more recently sociological theories have emerged that depict a more generalised state of risk and fear. As argued above, a key difference between panics past and present is that they have become an ever-present feature of modern society and, as such, it is more accurate to describe society as being in a permanent state of anxiety or 'panic'. Theories of 'risk' and a 'culture of fear' both analyse society from this point of view and are useful in helping to frame concerns about crime and disorder today. While appearing to be similar in their approach, however, Beck's theory of 'risk' and Furedi's theory of a 'culture of fear' are in fact very different. Indeed, following Furedi's understanding, Beck's approach can be understood as a form of amoral panicking itself.

Both Beck's theory of *Risk Society* (1992) and Furedi's *Culture of Fear* (1997) correctly describe how 'risk consciousness' has become widespread across society. Occasional eruptions of fear have been replaced by a more permanent cultural sense of unease. These theories both accept the significance of the fragmentation of society that has in part helped encourage this sense of insecurity; however, their explanations for why this has happened are poles apart. Where Beck often understands the sense of risk as a reaction to an objectively riskier society; Furedi to some degree follows the approach of moral panic theories, and argues that the culture of fear is more to do with the current state of subjectivity. However, for Furedi the generalisation of fear is not simply a ratcheting up of what went before, but rather is an expression of a fundamental loss of belief in humanity, progress and the idea of active moral subjects, which has developed out of the collapse of both left- and right-wing ideologies and the failure of the political and social experiments of the twentieth century.

Sheldon Ungar, examining the usefulness of the idea of a 'risk society' compared to past moral panic theories, correctly notes how 'new sites of social anxiety have emerged around environmental, nuclear, chemical and medical threats'. Consequently, 'the questions motivating moral panics research have lost much of their utility' (Ungar 2001: 271). Whereas moral panic research, Ungar argues, is concerned with exaggeration of the threat and the use of panics 'to engineer social consensus and control', with risk society, 'accidents being highly unpredictable and uncontrollable, the social constructionist concern with exaggeration is largely undermined as an analytical strategy'. Also, because a risk society has a 'roulette dynamic'—rather than more consciously created folk devils—then, for Ungar, the idea of risk society being used to develop social controls is questioned. Rather than moral order being created through 'risks', authorities can find themselves as carriers of 'hot potatoes' (Ungar 2001: 276).

Correctly, Ungar notes how the moral panic focus is more narrow in terms of looking at exceptional occasions of anxiety, whereas fearful events associated with risk are more ubiquitous (2001: 276). Moral panics are also often associated with a change in moral boundaries, whereas risks can emerge more from scientific findings. Also risks, for Ungar, are not developed 'top down' like many moral panics, but often emerge from a reaction to events like problems with nuclear reactors—which are made into issues by interest groups. Indeed risk society issues 'tend to involve diverse interest groups contending over relatively intractable scientific claims' (Ungar 2001: 277).

Rather than 'risks' being generated by an elite who attempt to promote an alternative moral order, Ungar accurately illustrates the way many risks emerge out with the traditional elite and can undermine rather than cohere the elite.

However, Ungar's understanding of risks being the product of 'highly unpredictable and uncontrollable' developments is questionable. Like Beck, Ungar often accepts the idea that these risks are *real*. Describing Beck's analysis, Furlong and Cartmel note that: 'Whereas modernity involved rationality and the belief in the potential offered by harnessing scientific knowledge, in late modernity the world is perceived as a dangerous place in which we are constantly confronted with risk' (Furlong and Cartmel 1997: 3).

For Furedi, a culture of fear has not developed because of any technical or global objective changes in production or communication. Rather, changes in society and the weakening of institutions have come at a specific time when there is a 'conservative sense of caution' (Furedi 1997: 9). In previous historical periods, Furedi argues, there was far more suffering, pain and disease than today. Despite there being various risks facing society, it is not the risks themselves but the pessimistic outlook within society that both inflates their significance and generates a sense of impotence in relation to social, scientific and even personal problems. This sense of impotence amongst the elite helps to explain why panics and 'risks' are rarely 'dampened down', as they were in the past, but become institutionalised.

Explaining this cultural sense of cautious pessimism, Durodie argues that there has been an:

> [U]nprecedented convergence of the political left's loss of faith in science and social transformation with the political right's traditional misgivings [that] have lent themselves to a pessimistic outlook leading to the rise of an exaggerated risk consciousness (Durodie 2002: 4).

How society reacts to technological changes is highly influenced by the cultural and ideological framework within which they emerge; and for Furedi, Beck's starting point for analysis upon these technical changes misses what is specific about late twentieth-century society. Rather than risks emerging in relation to global threats, Furedi identifies how the emergence of a 'risk consciousness' has occurred at every level of society and has impacted upon all relationships and institutions. That children are identified as being almost permanently 'at risk', for example, cannot be explained by global developments, or simply in relation to the individualisation of everyday life. Rather it is the end (or perhaps the suspension) of ideologies that held back the individuation of society for a century, which have collapsed and are central to understanding the culture of fear.

At a certain level of abstraction, what is being proposed here is that the idea of a 'risk society' is a reflection of the consciousness of the elite, which is then reflected back upon society. As such, the 'objective' risks identified by Beck, Giddens and others are a sociological expression of a loss of will of this elite—rather than an indication of any real increase of 'risks' in society.

Just as the enlightenment belief in science 'was a reflection and pronouncement of faith in humanity itself rather than merely in science' (Durodie

2002: 2), the loss of faith in science and the belief that the source of danger to society is not ignorance but knowledge (Beck 1992: 183) is the reverse— the loss of faith in humanity and of the capacity of human subjectivity to create social progress. All that is left for humanity is the question not of liberation, but of 'self limitation' (Beck 1996: 29). In a world of unintended consequences, 'Democracy in the sense that Lukacs described it, as "societal self-determination", is rendered impossible by "manufactured uncertainty"' (Heartfield: 2002: 81). Or as Furedi puts it, the picture portrayed by Beck is of a semi-conscious humanity desperately trying to control the destructive forces it has created (Furedi 2004: 133).

In this respect Beck's 'risk society' could be seen as another expression of amoral panicking by a sociological critic who sees a society under threat from technological developments rather than 'folk devils'.[18]

For both Furedi and Durodie, Beck's exaggerated sense of risk (Durodie 2002) reflects societies' own timidity and impotence towards social change and experimentation. With the loss of faith in human progress, what has emerged is a culture of self-loathing, which affects how every relationship or development in society is understood. Rather than embracing change, the left are now as conservative as the right and view change with suspicion and distrust. With a degraded image of 'man', many thinkers on the left have increasingly become preoccupied with images and issues associated with crime and abuse, discovering, as we have already seen, the endemic nature of violence across society.

Furedi's thesis notes that while a more conservative outlook has developed amongst more radical thinkers, at the same time many traditional values and norms of the right have also lost their consensus. Consequently without a social sense of the future and with the increased questioning of traditional norms, the result is a diminished sense of individual and social control (Furedi 1997: 68–9).

Within the 'politics of crime' a similar risk consciousness emerged—the new 'morality of safety' filled the vacuum of traditional morals and politics and now the demand was for 'crime to be taken seriously', for 'victims' rights' to be recognised, or for 'community safety' to be prioritised. Reflecting broad social and political trends, the emergence of this new 'morality' or amorality was encouraged by claimsmakers and campaigners from the left who promoted panics around child abuse, transformed crime and antisocial behaviour into a 'working-class issue' and discovered victims and vulnerable groups throughout society. Having given up on transforming society, the claimsmaking of many radical campaigners was reduced to demands to regulate, control and monitor individual behaviour. The loss of drive for social change within this process was replaced by a move to enforce social control.[19]

Within this cultural climate, even moral panics generated by conservative concerns about family and nation, are more likely to develop within the general framework of risk and safety. Indeed as noted previously, the

AIDS panic, while initially taking the form of a conservative panic about gays and promiscuity, was soon transformed into the modern-day form of panic around 'safe sex'. In general panics may still come and go, but more importantly there is a general and heightened sense of anxiety that affects almost all relationships, policies and practices in society. Rather than there being the occasional disproportionate outburst to social problems, there is a trend to exaggerate almost all social problems and a diminished sense of the capacity to overcome them. Instead of understanding 'risk' and 'moral panics' as separate developments in society—they can both be understood as part of a culture of fear—a culture that relentlessly reacts to new issues and concerns through amoral panics.

THE NEW THERAPEUTIC 'MORALITY' OF SAFETY

Despite the declining influence of traditional morality, the tendency to *moralise* has not declined. Indeed, the emergence of the 'politics of behaviour' suggests a more intensive scrutiny of individual behaviour has developed. Issues related to antisocial behaviour, crime, family life and relationships are central to many social problems that both capture the public imagination and excite political comment and action. However the dominant form that these problems take today relates not to tradition but to the amoral absolute of safety, while the justificatory basis (Beetham 1991) of this development is often in the form of therapeutic governance (Nolan 1998).

As Furedi argues,

> The marginalisation of traditional morality does not mean that society is without any system of values. On the contrary, the space left by the marginalisation of traditional morality has been filled by the system of values and notions of conduct associated with risk consciousness (Furedi 2002: 150).

That this new risk conscious outlook is rarely recognised as a form of moralising is explained by the 'value-free' basis upon which it is often promoted. Rather than ascribing a particular lifestyle as such, the new etiquette of safety is more self-consciously non-judgmental and relativistic. Almost any form of behaviour and outlook is acceptable within this etiquette—as long as it is safe and does not disturb the safety of others.

Despite being unconventional, this 'morality' is not purely 'new age' but also incorporates a number of traditional conservative themes, emphasising restraint and focusing on individual behaviour and responsibility.[20] Unlike traditional morality, however, that prescribed a 'single answer' to moral questions, the new etiquette of safety is more individualistically oriented and is therefore more able to relate directly to the contemporary experience of individuation (Furedi 2002: 163).

One key development within this more individualistically oriented etiquette is the emergence of the *Therapeutic State* (Nolan 1998), or of a *Therapy Culture* (Furedi 2004).

As the state comes to lack a moral or political basis of legitimation and engagement with the fragmented public, Nolan argues, a new set of 'cultural ideas and values that undergird the practical functions of the state' has emerged (Nolan 1998: 26). Reinforced by the 'demise of politics and social solidarity', social problems have subsequently been recast as emotional ones (Furedi 2004: 100). Social problems like crime, for example, have increasingly been understood in relation to the emotional sense of fear ascribed to it, while even welfare-related issues have become more therapeutic. Supporting this therapeutic framework, Giddens argues that economic benefits of welfare are virtually never enough—but rather, 'welfare institutions must be concerned with fostering psychological as well as economic benefits' (Giddens 1998: 117).

The state's increasing orientation towards a therapeutic model of intervention, Nolan observes, in the US has influenced civil case law, where emotional damages have outstripped other 'damages' cases dramatically since the 1980s; in criminal law where drug counselling and drug courts have develop an Oprah-esque relationship with the accused; in education where feelings of children—their self-esteem—is seen as one of the key guiding principles; in welfare where both the notion of emotional abuse and the reformulation of support around notions of dignity and self-esteem have increased; and in politics where connecting with the public has increasingly been established by politicians explaining themselves and their policies in terms of how they *feel* about them (Nolan 1998).

The significance of this development that has been replicated in the UK is, however, not simply in relation to the more emotionally oriented basis of contemporary culture, but that within this therapeutic outlook the individual is understood to be fundamentally vulnerable.

Actions and experiences that would have been ignored or understood as insignificant in the past are, within today's framework of therapeutic vulnerability, given a greater significance. Name-calling, for example, is now interpreted as a more serious form of 'bullying' for children, while the 'mischievous' actions of children are increasingly being redefined as forms of 'antisocial behaviour'—both examples being understood as having potentially long-term and significant implications for individuals and communities. Even crime itself has become problematised and given greater importance. As Furedi observed, in the 1970s crime surveys tended to suggest that the impact of crime was relatively short-lived and that only a small percentage of victims were affected by their experience of crime. However, more recently a radically different interpretation has been given to this experience, and through therapeutic language: 'Most studies highlight the acute stress, trauma and psychological damage suffered by victims of more serious crime' (Furedi 2004: 112).

The new etiquette of safety is able not only to relate to the individuation within society, but through the therapeutic culture a more vulnerable individual is both constructed and engaged with.

GRASSROOTS PANICS?

The panics and anxieties discussed above relate largely to the outlook and actions of the elite and of claimsmaking groups. However, for a 'culture of fear' to be a general societal trend, the sense of unease and the desire for safety and a more regulated society must also take hold within the public itself. The increased fragmentation of society has helped to ensure this development at the grassroots level of society—but this does not necessarily reflect a public that is in a 'panic'.

Discussing where moral panics are generated, Goode and Ben-Yehuda (1994: 143) have argued that most studies of moral panics incorporate an understanding of the role played by the elite, interest groups, and by the 'grassroots'. Indeed for moral panics to exist, there must at some level be an element of grassroots support for them. Whether or not the public 'panics' about issues there does appear to be a high level of fear and concern in society about a wide variety of issues. Child safety concerns in particular capture the public imagination and have had some impact on the emergence of what has been described as 'cotton-wool kids'.[21] There have also been reports of 'howling mobs' enraged by the panic about paedophiles—although as we will see the reporting of this is itself a bit of a panic.

Part of the explanation for the rise in grassroots anxieties and what is arguably a higher level of fear than existed previously is the increased level of individuation within society, a development that has been widely explored within sociology (Beck and Beck-Gernsheim 2002, Furedi 2001, Bauman 2000). The significance of this development is, for Thompson, that as the old structures and norms of society fragmented, an increasing amount of individual choice and diversity helped to generate more of a sense of being at risk (Thompson 1998: 88).[22]

The family, Thompson notes, at a time of declining communal values, has become 'all that is left of traditional community' (Thompson 1998: 88). The result of this modernisation process is that people have a sense 'that they are constantly going into a strange country and being at risk' (1998: 89). At the same time, the weakening of traditional beliefs and hierarchies, including family hierarchies, has increased the sense of risk concerning children and family relationships.

Furedi following Beck and Beck-Gernsheim's (1995: 37) point, takes this idea of the family as the last remaining 'institution of trust' one step further, arguing that because marriage itself has become a problematised area of life, today the last remaining 'institution' of trust is the bond between parent and child (Furedi 2001).[23] A world has emerged, argues Beck, where we have 'individuals within homogenous social groups', and communities 'dissolved in the acid bath of competition' (Beck and Beck-Gernsheim 2002: 33).

This emergence of a more 'liquid' form of modernity (Bauman 2000), in which relations of trust are reduced to the family and even to the bond between a parent and child, helps in part to explain the heightened levels of fear in society. However, individualisation has a long history within modernity and cannot in itself explain the emergent culture of fear. Fragmentation may have reduced trust at the level of the individual, but this has also been informed by a more pessimistic understanding of humanity more generally: a sense of pessimism and anxiety that has also been transmitted through the activities of safety-based claimsmakers, and by the development of laws and institutional practices that attempt to engage with this more fragmented individual through the prism of safety and fear.

A PANIC ABOUT A PANIC

Public 'panics', or perhaps more accurately their fear and insecurities, are today less an expression of a collective response to the challenge of social and moral norms than an example of the loss of these norms. Questions have already been raised here about the reality of the public 'panicking' in the past—something Cohen's own work challenged to some extent. However a more public and unified reaction (if arguably not a panic) was far more possible in the past than it is today. The nationalistic culture that allowed for a collective racist response to black 'muggers' amongst large sections of society in the 1970s for example is no longer dominant, nor is there, as Roiphe argued, a more unified, 'popularly accepted moral attitude' across society that can result in a coherent and collective response to events or incidents.

Despite a recognition by many that we are living in more 'post-modern' or 'liquid' times—there is at the same time, perhaps because of this loss of surety and connection between people and within society, an increasing concern about the potential of a 'mob' response to social problems. Today there is a new form of panic being generated by sections of the political and cultural elite—a panic about the public panicking.

Following the London 7/7 bombings in 2005, for example, there was an expectation of an Islamophobic 'panic' amongst the public. The police and politicians geared themselves up for an outburst of racist attacks. Officers were placed outside of mosques and warnings by chief police officers explained that the police 'would not put up with any hate crimes' (*Guardian* 12 July 2005). The Archbishop of Canterbury called for calm and warned against the temptation in some to make British Muslims a scapegoat, and a National Community Tensions Team began to monitor anti-Muslim incidents across the country. Left wing campaigners also covered major cities with posters promoting the need to 'Unite Against Islamophobia'. However, as the investigate journalist Brendan O'Neill observed, figures published by the Crown Prosecution Service for the year 2005–2006 (which covers 1 April 2005 to 31 March 2006, thus including the aftermath of the bombings) showed that there were prosecutions for only 43 cases of religiously aggravated crime. Only 18 of these crimes were committed against Muslims, and this represented a decline from 23 anti-Muslim crimes in 2004–2005. 'Far from being a backlash,' O'Neill argues, 'this figure is socially insignificant, representing a minuscule minority of overall crime for 2005–2006. The 'backlash' predicted by so many turned out to be a handful of mostly minor incidents carried out by drunks and losers'.[24]

More recently concern about 'Asian knife killings double in ten years' emerged. A *Times* article, with pictures of Asian men who suffered racial violence, was written with sub titles indicating what the story was about: 'Surge around the time of 9/11 attacks' and 'An anti-Muslim climate "likely factor"'. Islamophobia is on the rise was the point being made by even this 'right wing' newspaper. However, almost hidden in the final few paragraphs of the article other factors including an increase in Asian youth crime and of a greater number of young British Asians were mentioned. A spokesperson for the Home Office noted that, 'The details surrounding these homicides tell us that there is nothing to support the suggestion that the rise in 2001–02 had anything to do with 9/11', and that, 'In two thirds of the homicides the suspects were Asian too, and most involved domestic or local disputes. In the descriptions of cases there is no mention of 9/11 or any related topic whatsoever. Only one of the homicides was known to be racially motivated' (*Times* 26 April 2007).

In America, Wolfe has similarly noted despite the expectations to the contrary that, 'the September 11 attacks were met with relatively minimal outbreaks of Muslim bashing' (Wolfe 2003: 262).

A similar fear of the public and an expectation and portrayal of their violent and atavistic qualities was also illustrated in a story about a paediatrician whose house was mistakenly attacked by what was described as a 'howling mob'. Public anxiety about paedophiles had risen after the abduction and murder 8-year-old Sarah Payne, with calls for a Sarah's law—the equivalent of Megan's law in the US that allows the public to have information about the whereabouts of paedophiles. The tabloid Sunday newspaper the *News of the World* had subsequently published pictures of known paedophiles creating a debate about the dangers of inflaming the panic over 'paedos'. The fear based and exaggerated promotion of the paedophile threat by this newspaper was understood in 2001 to have helped create a lynch mob atmosphere when there were protests in local areas about paedophiles living there. One case in particular, a case that has now become a media folk tale about the dangers of the irrational mob, was of the paediatrician who was targeted by what the conservative *Daily Mail* described as a 'populace too ignorant and enraged to recognise the difference between paedophile and paediatrician'. There was indeed a heightened concern about paedophiles at this time, and some protests did occur—including one that resulted in a paediatrician being target. However, the stories of the lynch mob were themselves highly exaggerated with numerous stories misrepresenting where the incident occurred and what actually happened—including stories of a paediatrician being 'chased down the street', or having her office burnt down in 'righteous anger', and of a 'howling mob' stoning and fire-bombing a house. The reality, as Brendan O'Neill explains, was that a paediatrician had indeed been targeted in Newport, not Portsmouth or London, as had been reported—with 'paedo' being sprayed on her front door. As he notes the incident was indeed distressing for Dr Yvette Cloete, 'but there is no evidence that a mob was involved or of any evidence of any threats or incidents of physical pressure or violence'. The local police chief inspector, Andrew Adams, interviewed by O'Neill explained that 'there was no big mob' and that after the confusion had been explained to the community they had been outraged and 'supportive of the woman involved'. The 'paedo' graffiti, Adams believed was probably the act of youngsters, 'probably someone in the 12 to 17 age bracket'. But nevertheless, O'Neill argued, 'the story had taken on a life of its own, transformed into a dire warning about the hysterical mob who threaten the fabric of our nation'.[25]

The growing police vetting of all adults working with children, the development of sex offenders registers, and monitoring of paedophiles, have been developed by professionals, and 'child safety' has become an institutional framework for local authorities and within education. These developments have rarely come with evidence of an increasing problem of paedophilia or child abuse but they are seldom seen as 'panics' Contrasted to these highly significant changes to institutional practises that have an impact upon schools and youth clubs across the country—when a small group of 'locals' protest about the danger of paedophiles and some teenagers put graffiti on a house in Newport—a cautionary tale has emerged warning of the dangers to society of the irrational mob. Not only does this suggest that the 'panic' reaction to child safety is taking place within societies institutions and amongst the elite, it illustrates that the *today's panics are often not by the 'mob'—but about them.*

CONCLUSION

Amoral panics are a form of moralising without any wider system of meaning, and have emerged largely because of a collapse in the 'faiths' of the right and left, that cohered society in the past.

The changes from moral to amoral panics are summarised in Table 5.1.

The loss of a moral tale on the right and of the future oriented thinking of the left that framed the contested understanding of society for two centuries is no more. Consequently society has no narrative, and little sense of purpose that can engage even the elite with a historical sense related to what

Table 5.1 Comparison of Moral and Amoral Panics

Moral Panics	Amoral Panics
A minority concern or reaction to a specific event or change in society.	A universalised sense of anxiety felt across society to myriad issues.
Often dampened down by key sections of the elite.	Often encouraged and generated by the political elite.
Infrequently results in new laws and changes to institutional practices.	Has become central to major changes to law and institutional practices.
Promoted by old conservatives who defend the traditions of the past.	Promoted by 'new' conservatives with neither a belief in the future nor the past.
An attempt to defend a conservative morality associated with religion and nation.	A rejection of universal values and a promotion of the etiquette of individual safety.
Emerges at a time of political contestation between left and right.	Emerges with the collapse of both left and right.
Moral claims face a political challenge.	Amoral claims face little opposition.
Predicated on a belief in the possibility of a morally responsible individual.	Predicated on a diminished sense of the individual and the emergence of the 'vulnerable public'.
The 'Old Victorians' panic about the loss of moral absolutes.	The 'New Victorians' panic about absolutes.

has been or what is to come. The conservative belief of what *should* be and the radical ideals of what *could* be has been replaced by a preoccupation with what *is*. Without a coherent story or vision for society that informs and directs its institutions and its 'morality', the question of right and wrong has become confused. Moral purpose has diminished, while micro-moralising has increased as the question of 'society' is bypassed through an engagement with the individual through the issue of safety.

The new etiquette of safety actively avoids any attempt to uphold or promote a particular system of meaning in society that can unite people around the 'common good'.[26] Relying instead upon an engagement with the fragmented individual—amoral panics are by their nature 'anti-social'.[27]

Today, rather than panics being predicated upon an attempt to challenge and re-engage the public around moral absolutes, absolutes are themselves often seen as a problem because they 'exclude' individuals, they 'label' and damage them. Lacking a capacity to involve people in a wider project the demoralised elite attempt to therapeutically 'include' individuals—individuals who they recognise are already distant and disengaged from both politics and society. Absolute values and beliefs are consequently often seen to be both a barrier to this process of inclusion and a potentially dangerous basis for fundamentalism and conflict. *Lacking a coherent system of beliefs, beliefs themselves become a basis for elite panicking.*

A sense of panic—a defensiveness and reactionary response to events and changes in society—is no longer something that is sporadic, short lived and develop outside of key institutions. Rather, society could be said to be in a permanent state of panic. Key institutions in society are no longer grounded—they lack what Bauman would describe as a 'solid' foundation from which to direct their policies. For them, a panic response has become 'good practise' as well as a way to engage the public—a new basis of legitimation. Every major tragedy and atrocity over the last decade and half has, for example, led to new laws and initiatives that change the nature of institutions and their relationship with the public. Following the death of James Bulger, the Dunblane murders and the killing of Sarah Payne, new laws were developed—abolishing *doli incapax*, banning guns, creating school security systems, mass vetting of adults working with children and new anti-paedophile laws. Most recently, the abuse and killing of Victoria Climbie has resulted in 'the biggest reorganisation of children's services in England and Wales for 30 years' (*Guardian* 9 September 2003).

In the past, key section of the elite would often respond to events and 'panics' by dampening them down or opposing them, today the new elite is actively organised around the new amoral panics. The engagement with public fears and a perceived belief in the vulnerability of individuals means that if anything this framework for panicking and the attempt to regulate ever more areas of life can only increase.

This is not the age of the moral panic, it is the age of amoral panics.

6 Asocial Society

Never was the word 'community' used more indiscriminately and emptily than in the decades when communities in the sociological sense became hard to find in real life

(Hobsbawm 1994: 428).

INTRODUCTION

Many of the issues addressed here so far have attempted to challenge the 'myth' of antisocial behaviour: But of course bad behaviour is no myth. Indeed the 'collapse of community' that is widely discussed today would itself suggest that there has been a loss or at least a decline in social norms and arguably in relation to this a rise in the problematic behaviour between people. One could argue that behaviour is therefore worse today. If the 'social' has declined, how for example do we 'socialise' young people? This is a genuine problem but it is not a problem that can be properly understood through the issue of antisocial behaviour; in fact the preoccupation with, and the development of, the politics of behaviour has become a problem itself—and one that avoids the core problem, that we are living in an asocial society.

An asocial society is here understood to be one in which people have few connections with one another—not so much in terms of 'knowing your neighbours', although this is perhaps also more the case today as we go *Bowling Alone* (Putnam 2000)—but more especially in terms of people having few common values and beliefs that tie them to society and therefore to one another. There are few institutions in society that have the trust and confidence of the people—this is most evident in how politics and political institutions are engaged with—or more particularly how they are ignored or cynically treated. However this treatment is not novel to politics; how other key British institutions from the monarchy to the media and even to how unions are engaged with by the public indicates the more disconnected nature of the public itself. People are less grounded today—they are what could be described as—more 'liquid'.

People are more individuated and disconnected from society itself and there are few if any cohering beliefs and values that connect people or that can be called upon by the political elite to engage the public. This is a change from the past when in Britain and indeed many countries across the world issues associated with nationalism and socialism (or more accurately welfarism) both directed state policy and engaged the energy of the public. Today the 'social' has declined—but so too has the more coherent interconnections between people that directed their day to day lives.

Unfortunately rather than grappling with the 'social', and attempting to reformulate the 'common good', questions of society and of what connects people with one another have been sidestepped by politicians and state institutions. Consequently, the focus on behaviour has developed apace and a more therapeutic engagement with the isolated and more insecure individual has been institutionalised. The outcome of this development is that *asocial man* is being reinforced and the fragile diminished subject constructed. *In the process, our more introspective characteristics are actually being fortified against society by officialdom itself.*

THE MEANING OF 'ANTISOCIAL' BEHAVIOR

At a time when antisocial behaviour has become a key theme in politics and society, this development can appear to be a reflection of a government determined to enforce 'social' and 'moral' norms within society. However, in fact the opposite is the case. The rise of antisocial behaviour as a political issue reflects the loss, not the enforcement, of moral and political beliefs and a move towards understanding what is both social and antisocial behaviour with reference to how individuals feel.

Comparing the changing definition of the term 'antisocial' discussed in the introduction of this book we find that the modern term has lost its political content, it is more focused on the behaviour of children than on the beliefs and actions of adults and it also privileges the harm that is felt by individuals rather than to the damage to society itself. (It is no accident that at around the same time that this new definition was introduced into the *Oxford English Dictionary* in 1989 concerns about 'behaviour' were already growing—with for example the issue of school children bullying one another becoming a public and indeed political issue).[1]

The first use of the term 'antisocial', in 1802 and subsequently in 1844, identified by the *Oxford English Dictionary* and discussed in the introduction of this book, is highly political and referred to the moral and political standpoint of Republicans, who were perceived to be a threat to society and its social and religious/moral norms.[2] This definition of antisocial privileges the proposed beliefs of society against those who actively opposed them. In contrast, the more recent definition of antisocial in the 1989 dictionary has added to the idea of challenging the norms of society the following: *causing annoyance and disapproval in others: children's antisocial behaviour.* At the extremes, whereas the original use of the term antisocial was a denunciation of revolutionary Republicans, the modern equivalent is related to the misbehaviour of children. And where the first definition in denouncing Republican activities as antisocial sets up an alternative sense of the correct moral and political 'social' outlook, the latter meaning has a more limited political, moral or 'social' content.

Using the modern definition, what it means to be antisocial relates less to absolute 'social' norms and values of society, than to the offence and harm that antisocial individual acts may have upon other 'individuals'. The social content of the meaning of antisocial has largely been lost and been replaced by a concept that privileges and defends the individual from others. It is somewhat ironically a more asocial definition of what it means to be antisocial.

The concern with social order expressed in today's preoccupation with antisocial behaviour is not new. Indeed, nor is the anxiety about the loss of values and beliefs unique to late twentieth century society. Emile Durkheim for example, writing at the end of the nineteenth century, was largely motivated in his sociological study of religion to understand the moral vacuum left with the decline of tradition and religion. However, despite Durkheim's pessimism about the emerging individualism in society (Morrison 1995: 146), he maintained that 'there is something eternal in religion'. For Durkheim, this eternal something related not to religion as such, but to the centrality of society and the fundamental need for people to 'reaffirm the collective feelings and ideas that constitute its unity and its personality' (Durkheim 2001: 322). Where traditional forms of collectivity were in decline more secular forms would emerge. Indeed Durkheim was himself a French patriot, a firm defender of science, and has been described as a socialist—in this respect he embodied many of these secular forms of 'religion' that gave a collective coherence to much of twentieth century life and subsequently undermined the sense of a loss of social order which dogged Durkheim himself.[3]

Today the anxiety about a loss of social order in Britain and the concern with antisocial behaviour has re-emerged and become more universal following the collapse of many of these 'secular beliefs'. This sense of disorder is felt within the public and perhaps more acutely amongst the elite and has been encouraged by the decline of traditional morality—reflected in the confusion of 'moral language' and the inability of conservatives to promote a 'back to basics' outlook discussed in previous chapters. The 'new elite' lacks both traditional conservative values and 'secular religions' to cohere a society that it senses is out of its control. This sense of society being out of control is a reflection of the elite itself, which, as Bauman argues, has abdicated the responsibility of being the 'pilot' of society. This elite attempts to 'rule without burdening itself with the chores of administration, management, welfare concerns, or, for that matter, with the mission of "bringing light", "reforming the ways", morally uplifting, "civilizing" and cultural crusades' (Bauman 2000a: 13). Where past rules were set down by the 'captains' of society and 'displayed in bold letters in every passageway'—rules that could be followed or challenged—today, in comparison, 'the passengers of the 'Light Capitalism' aircraft . . . discover to their horror that the pilot's cabin is empty' (2000a: 59).

Perhaps more accurately, to use Bauman's analogy, the pilot is still on the aircraft but now engages the passengers not by morally uplifting them but by promoting a safe flight. On this journey clear signs about the purpose of the journey and the captain's rules on the trip have been replaced with no smoking signs, safety cards, warnings about mobile phone use, excessive drinking, antisocial behaviour and even peanut allergies, to help regulate the behaviour on this flight and ensure the passengers feel safe on their journey—*destination unknown.*

Whereas being antisocial in the past was understood as an affront to the values and institutions of society, today, even within the definition of 'antisocial' itself, the concern is not with society as such but with 'behaviour' of individuals and the harm done to individual 'victims' of this behaviour. Legitimation by today's pilots of society is accordingly gained in attacking antisocial behaviour, not with bold signpost of the rules of this society, but through the defence of individual safety. The society or 'community' that is being defended is, in effect, a conglomeration of individuals rather than a unified whole based on 'social' values and norms. Values have become relativised and few 'absolute' norms are accepted, except the asocial value of individual safety.[4]

THE PROBLEM OF BEHAVIOR

Within the definition of 'antisocial', it is noticeable that the modern emphasis is upon the *behaviour* of children, rather than the *actions* of adults. This new definition diminishes the conscious element within this form of behaviour. Where previously antisocial behaviour was understood to be acted out by conscious political adult subjects, today it has also come to relate to the relatively unconscious misbehaviour of children.

The definition of *behaviour* within the *Penguin Dictionary of Psychology* is: a generic term covering acts, activities, responses, reactions, movements, processes, operations etc., in short, any measurable response of an organism (Reber 1995: 86). Like this definition, which in part reduces behaviour to the reactions of an organism, the subjective human element within the understanding of 'antisocial' is today largely missing within the understanding of antisocial behaviour. To stretch the point, the more active understanding of the subject appears to have become—in the definition of antisocial to some extent and within society more generally—more passive: Here we no longer *act*, we *react*; we no longer produce our environment, we are products of it; we no longer determine our own fate, we are determined beings.

And in this respect it is less the thoughts and beliefs that we challenge in labelling someone as 'behaving' in an antisocial manner, but rather their 'thoughtlessness'—or their diminished capacity to think before they act.

Children, in everyday language, have often been described as being badly 'behaved'. But the term behaviour was rarely used with reference to adults themselves. This has changed and today it is not only children but adults who are infantilised through an understanding of their 'behaviour'. *This concern with the 'behaviour' of adults has increased as the capacity of the elite to engage their thoughts and beliefs has declined.*

Unlike terms that differentiated adult *criminal actions* from young people—who were labelled *juvenile delinquents*—today we have no equivalent term in common usage that differentiates the actions of adults from children's deviant activities. Rather, it is more the case that adults, like children, can be defined with the catch-all term 'antisocial behaviour'. Where the term juvenile delinquent separated adults from the world of children, privileging the idea of the adult subject and subsequently allowing a certain space for young people to be seen as 'behaving' in a manner related to their age and immaturity, today, through the categorisation of 'antisocial behaviour', we have an infantilisation of adult 'behaviour' and at the same time a more serious criminalisation of children.[5]

Within the previously defined 'juvenile delinquent' (which is still used as a term in law but rarely in public or politics), we had both labelling of a type of person, but also a sense of the capacity, with age and maturity, for a *progression* from 'abnormal' to 'normal' behaviour: a sense of *progress* embodied both within society and its capacity to socialise the young, and within the individual itself. This sense of social progress reflected in the individual is today more limited, at a time when 'causal interventions' must be 'condemned as an absurdity' (Mészáros 1995: xiii).

The distinction between subjective intentions and *behaviour* has been muddied and a more deterministic understanding of humanity has emerged, giving both a more limited sense of the individual's capacity to act consciously, while at the same time giving a more static sense of people and their capacity to change themselves or to be transformed by and transform society itself.

The underlying message—or fear—within the discourse of antisocial behaviour is, 'find me the antisocial child and I will show you the antisocial adult of the future'. And the age at which antisocial behaviour is being discovered by 'experts' is getting ever lower (note for example a recent discussion about nursery provision and the concern with the fact that 'antisocial behaviour' has been found to occur within 3-year-old children who attend nursery from an early age [*Times* 16 June 2005]). Rather than deviant actions being understood in part to be discrete immoral acts by individuals or as a reflection of the immaturity of young people, today we increasingly fear that 'types' of people are emerging who will be antisocial from cradle to grave. Antisocial behave is increasingly understood as a problem because it is believed to reflect what we *are*.

The case of the relatively recently labelled 'paedophile' is the best example of the discovery of a 'type' of person who is largely understood to have lost any moral capacity to 'act' in any other way than as a defined paedophile. This is similarly represented in the various discussions about 'cultures' of crime that give a sense of permanent distance between those who belong to these imagined 'cultures' and the rest of society (Calcutt 1996).

This deterministic understanding of individuals, as Furedi notes, goes way beyond that of classical social theorists like Marx and Weber, or thinkers like Freud, Mead and Dewey, all of whom recognised the constraints of society and culture in forging an individual's identity, but equally emphasised the 'element of interaction where individuals could exercise a degree of individual choice, though often in circumstances not of their own making'. In comparison, today's model of interaction 'has given way to an outlook where the individual is one-sidedly presented as a mere social product, whose action is almost never the outcome of choice, but of compulsion' (Furedi 2004: 124).

Like the behaviour of the antisocial individual, the victim of antisocial behaviour is also understood within a more diminished framework. As discussed previously, the idea that people are fundamentally vulnerable has helped to inform the issue of antisocial behaviour. Within the definition itself, the sense of human frailty is introduced in the modern meaning. The original meaning of 'antisocial' made no reference to damage being done to the individual: indeed there was no reference to the individual within this meaning, but rather to society and the beliefs and morals being challenged by antisocial Republicans. Within the modern definition of 'antisocial', however, the victim of this behaviour is privileged—in fact, what it is to be antisocial is directly related to the 'annoyance and disapproval in *others*'. Antisocial behaviour, in this respect, relates less to the actions of the perpetrator than to the subjective experience of those on the receiving end of it.

To a degree, even the definition that was introduced into the *Oxford English Dictionary* in 1989 could be said to be somewhat out of date in relation to the significance given to antisocial behaviour, which is today seen as being far more damaging and 'terrorising' to the individuals who live amongst 'neighbours from hell' in a 'yob culture'.[6] Taken to its extreme—an extreme which often informs political understandings of antisocial behaviour—a more accurate definition of 'antisocial' would relate not to the 'annoyance' but to the 'terror' caused by this behaviour.

With the decline in the 'social' and any positive sense of social change, the understanding of the individual has also been diminished and the understanding of their capacity and resilience to deal with conflict within everyday life has been weakened. This sense of individual and indeed public vulnerability is at the heart of the growing concern with the more petty aspects of behaviour within society. Seen less as *actors* in society than as being *acted upon*, today's understanding of antisocial behaviour relates to the *object* of this behaviour, rather than the *subject* who is acting in an antisocial manner.

The meaning and understanding of antisocial behaviour discussed above, despite the limited relation that it has with a wider moral or political understanding of social problems, is not *value free*. Today, the focus of concern within the new definition of antisocial is with *behaviour* seen to be a problem *to* the *individual* (and *then* to our 'society' of individuals). The modern meaning of antisocial behaviour privileges the *passive* recipient of the behaviour. The 'moral' weight of the term, and the legitimacy gained by those opposing it, comes with reference to the protection of the individual who is suffering at the hands of antisocial behaviour. However, at the same time, in addressing the antisocial actor, he himself is understood less as a conscious active agent than as a mere product of his environment and the 'behaviour' of those around him.

A contradictory consequence of this is that within a society where a more diminished or passive subject is the expected norm, responsibility for antisocial actions, despite the political vilification that accompanies this issue, is difficult to pin upon the individual who is understood to be more an organism that *behaves* than a conscious moral subject.

THERAPEUTIC BEHAVIOR

We have seen how the understanding of antisocial behaviour as a social problem has developed most significantly with the emerging understanding of the vulnerability of the individual in society. Psychological explanations of 'behaviour' have also become more influential in describing the somewhat determined actions of individuals deemed to be antisocial. Within this framework there is also a cyclical interpretation of this behaviour, with, for example, Farrington's research suggesting that the antisocial behaviour of mothers who drink and smoke while pregnant will result in the birth of antisocial children (Asquith et al. 1998: 5).

As well as the *physical* damage done by antisocial mothers, even more important in understanding the rise in the concern with antisocial behaviour is the rise of a therapeutic culture that both privileges the 'emotional self' but also understands the individual as being *emotionally vulnerable* and emotionally damaged. Rather than biological determinism, the dominant conservative understanding of humanity is developing around a belief in *emotional determinism*.

As Lasch argued in the late 1970s:

> The contemporary climate is therapeutic, not religious. People today hunger not for personal salvation, let alone for the restoration of an earlier golden age, but for the feeling, the momentary illusion, of personal well-being, health, and psychic security (Lasch 1979: 7).

Lasch believed that, 'Having displaced religion as the organizing frame-work of American culture, the therapeutic outlook threatens to displace politics as well, the last refuge of ideology' (Lasch 1979: 13). In the UK, the accelerated development of a therapeutic culture grew on the back of 'the thinning out of community attachments, the decline of systems of moral meaning', and was 'reinforced in the 1980s by the demise of politics and social solidarity' (Furedi 2004: 100). Subsequently, social problems have been increasingly recast as emotional ones. Two decades on, Lasch's predic-tion appears apposite.

This turn inwards into the individual to find meaning however, is not simply of concern to the 'elites' and social institutions, but also engages with the more fluid and isolated individual within society. As Bauman notes, compared to Durkheim's sense of individuation, which in hindsight appears to be grounded in a 'land of solid modernity', today the individual and indeed 'the body' appears—in comparison with almost all social institutions and bonds of solidity—to be the 'last shelter and sanctuary of continuity and duration' (Bauman 2000: 183).

The therapeutic turn not only transforms the understanding of the individ-ual and society, but the in-built belief in the fragility of this emotional 'state' leads to the presumption of the need to protect people from an increasing array of potential harms. By one-sidedly engaging people as fragile, emotion-ally constituted individuals almost all relations, with parents, peers, neigh-bours, workmates and so on have become understood as sites of harassment, harm and abuse. In this respect, antisocial behaviour is all around us.

For Bauman, having lost the solidity of the past, liquid modernity attempts (unsuccessfully) to engage with and relate to the individual as a 'body' within a 'community', both being 'the last defensive outposts on the increasingly deserted battlefield on which the war for certainty, security and safety is waged daily with little, if any respite' (Bauman 2000: 184).

Through today's therapeutic culture, 'well-being', as Hoggett argues, 'is defined essentially in mental-health terms'. This, Furedi argues, results in the citizen being 'transformed into a patient', and the 'private feelings of people [becoming] a subject matter for public policy-making and cultural concern' (in Furedi 2004: 197).

The objective measurement of 'breaking the law' is, to a degree, by-passed in an attempt to engage with the emotional feelings of the victim, and laws develop to encourage 'respect'. Part of the 'respect' offered by the state is increasingly to accept that if an individual 'feels' that there is a problem, then there is one. Antisocial behaviour subsequently becomes, not about objective actions defined as 'illegal' by society, but more about the subjective sense of the victim.

An example of this development can be seen in the changes in the way the police record incidents of racism: Speaking on BBC Radio 4, ex-Chief Constable David Westwood explained that all racist reporting needed to be recorded—regardless of the evidence. As he said, 'it's about each individual respecting other individuals', you record that people 'believe' there was racism, and have to 'accept that someone feels aggrieved', otherwise you 'turn them right off', you 'doubly traumatise' the individual.[7]

Rather than a rise in traditional morality, within this therapeutic culture, and in relation to antisocial behaviour, we find a remoralisation of behaviour in relation to the emotional sensitivities of the public. 'Antisocial behaviour' relates less to conventional criminal acts—to economic damage or physical harm—than to issues understood to disrupt the sensibilities of the individual and the 'community'. Graffiti, for example, may still be a problem of criminal damage, but its significance for the governing of communities is with the sense of disorder—felt most acutely at the level of the individual victim's emotional state of well-being.[8]

Even the definition of the term antisocial behaviour and the implementation of initiatives to tackle the problem recognise that what is deemed to be antisocial is often dependent upon subjective factors and interpretation. The Crime and Disorder Act defines antisocial behaviour as 'conduct, including speech, which has caused, or is likely to cause, alarm or distress to one or more persons'. Being 'anti-social' therefore, and somewhat ironically, relates not to wider social norms as such but more particularly to the impact that this behaviour has upon the feelings of individuals. Antisocial behaviour is therefore often measured in relation to the level of fear, anxiety or stress that is (or is assumed to have been) felt by the public. The subjective component of the meaning of antisocial behaviour, coupled with the centrality of vulnerability, gives it a high level of flexibility and means that an ever-greater array of forms of behaviour can be interpreted as being antisocial.

At the level of social policy, then, the aim in tackling antisocial behaviour is not connected to *creating* a positive sense of the 'social', but rather in allowing individuals to be 'liberated from fear'. The positive 'sense of community' comes about not through political or moral purpose and unity, but via the agglomeration of individuals' feelings of safety—with this being accomplished, it is assumed, by the eradication of antisocial behaviour.

ASOCIAL ENGAGEMENT

In 2003 the Antisocial Behaviour Bill was introduced to the House of Commons by David Blunkett who described the legislation as something that would 'empower people across the country once and for all' by getting to grips with the, 'scourge that bedevils their communities: the antisocial behaviour that makes other people's lives a misery'. As Burney notes, the Bill was accepted almost without exception by the opposition MP's. The late Labour MP Tony Banks summing up well the mood of the Bill for politicians stated that:

> The Bill unites all honourable Members, because every one of us can point to examples in our constituencies of people coming to complain

to us about antisocial behaviour, and we share our constituents' anger and frustration, and fear for them. Perhaps we should call this a 'letting off steam Bill' as far as Members of Parliament are concerned (Burney 2005: 34).

The Bill itself brought in new powers against crack houses, fireworks, airguns, misbehaving tenants, spray paint, parents of truants and powers to disperse groups of two or more people from certain areas. It was a 'grab-bag collection' of issues associated with 'community empowerment and responsibility' (Burney 2005: 35). These new powers are interesting in themselves, but more interesting perhaps was the tone of the 'debate' in parliament— the 'frustration' being expressed by politicians and the underlying form of engagement taking place here between people who 'complained' and their MPs. Complaints that at another time may have gone to local councillors, the local police, perhaps the Citizen's Advice Bureaus or even to neighbours themselves had ended up in parliament where MPs like Tony Banks were able to empathise with their constituents' anger and frustration and to advocate on their behalf.[9]

The changing nature of politics that is expressed in this developing form of advocacy for victims of antisocial behaviour is something Labour MP Frank Field had alluded to in his book *Neighbours from Hell* where he explained:

> What my constituents see as politics has changed out of all recognition during the 20 years or so since I first became their Member of Parliament. From a traditional fare of social security complaints, housing transfers, unfair dismissals, as well as job losses, constituents now, more often than not, ask what can be done to stop their lives being made a misery by unacceptable behaviour of some neighbours, or more commonly, their neighbour's children (Field 2003: 9).

There seems to be little doubt that the complaints discussed by Field have indeed become an issue—whether or not his constituents saw these complaints as 'politics' as Field states is less clear. Today this may be the case but this must in part be due to the politicisation of behaviour by politicians like Field himself. What is perhaps more relevant is that what a Labour MP see as politics has changed out of all recognition. If Frank Field was being a little more self critical he may have observed that the issues of social security, unfair dismissals and job losses were social problems that the Labour Party in the 1980s found difficult to resolve and indeed it seems to be no accident that the decline of these issues as 'social problems' and the rise of the politics of antisocial behaviour occurred at the same time. Through the 1990s the more fragmented public may have become more engaged by private *troubles* but it was politicians and in particular Labour politicians who constructed and promoted the issue of 'antisocial behaviour'.

The Labour Party MPs mentioned above present their concern about antisocial behaviour in a one-sided fashion—as a mere reaction by themselves to public concerns. However this misrepresents a process that involved the transformation of the Labour Party itself—from a welfarist party connected to the unions and the labour movement—into an organisation that was more detached from any constituency in society and which began to engage with individuals through their sense of vulnerability. This was a process that developed within the Labour Party—but more generally influenced the changing nature of state institutions themselves and their engagement with the public. It is no accident for example that the legal basis for the development of antisocial legislation came out of social housing and the changing role of local authorities as social landlord; their new role motivated a shift away from issues associated with housing in a welfare context and towards an engagement with tenants complaints and the management of their behaviour on estates. Previously 'social' issues regarding housing had been framed within a political context: through the 1980s and 1990s this was replaced by a more individuated relationship between tenants and councils. As Cummings observes, 'The transformation of the housing issue from provision of homes to the regulation of behaviour has been quite startling' (Cummings 1997: 5). The subsequent mass of legislation to deal with the 'problem of behaviour' is an illustration of the new relationship developing between the individual and the state—it is 'legislation made for a fragmented society' (Cummings 1997: 6).

The political elite in the 1990s found that they were disconnected from the public and lacked any wider political framework that could engage the electorate. Public institutions that had previously been part of the 'welfare state' were equally cut adrift from a coherent framework of operation and from the public itself. Consequently a new relationship in politics and within these institutions of society developed that attempted to engage with and build trust with individuals. Relating to the more fragmented insecurities in society 'safety' became a dominant framework of engagement. Through the issue of crime and antisocial behaviour the Labour government attempted, as David Blunkett explained, to develop 'trust and security in society' and to 'respond to people's sense of insecurity at a time of rapid social change'. Tony Blair has similarly explained that his crime strategy is a 'personal crusade' that he hopes will 'build a new partnership with the decent law-abiding citizens to improve the quality of life in every neighbourhood'.[10] The issue of antisocial behaviour may have a reality on the ground—but it was the changing nature of institutions and of politics itself that led to an engagement with this behaviour as a new basis upon which legitimacy could be established.

ASOCIAL INDIVIDUAL

The number of books on 'manners' for both adults and children that have been published in the last decade indicates that there is a certain concern and indeed confusion about the nature of relationships and the expectations of 'good manners'. One of the most popular of these books is *Talk to the Hand*. Written by the best-selling author Lynne Truss, this often light-hearted look at *The Utter Bloody Rudeness of Everyday Life* manages to identify many of the contradictory aspects of behaviour in modern Britain (Truss 2005).

Truss's key insight is to argue that we live in a 'hamster ball' society, a world made up of individuals living in their own private bubbles. Here, she gets very close to describing the real problem we face today: not a problem of antisocial behaviour but rather the problem of living in an asocial society. In other words, ours is a society that lacks the capacity to connect people with one another through a system of meaning. Looking at the problem in this way can be helpful, as it shifts the debate away from the one-dimensional focus on antisocial behaviour, and it shines some light on some of the genuine and new problems with behaviour between people today.

Bauman has similarly noted the emergence of this bubble world—a world where the individual has been removed from and indeed often attempts to escape from the *public*, re-creating 'communities' online from the safety of the bedroom (Bauman 2004: 25). In our more fragmented world, where the purpose of society is unclear and our individual role within it even more so, there have emerged new forms of introspection and a trend for people to play by their own rules: 'Hey, my bubble, my rules'. This is a world where we walk around in our own private bubble, and the 'public' becomes something of an obstacle in our way as we listen to our iPods or text our friends. When we live such bubbled existences, then standards and manners look more and more like they are being enforced upon us from without, and thus we become more inclined to give them the finger. 'Authority', Truss notes, 'is largely perceived as a kind of personal insult'.

This sense of distance and separation between the individual and society rings true, where personal concerns override public interests, where our business is nobody else's, where the separation between public and private seems to have broken down. As Truss observes, 'It's as if we now believe, in some spooky virtual way, that wherever we are, it's home'. Describing the way we have become disconnected from one another and increasingly inwardly focused, Truss argues that 'The once prevalent idea that, as individuals, we have a relationship with something bigger than ourselves, or bigger than our immediate circle, has become virtually obsolete'.

ASOCIAL ANXIETY

Concerns about declining manners and behaviour addressed by Truss and others often point to the individualistic and selfish nature of society to explain this development. However there is an alternative explanation—the rise of the therapeutic society. This is a society based not on selfishness and greed, but rather one in which the mantra 'talk to the hand' expresses an inward-looking and rather fragile sense of the self: a defensive retreat into the world of self-esteem. And it is this retreat of the vulnerable individual that can also help to explain not just 'problems of behaviour' but perhaps more importantly why we as individuals are so outraged by antisocial behaviour.

Isolated in our own bubble, we may find that other people are occasionally rude to us—but more significantly, we are also inclined to have an exaggerated sense of their behaviour as problematic or threatening. Truss herself notes this observing that people in Britain still queue quietly, and she cites the work of Kate Fox, a researcher who walked around bumping into people and discovered that the vast majority of them said 'sorry'. Fox concluded that manners had not declined in Britain.

Despite Truss' concerns about the changing nature of relationships between people, she also—if only every now and then in the book—recognises that most of the people most of the time are not antisocial or rude but are generally polite to one another. 'And yet', she notes, 'if you ask people, they mostly report with vehemence that the world has become a ruder place. They are at breaking point. They feel like blokes in films who just. Can't. Take. Any. More.'

Unlike the myriad government ministers who relentlessly take the preoccupation with antisocial behaviour at face value, Truss (perhaps because of her own preoccupation with 'standards' reflected in her previous book about the declining adherence to grammatical rules) has the presence of mind to recognise a contradictory situation: people are often still civil to each other but seem to believe that everyone else is being rude. 'So what on earth is going on?' she asks.

What is going on is that the 'bubble world' we are living in has a pretty thin skin; it encircles a rather anxious and vulnerable *therapeutic me*. There has been a shift in recent years from the idea of public man—a strong-willed citizen who can make decisions and take actions by himself—to therapeutic man, where we are increasingly seen as fragile, potentially damaged, and in need of help from apparently benign authorities to manage not just our day-to-day lives but also our innermost emotions and feelings. Behind today's therapeutic mindset there lurks the idea that humans are frail and weak; that we need constant protection from others and from the challenges thrown up by life itself.

In *Therapy Culture* Furedi notes how terms like 'self-esteem', 'trauma', 'stress' and 'syndrome' have exponentially increased within newspapers since around 1993 as the understanding of social problems shifted onto the perceived 'emotional deficit' in society: An, 'invisible disease that undermines people's ability to control their lives', and one that was predicated upon an, 'intense sense of emotional vulnerability' (Furedi 2004: 5). As this understanding of people becomes institutionalised and normalised it influences how we understand ourselves, what we expect from ourselves and how we experience the behaviour of other people.

The therapeutic culture coupled with the more fragmented society we live in has resulted in the 'antisocial behaviour' of even young children being experienced as more serious than it would have in previous times. Already feeling somewhat vulnerable, in our disconnected society, where one of the few positive connection we have with other people is through polite exchanges we experience as we drift past one another, politeness has become more significant, not less. We may not all practice it, but, almost to a man, we are concerned about it—and when politeness is not forthcoming, we react in a more extreme way to this perceived snub. We 'rage', or more often we are simply internally outraged.

Consequently, our overreaction to 'antisocial behaviour' is often not directly determined by the behaviour of the 'antisocial' person; rather, it is when our fragile world of politeness breaks down that we seem to sense the more fundamental problem of our isolation and lack of connection with those around us. In this respect, experiencing or witnessing 'antisocial behaviour' seems to expose our sense of alienation within today's asocial society. *When politeness is all we have connecting us to others, incivility takes on an exaggerated significance.*

Truss presents in a humorous fashion a genuine feeling of anger we often sense at other people's lack of politeness and 'respect'. Holding the door open for people who refuse to say thank you, Truss notes her own sense of wounded dignity. 'You feel obliterated', she writes. 'Are you invisible, then? Have you disappeared?' She continues:

> Instead of feeling safe, you are frightened. You succumb to accelerated moral reasoning. This person has no consideration for others, therefore has no imagination, therefore is a sociopath representative of a world packed with sociopaths. When someone is rude to you, the following logic kicks in: 'I have no point of connection with this person. . . . . . A person who wouldn't say thank you is also a person who would cut your throat. . . . Oh my God, society is in meltdown and soon it won't be safe to come out.' Finally you hate the person who did not say thank you (Truss 2005: 54).

FUTURE SHOCK

At a broad cultural level, the climate of political cynicism—which has seen the fall in voter turn-out, the huge decline in party political activists (Heartfield 2002: 202), and the development of political parties as some of the least trusted organisations in society (MORI 2001)—has helped to create a climate of pessimism about the future and a diminished sense of collective and also individual possibilities. As Furedi argues, the significance of the collapse of politics reflects not simply a form of apathy on an otherwise healthy civil society, but rather: 'Cynicism and suspicion towards politics ultimately represents cynicism and suspicion towards one another' (Furedi 2005: 2).

This 'cynicism and suspicion' of others has resulted, for example, in the increasing concern amongst parents and grandparents about 'what the future will be for our children'. Part of the more pessimistic view about life for the next generation has come from an increased fear of crime and antisocial behaviour that is understood to be blighting children's future (Barnardos 1995a). But this fear has also resulted in a more negative image of young people themselves, an image that preoccupies the imagination both here and abroad. A recent survey on public attitudes to youth and youth crime in Scotland, for example, found that despite the statistical fall in youth crime, of those interviewed 69% believed that youth crime had increased and only 2% believed it had fallen.[11] Describing the misanthropic outlook towards young people in the US and the fear of 'violent youth', Zimring notes that:

> A modest expansion in the size of the youth population is regarded as unqualified bad news. It is never alleged that more than a small propor-tion of this population will be involved in serious criminality, but this is the only subject to be considered in congressional debate. From this perspective, an entire generation of future adolescents is considered to be bad news, so that the larger the size of the cohort, the bigger the so-cial and government problems will result (Zimring 2000: 179).

Similarly Zimring notes the profound pessimism of James Q. Wilson, who in the mid seventies had been pessimistic about the state of crime but had by the mid nineteen nineties become even more despairing about the future. In 1995 Wilson's sense of doom was expressed thus:

> Meanwhile, just beyond the horizon, there lurks a cloud that the winds will soon bring over us. The population will start getting younger again. By the end of the decade there will be a million more people between the ages of fourteen and seventeen than there are now; this increase will follow the decade of the 1980s when people in that age group declined, not only as a proportion of the total but in absolute numbers. This ex-tra million will be half male. Six percent of them will become high rate, repeat offenders—30,000 more young muggers, killers, and thieves than we have now. Get ready (Zimring 1998: 49).

This more cynical and pessimistic sense of the future has arguably trans-formed the way young people in particular are understood—as without a positive sense of social meaning and developing possibilities, the lives of the future generation comes to be seen as more directionless and out of control. In the past, when there was a greater understanding of where young people would fit into society and also what the role of adults was in this process

(Furlong and Cartmel 1997: 110), a more relaxed attitude was taken to forms of behaviour that are today seen as being antisocial. Without a sense of social progress or a vision of the future, the trend in politics and society more generally has been to lose the optimistic belief that young people will 'grow out of crime' (Squires and Stephen 2005: 21), or that their energy will be harnessed in socially useful ways—within the workplace, by 'serving their country' (or indeed their class), or in looking after themselves and their family. Even the language used to describe young boys and men in particular has changed, as 'mischievous' and 'boisterous' behaviour has become reclassified as aggressive and antisocial, while being tough and assertive has become 'macho' and 'abusive'.

In a society that lacks a positive vision of the future, and is preoccupied with preventing harm rather than creating good, the 'bad behaviour' of young people has become exaggerated as a social problem. In this respect it is not the behaviour of young people itself that has resulted in the concern with antisocial behaviour, but rather that *within this more pessimistic cultural climate the image of the 'antisocial yob' has become a metaphor for a loss of social control in a society that lacks direction and purpose.*

In a world where people had a strong sense of connection with society—with institutions, organisations and beliefs, and consequently with one another—the irritations of everyday life would not be considered to be of such life-changing importance; they would not be read as signs that society must be in 'meltdown'.

The world of 'my bubble, my rules' may have resulted in the emergence of a 'me generation', but it is a therapeutic me rather than a self-interested or ambitious me. British society has become more introspective—a society where individuals are less aware of any social mores beyond their own selves, and, perhaps more significantly, appear prone to overreacting to those around them. Thus, we seek refuge in our own private world and it is within this private world that the government has attempted to engage the 'public'.

Today there is little aspiration to recreate the social. Rather we discuss 'community' or even 'communities'—an empty space engaged with by the elite who endeavour to give us a 'quiet life' and encourage us to leave other people alone. Antisocial behaviour is itself a term that equates the fundamental values of society with not disturbing others—or with 'being nice'. But within this focus upon the asocial individual, despite the demand for common decency and behaviour between people, the necessity for beliefs and values that give social connections a wider meaning are avoided.

In the criminal justice system, the authorities' engagement with the vulnerable individual has grown rapidly in recent years. Now, rather than law being enforced by the state against the criminal, on behalf of all of us and of society itself, we have victim-centred justice—a form of 'justice' that really endorses the idea of 'my bubble, my rules', or in this case, 'my feelings, my law'.

ASOCIAL RESPECT

Ironically, even within the British government's Respect Agenda, the asocial outlook is encouraged rather than challenged; a kind of NIMBYism of the self is reinforced by New Labour's version of 'Respect'.

The government's *Respect Action Plan* may sound like an old-fashioned attempt to instil good moral values in society. It also appears to be all about creating a more social society, with catchy subtitles such as 'Everyone is part of everyone else', and 'The whole is greater than the sum of its parts'. However, hidden within the very meaning of 'respect' promoted here, is the same asocial and equally amoral outlook that is coming to dominate politics and social policy more broadly.[12]

Until recently, the idea of respect related to experience and achievement. Adults, for example, deserved respect from children due to the socially accepted notion that they, as mature, active subjects, the people who made society, should be looked up to by their less mature charges. Particular individuals were given respect for great things they had done: we looked up to our heroes as people who had achieved something important. Respect was a socially ascribed category, something that was *earned*: it represented a judgement of certain individuals based on what they had done. There may have been battles over who should be seen as deserving of respect, with disagreements between conservatives and radicals, but all sides tended to celebrate the actions and attributes of certain individuals and institutions.

Today, by contrast, the idea of respect is devoid of content or of character. Everyone, we are told, should be respected—adults and children alike. Respect young people, the children's commissioner tells us, and they will respect you (*Guardian*, 19 January 2006). In his book *Respect*, the sociologist Richard Sennett asks how the professional classes might *give* respect to the poor (Sennett 2004). Here, respect has become something handed down from above, often just for being who you are, rather than a set of values that we aspire towards that can take us beyond our 'selves'.

'Give respect get respect'—that is the title of the opening chapter of the *Respect Action Plan*. It quotes young people defining respect in the following ways: 'Being able to be the way I am without being bullied or skitted. And vice versa'; 'Not offending or damaging someone else's feelings or property'. This is a highly individualised, fragile and negative vision of respect. Rather than respect embodying values of achievement and character—something which, in the process of aspiring to, can help us change ourselves, to mature and gain self-respect—it has become something we demand simply for *who we are*.

In the framework of today's preoccupation with antisocial behaviour, the demand for respect has become little more than a call to be nice to one another. To translate, 'Give respect get respect' really means 'Be nice and others will be nice to you'. Rather than respect being a form of social judgement, we are told to be non-judgemental, to respect people for who they are. Indeed, we are actively encouraged to respect an individual's self-esteem, which is seen as being easily damaged by any apparently hurtful social judgements. In essence, this is little different from the sentiment of 'talk to the hand', or the outlook of the child who challenges your right to question his behaviour by arguing, 'I know my rights'.

Broken down to its basic elements, the idea of respect today is really: 'Respect my bubble, my rules and I will respect yours.' Rather than the individual being drawn out of himself through values that relate to society, society is validating the inward-looking and insecure outlook of the 'therapeutic me'.

The government's Respect Agenda is based on the idea that the state must protect vulnerable individuals. 'Respect' has become little more than the protection of one individual from the 'abuses' of others. It is not about saying 'respect me, because I have done something to deserve it', nor is it about respecting adults because they know best; rather, it is a demand that we should respect everybody because if we don't then we will undermine them and their self-esteem. In other words, respect is now defined by the need to curb 'bad behaviour' and defend the vulnerable, rather than by ideas of what it is to be a good and strong-willed character who has achieved a status that deserves recognition. By saying everyone should be respected—young and old alike—the government actually undermines the idea of respecting adults and infantilises the notion of respect itself.

At a time when respect for the institutions of society is in decline, the British government is attempting to engage with the bubble world of the individual. In the process, respecting others has become contentless. Any sense of the 'social' informed by moral or political norms has been diminished, and today's political elite instead promotes a respect agenda in which there is no sense of society beyond the feeling of the 'therapeutic me'. Through this process people are encouraged to have respect for the 'self' rather than actively achieving self-respect. And showing good manners become little more than an acquiescence to the vulnerable individual: 'respect' for the therapeutic self.

ENCOURAGING IMPOTENCE

Traditionally, respect was given to adults because of their capacity to *act*. Today, respect is about not acting—about not harassing, upsetting, abusing, alarming or offending the vulnerable individual. There is no sense of individual capacity or of social responsibility, except in ensuring that our actions do not harm others.

Protecting the diminished subject—the fragile individual—is the basis for myriad antisocial behaviour initiatives. Disastrously, this approach takes the asocial self as the starting point and consequently reinforces the problem of the asocial society.

Rarely, if ever, are people encouraged to take responsibility for the behaviour of others. Rather, a framework is being established that encourages us all to resolve the irritations of everyday life—of noisy neighbours, rude commuters, rowdy kids and aggressive customers—by contacting the authorities to deal with these problems on our behalf. This both discourages the establishment of social norms by the public itself, and also adds to the sense of individual impotence.

Until recently, antisocial behaviour was understood as a problem to be resolved by people themselves. When children swore and dropped litter or neighbours were noisy, people were expected to take a socially responsible approach and act themselves to discuss and resolve such behaviour. Today we are less inclined to act; indeed we are discouraged from doing so. The various antisocial behaviour laws and programmes being introduced tell us the authorities will do it for us. Now there is a whole range of community wardens, police initiatives and helplines that we can contact to ask for help in dealing with any problems we have with other people's behaviour.

When we fail to take responsibility for these problems—which we know, in our hearts, that we should be doing something about—then we diminish our sense of ourselves. *By not acting we both sense and reinforce our own diminished subjectivity.*

Despite New Labour's proclivity to replace a sense of purpose with an ever-growing list of statutes, laws cannot resolve society's problems. Lynne Truss notes that when a policeman kindly asks you to get out of your car, regardless of how politely this is done, it is not a form of good manners but of force. Manners, she notes, cannot be enforced. Today, through the process of relating to others through third-party mediators, individuals are actually being de-socialised. One consequence is that we increasingly feel comfortable engaging with others only within a regulated environment—such as in the exchange between a customer and a shopkeeper—rather than through a free exchange with members of the *public*.

Ultimately, despite some real issues of behaviour in our hamster ball world, the preoccupation with antisocial behaviour has emerged because of the loss of connection we feel with society and with those around us. This is something that is being reinforced by an asocial elite which lacks a social sense and which is equally disengaged from 'public' life. By engaging with the asocial individual through his or her fears, not only is the 'my bubble, my rules' outlook not overcome but the fragmented nature of society is reinforced.

Rather than examining how we can stop people being antisocial, the real question today is how can we create a 'pro-social' society; how can we burst the bubbles many of us seem to be living in? With this starting point there is the capacity to move beyond the myopic focus on antisocial behaviour, to raise the expectations of individuals to act for themselves, and also to identify how today's elite is actually codifying rather than transforming the asocial nature of society.

Notes

NOTES TO PREFACE

1. Across the Western world there is a similar trend towards the increasing regulation of society coming with, for example, a dramatic increase in the number of police officers—where Australia holds the record, with an increase of 97% since 1970 (Braithwaite 2000: 53)—and as Bauman observes, there has been a fast growing number of people in prison or awaiting prison sentences, in almost every country (Bauman 2000b: 33).
2. This refers to C Wright Mills' discussion about how fragmented personal *troubles* were coming to dominate what were previously *public issues* (Mills 1968).
3. Bentham's pursuit of individual liberty was however one sided, and the growing interest in developing a police force also related to the fear of the 'gentry' who observed the 'awakening of the labouring classes' following the French Revolution.

NOTES TO CHAPTER ONE

1. Media search of Lexis Nexis on 1 May 2007 for 'antisocial behaviour' within the *Guardian* newspaper.
2. See Dolan Cummings' introduction to O'Malley and Waiton's *Who's Antisocial: New Labour and the Politics of Antisocial Behaviour* (2005: 6).
3. See Chapter 1 of Burney's *Making People Behave* (2005).
4. There was also a psychological footnote added in the 1989 definition—*Psychiatry sociopath*.
5. For some the growing concern with harmful behaviour is justified and relates to the changing form of behaviour itself. Stuart Jeffries for example argues, 'That growing vulgarisation points up a problem for Mill's principle—what one person believes causes harm or thinks intolerable will be very different from another. But surely vulgarity and rudeness harm others and steadily make our culture uncivilised? Mill's principle needs to be recast for a new age' (*Guardian* 19 September 2005). Why Mill's principles need to be recast is unclear. Mill and those of his generation did not accept vulgarity and rudeness—but they did expect individuals to be able to deal with these issues without the use of the state and the law. What Jeffries approach represents is perhaps less the growing problem of behaviour than of a growing fragility within society and an increasing reliance on the state to resolve problems that individuals were previously expected to be able to deal with.
6. This new branch of criminology is called Zemiology from the Greek Zemia meaning harm. See Hillyard's *Beyond Criminology: Taking Harm Seriously* (2004). Reducing everything from unemployment to murder as a form of 'harm' risks

losing what is specific and very different about these social problems. It also risks reducing almost all human experiences to the 'damage done' to people: Being harmed now becoming central to what we are and how we understand ourselves. Ironically this approach replicates the very framework that governments have adopted to develop their policies around crime and antisocial behaviour.

7. The development of antisocial behaviour in its present legal form has its origin within the state housing sector. A key role for government and the state within the welfare system was to provide decent affordable housing and issues of controversy often related to the standard of housing and the cost of it. However in the 1980s and the 1990s the issue of antisocial tenants emerged and the role of housing managers began to shift away from the issue of quality housing towards managing the quality of relationships between people. This can be understood as both a changing relationship between people and, perhaps more significantly, as a transformation in the role of the state itself away from the 'social' issue of housing, towards the micro-managing of behaviour.

NOTES TO CHAPTER TWO

1. 'Social problem' is in speech marks here to indicate what is understood in this book to be the socially constructed nature of the 'social problem' of antisocial behaviour.
2. See the *Guidance on Crime and Disorder Act: Local Child Curfews* (1998).
3. The justificatory framework of policies relates to the notion of state legitimation. See work by Beetham (1991) and Nolan (1999).
4. This figure shows the results from the *Times*' own website for the term antisocial behaviour from 1984 to 2001, and the term antisocial behaviour in a Lexis Nexis media search of the *Guardian* newspaper.
5. It should be noted however that despite the number of laws developed allowing local curfews relatively few councils have used these powers to date.
6. Chief Constable John Orr, speaking at the launch of the Hamilton Child Safety Initiative, Thursday 23 October 1997. Subsequent quotes used attributed to John Orr if not otherwise stated are from this speech.
7. Tom McCabe, speaking at the launch of the Hamilton Child Safety Initiative, Thursday 23 October 1997. Subsequent quotes used attributed to Tom McCabe if not otherwise stated are from this speech.
8. Sandy Cameron, Executive Director of Social Work, speaking on Sky Scottish 26 October 1997.
9. Tom McCabe, Labour Leader of South Lanarkshire Council, speaking on Sky Scottish 26 October 1997.
10. Sandy Cameron, Executive Director of Social Work, speaking on Sky Scottish 26 October 1997.
11. This aspect of the 'at risk' young person appears to have been integrated into the CSI by the social work department themselves, giving a more 'caring' framework for the initiative. The social work department, while playing no role in the enforcement of the initiative, had worked closely with the police in the development of the curfew prior to its introduction.
12. Here, *typical* is used to refer to what Joel Best has described as a process of 'typification'—a process whereby an extreme example is used to depict what *the* problem is, namely, what is typical (Best 1990).
13. Tom McCabe is now the Labour Party's Finance Minister in the Scottish Executive. It is perhaps telling that McCabe could passionately denounce the very idea of a curfew while becoming part of a government that has subsequently passed a whole range of curfew powers that can be used against young people.

What appeared to be a point of principle—something that was in direct opposition to his view of a 'new millennium' seems to have been mere words devoid
of principle and accountability.

14. There was however one occasion when public fears were actually challenged
by the head of the council. This was in relation to the £3 million Universal
Connexions youth café that had been set up as part of the CSI package—not
only to remove young people off the streets, but to give them something to do
and somewhere to go. A year after the curfew had been introduced, the success
of this new youth centre meant that a large numbers of young people would
gather outside it—a development that led to complaints from neighbouring
adults. However, this time, rather than engaging with the concerns and fears
that these adults had, perhaps setting up another forum to discuss community
safety, or introducing another curfew, a somewhat frustrated Tom McCabe
dismissed the local concerns and stated that the area was, 'never that quiet
anyway' (*Hamilton Advertiser* 24 December 1998). Despite the promotion
of community participation around the issue of safety it appeared that this
was something that could be engaged with or ignored by local politicians.
The genuine active 'participation' of the public and the accountability of these
politicians to this public in this respect is highly questionable. The public could
be 'empowered' by politicians through their initiatives but appeared to have
little independent power of their own.

15. Two Sides to Every Story 'Proximity Conference': Bridging the Gap Between
Young and Old Conference, 10 November 1997, former Strathclyde Regional
Council Headquarters, Glasgow.

16. South Lanarkshire Council prior to the curfew had hired the System 3 survey company to find out what concerns and issues were of relevance to local
people (System 3 1996). Following this, the 'First Citizens' Jury in Scotland'
was set up to address the issues of community safety and it was this jury that
was later said to have come up with the idea of the curfew (South Lanarkshire
1997a). Subsequently research with young people was carried out in schools
in Hamilton to assess the thoughts of young people about the curfew. Also the
police hired researchers from Strathclyde University to assess the effectiveness
of the curfew not simply in reducing crime but in improving the public sense
of safety (McGallagly et al. 1998)

17. A 'phone-in' opinion poll run by the local *Hamilton Advertiser* 16 October
1997 showed that 95 per cent of the public supported the curfew—this was
something referred to by Chief Constable John Orr in his launch speech.

18. During the curfew the police themselves kept a record of the thoughts of the
young people who they picked up on the street, which showed that a majority
supported this initiative. The exact figures of support by these young people
has been questioned and the usefulness of statistics collected by the police
from young people taken home can be questioned (see Springham 1997).

19. Part of the reason for Robertson making this claim was that he had suggested
setting up Citizens' Juries to test public opinion on local issues. Often projected
as a more democratic attempt to 'listen to the people', this approach to social
policy development and the growth of the use of consultants in local government also suggests a level of disengagement felt by politicians and local authorities from the public. That Robertson could claim—without any challenge to
this claim, at least within politics and the media—that the idea for a curfew
had come from the Citizen's Jury, despite this not being the case, also suggests
a one-sided dimension to this group of 'citizens' whose 'voice' could be falsified
and used by politicians with little recourse for those involved with this group.

20. The various children's charities mentioned above, that opposed the curfew,
appealed to a number of clauses within the UN Convention on Human Rights,

which protected children's right to freedom of association, to leisure, and to families to be treated with respect. However, given these groups' acceptance of the problem of young people being at risk and of the abusive nature of the family, these arguments were somewhat contradictory with the idea of individual and family freedoms. For both those for and against the curfew, within the objectified 'at risk' framework the freedom of families to make their own decisions, and of young people to associate freely, was to a degree seen as a problem in and of itself. Unregulated activities, after all, carry within them unpredictable outcomes and risks that make them, within a precautionary framework, intrinsically unsafe.

21. Allison McLaughlan of the *Daily Record* summed up the feeling of those promoting the curfew when she described the Scottish Human Rights Centre as 'nutters'. 'It's OK for liberals to be standing sayin, 'Oh aye, it's infringing people's human rights'', McLaughlan said, 'but what about the rights of people who are getting their windows panned in' (*The Face*, June 1998).

22. As Rose has argued, the emergence of the governance through 'community', predicated on a more micro-management form of crime prevention, has over recent years become understood as a 'cure for all ills' (N. Rose 1996: 331).

23. Gilling also identified that the move to community safety developed under the Conservative government, with the primary problem being understood to be economic, 'the Conservative solution being a market one'. With the creation of *Safer Cities* it was believed, enterprise, community activity and personal responsibility could flourish (Gilling 1999: 5)

24. Rose rightly observes that the process of governance through the 'community' developed as a 'new plane or surface upon which micro-moral relations among persons are conceptualised and administered', and where 'a whole series of issues are problematised' (N. Rose 1996: 331).

25. Rose in particular has a critical recognition, for example, of the therapeutic interventionist element of responsibilisation and the development of new relations of governance through 'community' professionals (N. Rose 1996: 348; 1999). However, the idea of responsibilisation also relates to the individual and his behaviour. Here it is this aspect of the notion of responsibility and responsibilisation that is examined.

26. This is not to argue that a more individualised aspect of crime prevention has not developed in a technical sense—whereby individuals take more responsibility for private security measures. But within the realm of human consciousness and interpersonal or public action, rather than autonomous self-governing individuals developing, we see a promotion and emergence of diminished subjective engagement with the community within an ontological framework of the vulnerable individual.

27. Even at the level of intergenerational communication, the Bridging the Gap conference, mentioned above, can be seen as an example of how past informal relationships between the generations were formalised: a mechanism that has increasingly been understood to be the way forward for helping to recreate a sense of community. A number of conferences around the UK have developed over the past seven years connected to 'intergeneration' reconnecting. One such conference in Keele explained that, 'Participants took part in a variety of workshops on issues such as citizenship, fear of crime, reminiscence, effective intergenerational practice, building healthy communities and intergenerational mentoring. Participants also had the opportunity to see displays on a wide variety of intergenerational initiatives' (www.bgop.org.uk/pages/events_past019.html).

28. See Labour MP Frank Field's book *Neighbours from Hell: The Politics of Behaviour* (2003) where he promotes the need for the police to play the role of surrogate parents.

29. http://www.centre21.org.uk/agenda/agenda2000/articles/tough.html.
30. The specific activities of young people were often referred to—especially by the tabloid press—as a problem in and of itself. However, for those promoting the curfew, the underlying problem being engaged with was the more generalised concern about fear which was understood to be an almost permanent emotional state of the adults living in the targeted areas.
31. See Furedi (2004: 136) where he notes that, 'The 'self at risk' is a construction of cultural norms that regard people's fears as itself a source of risk.
32. Here the focus of the therapeutic outlook has been focused on the issue of the fear of crime. However, this was equally significant in the attempted engagement made with young people and parents, i.e. the fear felt by these groups was understood as the core basis of connection and of the legitimation of the curfew.
33. Visiting Hillhouse, the largest of the curfew-targeted areas, for the first time, I was struck by the unexceptional appearance of the estate. In conversation with local adults and the primary school teachers working in the area, they too appeared somewhat bemused by the initiative and the international media attention it had received. In an article examining the curfew, the music magazine *The Face* gave an apt, if somewhat dramatised, picture of Hamilton—a picture that was equally applicable, if without the 'guns', 'hatchets' and 'heroin', to the Hillhouse estate: 'There are knives, guns, hatchets, heroin, booze and unemployment problems throughout the vale of Hamilton, but it's nowhere near as grim as Glasgow's Easterhouse or Castlemilk. Or Manchester's Moss Side or Pill in Newport and a thousand other places in Britain and beyond. Places you can probably see from your own bedroom window' (*The Face*, June 1998). Hillhouse was an area of relative poverty, with a couple of small streets with largely boarded-up windows and a population of 2,400. Public sector housing made up 80 per cent of houses in the area compared to 44 per cent throughout the region of South Lanarkshire, with a greater percentage of young people and single parents living in them. Despite the murder of a Hillhouse boy two years prior to the introduction of the curfew, as the local police repeatedly informed the press, it was not an area with a particularly high crime rate. Hillhouse was in no sense a ghetto
34. A number of these 'child safety' issues referred to by the police were incidents of children for example who were selling newspaper while being 'inappropriately dressed'. Examples like this—that a generation previously would not have been seen as significant or a cause for concern, and certainly not an issue for the authorities—suggested that it was the classification of 'children at risk' perhaps rather than the activities of these children that had changed.
35. The myth of the problem of under-10-year-olds is of particular significance given the later development of curfew legislation across the UK targeting this age group—something that was justified in part with reference to the success of the Hamilton curfew.
36. The idea of the *public*, here relates to C. Wright Mills' (1967) understanding of active engaged individuals, discussed in Chapter 4.

NOTES TO CHAPTER THREE

1. The collapse of labour movements throughout the world, and the economic 'victory' of the free market has had a profound impact upon society. However, this 'victory' did not result in a confident free market elite emerging, but interestingly the loss of the political opposition of the left appeared to undermine the confidence of the conservative elite itself. From this point on a

more negative interpretation of capitalism developed—even within this elite itself. The concern about 'greed' for example, was not simply a left-wing reaction in the 1990s, as Philips observed with reference to the United States, 'Many conservatives, including President George Bush himself, were becoming defensive about great wealth, wanton money-making greed'. As Heartfield argues, at this time the capacity of the market to inspire was in decline and concern about 'fat cats' in the West, the 'lawless' free market states of the East, and the inhumanity of capitalism in China, grew (Heartfield 2003: 271–89).

2. Where the petty criminal acts of children were mentioned, the target was not simply with this behaviour itself, nor the impact it had on individuals, but rather with the 'soft liberal' moral values—held by teachers and social workers—that it was assumed were the cause of undermining British Victorian values of discipline, hard work and a 'stiff upper lip' (Pearson 1982).

3. See Jenkins (1992), *Intimate Enemies*, for a discussion on this.

4. However, we will go on to see, the push for child safety and victim centred justice came not just from the right—but perhaps more significantly from feminist and radical activists. See for example Philip Jenkins, *Intimate Enemies*, and the discussion about the role of feminism in promoting the social problem of child abuse and satanic abuse (Jenkins 1992).

5. The distinction drawn in this chapter between the political use of crime by Margaret Thatcher and the micro-political approach of John Major, is overly demarcated, and is done more to indicate what was different about these two approaches in the decades of the eighties and nineties. In reality however, by 1987 the labour movement had largely been defeated, with the loss of the miners strike and the third consecutive election defeat for the Labour Party. With the demise of labourism the purpose and coherence of 'Thatcherism' regarding law and order also began to wane. Ironically, with the defeat of the 'enemy within' the Tory's belief that they could resolve the problem of crime actually declined, and they stopped 'claiming that their policies would reduce the incidence of crime' (Downes and Morgan 1997: 290). Now crime became understood more as a problem in and of itself rather than the through the political and moral prism of 'Thatcherism', and with the loss of political purpose it became understood to be more not less of an intractable problem, something that had origins 'deep in society'. The Thatcherite framework for addressing the issue of crime remained to some extent but became less and less relevant, while the understanding of crime as an everyday problem of behaviour began to emerge. Rather than engaging with the political fight against demonstrators and disruptors, the Conservatives began to engaged more with the issue of crime as a problem in and of itself. Fighting crime, rather than the 'enemy within' became a, 'task for everyone' to be involved with. For Downes and Morgan, this de-Politicisation of crime (and indeed the growing acceptance of crime as a problem by the Labour Party) represented a display of, 'greater realism and restraint'. This is true. However, the growth of realism should perhaps more readily be understood as a growth of pessimism and a loss of purpose within politics—something that both undermined the political elite's coherence and sense of political order, and led to the growing feeling that society was itself out of control.

6. Crime was certainly an issue that the Conservative government used in the 1980s, however, as Dunbar and Langdon note, it was not an issue that was, 'very prominent in either of the general elections of 1983 or 1987' (Dunbar and Langdon 1998: 100).

7. Reference http://www.rethinking.org.uk/facts/system.shtml [accessed 29 Nov. 2005].

8. The articles discussing community safety at this time were written with reference to the victim research being carried out examining the impact of racial
   harassment and also general crime concerns of burglary and robbery. This
   research was not simply academic but was a form of action research adopted
   by the council, 'in the hope that it will show [local people] how to defeat
   burglars and robbers' (*Times* 24 November 1987). Left realist, feminist criminologists and activists including Jock Young carried out this research. Still
   focused on specific areas and particular groups, this approach grew in the late
   1990s to incorporate the entire population.
9. The extreme examples of the shooting of school children in Dunblane and the
   killing of the head teacher Philip Lawrence were sited as evidence, which *typified* the problem of 'an explosion of crime and disorder'.
10. 'Community safety' as a term used in the press with reference to crime notice-
    ably increase in its significance in the mid 1990s, and a more pronounced
    increase followed the election of New Labour in 1997. From zero articles in
    1986 and four in 1987 this increased to 61 in 1995 and by 1998 there were
    over 900 articles related to community safety and crime (Lexis Nexis media
    search of all British newspapers from 1984 that contained the words 'com-
    munity safety' and 'crime').
11. Writing in 2003, one Labour MP described the changing relationship with the
    electorate:

    > What my constituents see as politics has changed out of all recognition
    > during the 20 years or so since I first became their Member of Parliament.
    > From a traditional fare of social security complaints, housing transfers,
    > unfair dismissals, as well as job losses, constituents now more often than
    > not, ask what can be done to stop their lives being made a misery by the
    > unacceptable behaviour of some neighbours, or more commonly, their
    > neighbours' children (Field 2003: 9).

12. James Q. Wilson's book *Thinking about Crime* (1975), written from a con-
    servative perspective, was even more influential in questioning the idea that
    the 'causes' of crime could be tackled, leading to a pragmatism and technical
    approach to crime reduction
13. The idea that the fear of crime was irrational was advocated within the first
    British Crime Survey (Hough and Mayhew 1983). Developed in part because
    of the loss of statistical credibility in official crime statistics, the BCS, by dis-
    covering the 'dark figure' of crimes that went unreported to the police, helped
    to develop a focus upon the victims of crime and more specifically the victims
    of minor and middle range offences. Despite this, left realist and feminist crim-
    inologists argued that crimes against women and minor incivilities against
    'vulnerable groups' remained hidden.
14. The term 'vulnerable groups' is telling in and of itself, in that it ascribes the
    status of vulnerability to an entire section of society, the commonality between
    these people being subsequently understood through this label of being vul-
    nerable. By the very nature of *being* a child, or elderly, or a woman you *are*
    vulnerable—regardless of how you understand yourself or experience life—
    and are therefore in need of protection.
15. Also see Simon Jenkins's critique of the Conservative governments in *Account-
    able to None: The Tory Nationalisation of Britain* (1995).
16. Writing in 1989 a *Guardian* columnist noted that the 'conventional wisdom'
    within the Home Office and policing circles was that the, 'risk of crime is
    much lower than the public suspects . . . and that the mass media have contrib-
    uted to irrational fears, particularly amongst women and the elderly' (Hunt
    1997: 640).

NOTES TO CHAPTER FOUR

1. This loss of a sense of human agency has been objectified and theorised by Ulrich Beck's understanding of a risk society (1992).
2. The understanding of Thatcherism for explaining the transformation within the working class was developed systematically within the radical journal, *Marxism Today*, a journal within which significant individuals who went on to influence the emergence of New Labour wrote, including Tony Blair (if infrequently), Geoff Mulgan and Charles Leadbetter (Finlayson 2003: 117).
3. Hayes and Hudson (2001: 11) described the notion of Essex Man as a 'crude lifestyle caricature', which was an 'implausible attempt to define a new group of workers with a Thatcherite ideology'.
4. The discovery by the Birmingham School of youth subcultures as sites of resistance reflected in part a more diminished view of what 'resistance' was—with often apolitical young people's clothes styles and their 'culture' being elevated in significance as a form of opposition to the values of capitalism. With a declining belief in the radical possibility for change critics like Stuart Hall found meaning and significance in culture—something that represented in reality the retreat from politics.
5. TINA was a term used to describe the idea promoted by Margaret Thatcher that There Is No Alternative to the market.
6. See for example the NSPCC's research *Child Maltreatment in the UK* (2000) where this approach is adopted.
7. The programme took place on Thursday 21 April 2005, on BBC 1 television.
8. In a sense what Mills was discussing was the classic liberal understanding of democracy: a democracy that he recognised was problematic in terms of where power lay in society and the subsequent role of public institutions. However, his discussion of a *public* is nonetheless a useful starting point to contrast the changing nature of politics in late twentieth century Britain.
9. See *New Statesman* 7 July 2003 where the legislative fever of the Labour governments was observed by Nick Cohen, who described the '661 new crimes' created by the Labour governments since 1997.
10. This development also helps explain the emergence of therapeutic politics, as Heartfield notes: 'Where the people are no longer constituted through the political process as a people, but remain instead atomised individuals, the state cannot represent the general will. In such conditions modern elites relate to the electorate on a more personal basis, in which circumstance, the expression of love is more appropriate' (Heartfield 2002: 200).
11. The 'vital ingredient', of 'fear of crime', 'discovered' in the 1980s (Gilling 1999: 1), was one of the key developments which led to a move towards a more therapeutically oriented approach to crime which became increasingly central to law and order issues as the 1990s progressed. One example of this, is the publication of *Anxieties about Crime: Findings from the 1994 British Crime Survey* (Home Office 1995). That the Home Office researchers decided to write a specific paper on anxieties about crime reflected the growing centrality of emotional indicators as central to the understanding of the social problem of crime.

NOTES TO CHAPTER FIVE

1. The conference "Moral Panics: Then and Now" was a British Academy discussion on the 9th March 2007 between Stanley Cohen, Stuart Hall and David

Garland. It is available online at http://www.britac.ac.uk/events/2007/moral-panic/index.html.

2. Cohen's work on Mods and Rockers was developed from labelling theory that emerged in the USA in the fifties and sixties (Lemert 1951; Becker 1991 [originally published in 1963]). Labelling theory, rather than taking the deviant as a given by his actions and studying this, looked at how the very process of labelling came about, and what impact labelling an individual or group had on the accused.

3. This, he argued, in the 1960s was something felt most acutely by the lower middle class, as the 'work ethic' was seen to be displaced amongst the young by a 'New Hedonism' (1978: 157).

4. Many on the right attacked extremists, demonstrators, squatters, black power activists and student radicals. Militant trade unionists were also attacked and new laws like the Industrial Relations Act introduced. The demonstration against this act was depicted at the time as a demonstration of rowdies and anarchists 'promoting the downfall of law and order' (1978: 284).

5. Explaining how society 'creates' deviance, Becker notes that '*social groups make deviance by making the rules whose infraction constitutes deviance*, and by applying those rules to particular people and labelling them as outsiders. From this point of view, deviance is *not* the quality of the act the person commits, but rather a consequence of the application by others of rules and sanctions to an "offender"' (Becker 1991: 9).

6. This form of social constructionism, known as contextual constructionism, informs the work within this book. For a discussion about the conflicting methods of strict and contextual constructionists, see Spector and Kitsuse (1987) and Best (1990: 189)

7. Indeed, reading *Policing the Crisis* one is struck by the extent to which this is not a book about moral panics at all (as it has become seen as), but rather a book about class conflict and racism—and the highly charged political use of moral issues as part of a wider political battle between 'forces of conservatism' and the 'enemy within'.

8. The interest group theory has been developed most in the US, due, Thompson believes, to existing fields of research in this country around social movements and collective behaviour studies. These social movements are defined as those groups that do not have the influence of established pressure groups and therefore, in part, because they need to attract attention to their issue of concern, are prone to present these concerns in terms of outrage and moral indignation (Thompson 1998: 19).

9. The defence of tradition—and particularly the notion of a national tradition—is explicit within these statements and have been part of the conservative outlook in Britain since the French Revolution. See for example Edmond Burke's *Reflections on the Revolution in France* (1999).

10. The 'back to basics' campaign was launched by Prime Minister John Major in 1993. Notorious for its 'high moral tone', it has been understood as a failed attempt to re-launch the Conservative government.

11. Fitzpatrick sees the Aids panic really taking off with this government campaign, but rather than being a traditional 'moral' panic what Fitzpatrick describes could be seen as more of an 'amoral' panic. With reference to work by Susan Sontag, he notes that, 'Sontag recognised that the wider AIDS panic connected with a public mood of restraint, 'a positive desire for stricter limits on the conduct of personal life', encouraging attitudes such as 'Watch your appetite. Take care of yourself. Don't let yourself go' (Fitzpatrick 2001: 9).

12. The family by the 1990s was understood to be 'in crisis'. This incorporated both the conservative concern about the 'underclass'—of the rise of single parents

and loss of morality, but perhaps more importantly, a radical understanding of the family as a site of abuse and violence. Hunt discussing the fall out after the killing of James Bulger notes that, the 'generalised concern that parents have lost either the will or the capacity to control their children', was coupled with the understanding that, 'those who pose the source of danger to children are no longer dangerous strangers, but treacherous intimates, parents themselves and those in positions of trust such as the clergy, youth leaders, sports coaches and the like' (Hunt 1999a: 212). In reality, the tendency to panic in the 1990s was becoming more general across the political spectrum, reflected in the move by those on the left to become more preoccupied with issues of, violence and abuse, within a broader sense that humanity and human relationships and actions were destructive and needed to be regulated. A new 'tolerant' form of 'morality' was being established here—by those whom Himmelfarb described as the 'New Victorians'. Radical political issues of the 1970s and 80s now took on an increasingly moralistic dimension, as Himmelfarb observed in 1995, 'More recently still, efforts have been made to expand paternalism still further: to prohibit pornography, "hate speech," "sexual harassment," and "date rape," and to require employees, students, and professionals to attend "sensitivity" and "consciousness-raising" sessions to correct their supposed racism, sexism, and homophobia' (Himmelfarb 1995: 259).

13. Like the underclass, single parents and muggers.
14. See *Knife Culture? Cut the Crap* (http://www.spiked-online.com/Articles/0000000CA825.htm).
15. 'Binge drinking' as a term used in the UK press has emerged in a similar way to term 'antisocial behaviour'—first used in 1988, by 2006 there were 3131 newspaper articles that used the term.
16. See Theodore Dalrymple's *Romancing Opiates: Pharmacological Lies and Addiction Bureaucracy.*
17. See http://www.spiked-online.com/index.php?/site/article/128/.
18. See Beck in Lash et al.'s *Risk, Environment and Modernity: Towards a New Ecology* (1996).
19. The concern with social control as the aim for social policy and political interventions is expressed clearly by leading sociologist and New Labour adviser Anthony Giddens, in his book *The Third Way*. Giddens' concern for social order is reflected in his proposals, which lose any principle and become simple pragmatic judgements about the best way to maintain order in society. Meritocracy, for example is discussed in wholly negative terms and is questioned because of its potentially destabilising impact on 'social cohesion' (1998: 102).
20. Although what is meant by responsibility has changed and diminished.
21. The idea of cotton-wool kids relates to children who are over-protected by their parents.
22. Individuation within modern society has a long history but only in the last few decades has the sense of 'risk' become more of a general phenomenon. It is not simply the fragmentation of 'structures', but the decline of political and ideologies that have encouraged this development. However, it is also the construction of social problems and institutional norms around a risk or safety based framework that have helped to 'formalise informal relationships' a process that has encouraged the individuation and sense of distance between people in society. This will be discussed in the final chapter.
23. This helps in part to understand the notion of 'paranoid parenting', and the strength of the amoral absolute of child safety, discussed in later chapters.
24. See article at http://www.spiked-online.com/index.php?/site/article/2271/.
25. See BBC online article—http://news.bbc.co.uk/1/hi/magazine/4719364.stm.

26. See Philip K Howard's *The Collapse of the Common Good* (2002)—a book examining the legalisation of American society and the consequent development of the 'avoidance of risk' as the basis of organising society.
27. The profound concern about child abuse and paedophiles that has become the most significant influence upon new laws and procedures in regulating relationships between adults and children has developed as part of the new 'moral' absolute of child safety. However, this preoccupation with child abuse should be understood as the morality of the lowest common denominator.

NOTES TO CHAPTER SIX

1. In 1986 there were 17 articles in the *Guardian* newspaper referring to bullying in schools; this had risen to 116 articles by 1996 and 201 in 2006. In the 1990s the first national anti-bullying campaigns were also launched both within education and through independent charitable organisations.
2. 1802 J. Mackintosh in *Memoirs* (1835) I. Iv. 176 A collection of all the rebellious, antisocial, blasphemous . . . books . . . published . . . during . . . the Revolution. 1844 *Dublin rev.* Mar. 34 The dark, malignant, atrocious, and utterly anti-social character, which the Republican party in its contest with the new government has exhibited (*Oxford Dictionary* 1885).
3. Also see Furedi (1992: 90–97).
4. The safety of children—especially with regard to the issue of child abuse and paedophiles—is one of the few 'absolute' values that British society feels confident to uphold. But this is a particularly negative and low-level common denominator around which to develop a web of meaning.
5. Note for example the change in the law related to *doli incapax* discussed previously.
6. See for example Frank Field's description of antisocial behaviour, which he believes is as significant a threat as international terrorism (Field 2003).
7. BBC Radio 4, July 26th, 2005, *On the Ropes.*
8. Tony Blair described anti-social behaviour such as vandalism, graffiti and fly tipping as 'probably the biggest immediate issue for people in the country'. It will be the centrepiece of the Queen's speech on November 13, he added during a visit to Newham in East London (*Guardian* 14 November 2002). On November 4th, 2002, Tony Blair argued that the clutch of bills to deal with crime and antisocial disorder at the heart of the Queen's speech was designed to create a 'victim justice system' rather than the present 'criminal justice system' (*Guardian* 4 November 2002).
9. That Banks described the process of discussing the Bill as 'letting off steam' added a curiously therapeutic element to the parliamentary discussion itself for the MPs involved.
10. See http://www3.labour.org.uk/news/tbcrimespeech.
11. See Scottish Executive Publications (2005).
12. See http://www.homeoffice.gov.uk/documents/respect-action-plan.

Bibliography

Allen, R. (2004) 'Classic Text Revisited . . . Hooligan Geoffrey Pearson, 1983'. *Young People Now*. January 21–27.

Amis, D. (1997) *Adolescence, Risk and Independence: Preliminary Findings*. London: Families for Freedom.

Anderson, S. (1992) *Loss of Virtue: Moral Confusion and Social Disorder*. London: Social Affairs Unit

Anderson, S. and Leitch, S. (1996) *Main Findings from the 1993 Scottish Crime Survey*. Edinburgh: Scottish Office Central Research Unit.

Angrosini, M. and Mays de Perez, K. (2000) 'Rethinking Observation: From Method to Context', in Norman Denzin and Yvonne Lincoln's *Handbook of Qualitative Research: Second Edition*. London: Sage.

Asquith, S. et al. (1998) *Children, Young People and Offending in Scotland*. Scotland: The Scottish Office Central Research Unit.

Barnardos (1995a) *The Facts of Life: The Changing Face of Childhood*. London: Barnardos.

Barnardos (1995b) *Listen to Children: Children, Ethics and Social Research*. London: Barnardos.

Barnardos (1995c) *Playing It Safe*. London: Barnardos.

Bauman, Z. (2000a) *Liquid Modernity*. Cambridge: Polity Press.

Bauman, Z. (2000b) 'Social Uses of Law and Order', in *Criminology and Social Theory*. Oxford: Oxford University Press.

Bauman, Z. (2004) *Identity*. Cambridge: Polity Press.

Beck U. (1992) *Risk Society: Towards a New Modernity*. London: Sage.

Beck, U. (1996) 'Risk Society and the Provident State', in S. Lash et al. (eds.) *Risk, Environment and Modernity*. London: Sage.

Beck, U. and Beck-Gernsheim, E. (1995) *The Normal Chaos of Love*. Cambridge: Polity Press

Beck, U. and Beck-Gernsheim, E. (2002) *Individualisation*. London: Sage.

Beck, U., Giddens, A. and Lash, S. (eds.) (1994) *Reflexive Modernisation: Politics, Tradition and Aesthetics in Modern Social Order*. Cambridge: Polity Press.

Becker, H. (1991) *Outsiders: Study of the Sociology of Deviance*. New York: Free Press.

Beetham, D. (1991) *The Legitimation of Power*. London: Macmillan.

Bell, D. (1962) *The End of Ideology*. New York: Collier Books.

Ben-Ami, D. (2001) *Cowardly Capitalism: The Myth of the Global Financial Casino*. West Sussex: John Wiley and Sons.

Bennett, A. (2001) 'Contemporary Youth Music and Risk Lifestyles', in Joel Best (ed.) *How Claims Spread: Cross National Diffusion of Social Problems*. New York: Walter de Gruyter

Berger, P. (1965) 'Towards a Sociological Understanding of Psychoanalysis', *Social Research* 32, pp. 26–41.

Best, J. (1993) *Threatened Children: Rhetoric and Concern about Child-Victims.* Chicago: University of Chicago Press.

Best, J. (1995) *Images of Issues: Typifying Contemporary Social Problems.* New York: Walter de Gruyter.

Best, J. (1999) *Random Violence: How We Talk about New Crimes and New Victims.* Berkley: University of California Press.

Best, J. (2001a) *Damned Lies and Statistics: Untangling Numbers from the Media, Politicians, and Activists.* Berkeley: University of California Press.

Best, J. (ed.) (2001b) *How Claims Spread: Cross National Diffusion of Social Problems.* New York: Walter de Gruyter.

Best, J. (2004) *Deviance: Career of a Concept.* Belmont: Wadsworth.

Blatchford, P. (1999) 'The State of Play in Schools', in M. Woodhead et al. (eds.) *Making Sense of Social Development.* London: Routledge.

Blears, H. (2004) *The Politics of Decency.* London: Mutuo.

British Journal of Criminology 1984, Review Symposium. Vol. 24, pp.195–205.

Bottoms, A.E. (1977) 'Reflections on the Renaissance of Dangerousness,' *Howard Journal*, Vol. 16, pp. 70–96.

Bowling, B. (1999) 'The Rise and Fall of New York Murder: Zero Tolerance or Crack Decline?' *British Journal of Criminology*, Vol. 39, No. 4.

Box, S. (1983) *Power, Crime and Mystification.* London: Tavistock.

Braithwaite, J. (2000) 'The New Regulatory State and the Transformation of Criminology', in *Criminology and Social Theory.* Oxford: Oxford University Press.

Bronfenbrenner, U. (1967) 'The Psychological Cost of Quality and Equality in Education'. *Child Development* Vol. 38, No. 4, pp. 909–926.

Brook, L. and Cape, E. (1995) 'Libertarianism in Retreat', in Roger Jowells (ed) *British Social Attitudes: The 12th Report.* Dartmouth: Dartmouth Publishing Company.

Buck-Morss, S. (2000) *Dreamworld and Catastophe: The Passing of Mass Utopia in East and West.* Cambridge, MA: The MIT Press.

Burgess, A. (2004) *Cellular Phones, Public Fears, and a Culture of Precaution.* Cambridge: Cambridge University Press.

Burke, E. (1999) *Reflections on the Revolution in France.* Oxford: Oxford University Press.

Burney, E, (2005) *Making People Behave: Anti-social Behaviour, Politics and Policy.* Devon: Willan.

Calcutt, A. (1996) 'Uncertain Judgement: a Critique of the Culture of Crime', in Suke Wolton (ed) *Marxism, Mysticism and Modern Theory.* London: Macmillan.

Calcutt, A. (1998) *Arrested Development.* London: Cassell.

Campbell, B. (1993) *Goliath: Britain's Dangerous Places.* London: Metheun.

Christensen, P. and James, A. (2000) *Research with Children: Perspectives and Practices.* London: Falmer.

Cohen, S. (1971) *Images of Deviance.* Harmonsworth: Penguin.

Cohen, S. (1985) *Visions of Social Control.* Oxford: Polity Press.

Cohen, S. (1988) *Against Criminology.* Oxford: Transaction.

Cohen, S. (2002) *Folk Devils and Moral Panics: The Creation of the Mods and Rockers.* London: Routledge. [Orig. published 1972]

Coleman, C. and Moynihan, J. (1996) *Understanding Crime Data.* Buckingham: Open University Press.

Coleman, J. (1999) *Key Data on Adolescence.* Brighton: Trust for the Study of Adolescence.

Collins Modern English Dictionary (1986) London: William Collins Sons & Co. Ltd.

Cook, D. (2000) 'Safe and Sound? Crime, Disorder and Community Safety Policies', in Margaret May, Robert Page and Edward Brunsdon (eds) *Understanding Social Problems: Issues in Social Policy*. Oxford: Blackwell Publishing.

Corbett, C. and Hobdell, K. (1988) 'Volunteer-based Services to Rape Victims: Some Recent Developments', in M. Maquire and J. Pointing (eds) *Victims of Crime: A New Deal*. Milton Keynes: Open University Press.

Cretney, A., Davis, G., Clarkson, C., and Shepherd, J. (1994) 'The Failure of the "Offence against Society" Model'. *British Journal of Criminology*, Vol. 34, No. 1, pp. 15–29.

Critcher, C. (ed) (2006) *Moral Panics and the Media*. Berkshire: Open University Press.

Cullen, J. (1996) 'The Return of the Residuum', in L. Revell and J. Heartfield (eds.) *A Moral Impasse: The End of Capitalist Triumphalism*. London: Junius.

Cummings, D. (1997) *Surveillance and the City*: Glasgow: Urban Research Group.

Cummings, D. (ed.) (2006) *Debating Humanism*. Exeter: Societas.

Dalrymple, T. (2006) *Romancing Opiates: Pharmacological Lies and Addiction Bureaucracy*. New York: Encounter.

Davis, H. and Bourhill, M. (1997) '"Crisis": The Demonization of Children and Young People', in Phil Scratton (ed.) *'Childhood' in 'Crisis'?* London: UCL Press Limited.

Davis, R., Lurigio, A. and Skogan, W. (1997) *Victims of Crime: Second Edition*. Thousand Oaks, CA: Sage Publications.

Deane, A. (2005) *The Great Abdication: Why Britain's Decline is the Fault of the Middle Class*. Exeter: Imprint Academic.

Dennis, N. (ed.) (1997) *Zero Tolerance: Policing a Free Society*. London: The IEA Health and Welfare Unit.

Dionne, E.J. (1992) *Why Americans Hate Politics*. New York: Simon & Schuster.

Downes, D. and Morgan, R. (1997) 'Dumping the "Hostages to Fortune"? The Politics of Law and Order in Post-War Britain', in M. Maguire, R. Morgan and R. Reiner (eds) *The Oxford Handbook of Criminology*. Oxford: Oxford University Press.

Dunbar, I., and Langdon, A. (1998) *Tough Justice: Sentencing and Penal Policies in the 1990s*. Oxford: Blackstone Press.

Durham, M. (1991) *Sex and Politics: The Family and Morality in the Thatcher Years*. London: Macmillan.

Durkheim, E. (2001) *The Elementary Forms of Religious Life*. Oxford: Oxford University Press.

Durkheim, E. (2002) *Suicide: A Study in Sociology*. London: Routledge.

Durodie, B. (2002) 'The Demoralization of Science'. Demoralization: Morality, Authority and Power Conference, Cardiff University, 5 April.

Embry, D.D. (2002) 'The Good Behavior Game: A Best Practice Candidate as a Universal Behavioural Vaccine'. *Clinical Child and Family Psychology Review*, Dec., Vol 5, No 4, pp. 273–297.

Etzioni, A. (1997) *The New Golden Rule: Community and Morality in a Democratic Society*. London: Profile Books.

Fairclough, N. (2000) *New Labour, New Language?* London: Routledge.

Farrall, S. and Gadd, D. (2004) 'Research Notes: "The Frequency of the Fear of Crime"'. *British Journal of Criminology*, Vol. 44, pp. 127–132.

Farrall, S., Bannister, J., Ditton, J. and Gilchrist, E. (1997) 'Questioning the Measurement of the "Fear of Crime": Findings from a Major Methodological Study'. *British Journal of Criminology*, Vol. 37, No. 4, pp. 658–666

Farrington D.P. (1997) 'Human Development and Criminal Careers', in M. Maquire, R. Morgan & R. Reiner (eds), *The Oxford Handbook of Criminology: Second Edition*, pp. 361–408. Oxford: Clarendon.

Farrington, D.P. (2002) 'Developmental Criminology and Risk-Focused Prevention', in M. Maquire, R. Morgan & R. Reiner (eds), *The Oxford Handbook of Criminology: Third Edition*, pp. 657–701. Oxford: Oxford University Press.

Farrington, D.P., Lambert, S. and West, D.J. (1998) 'Criminal Careers in Two Generations of Family Members in the Cambridge Study of Delinquent Development.' *Studies in Crime and Crime Prevention*, Vol. 7, pp. 1–22.

Feeley, M. and Simon, J. (1992) 'The New Penology: Notes on the Emerging Strategy of Corrections and its Implications', *Criminology*, 30, pp. 449–74.

Feeley, M. (2003) 'Crime, Social Order and the Rise of Neo-Conservative Politics'. *Theoretical Criminology*, Vol. 7, No. 1, pp. 111–130.

Field, F. (2003) *Neighbours from Hell: The Politics of Behaviour*. London: Politico's.

Finlayson, A. (2003) *Making Sense of New Labour*. London: Lawrence and Wishart.

Fitzpatrick, M. (2001) *The Tyranny of Health: Doctors and the Regulation of Lifestyle*. London: Routledge.

Fitzpatrick, M. (2004) *MMR and Autism: What Parents Need to Know*. London: Routledge.

Fitzpatrick, M. and Milligan, D. (1987) *The Truth about the AIDS Panic*. London: Junius.

Flint, J. (2002) 'Social Housing Agencies and the Governance of Anti-social Behaviour'. *Housing Studies*, Vol. 17, No. 4, pp. 619–637.

Fontana, A. and Frey, J. (2000) 'The Interview: From Structured Questions to Negotiated Text', in Norman Denzin and Yvonne Lincoln (eds.) *Handbook of Qualitative Research: Second Edition*. London: Sage.

Fukuyama, F. (1992) *The End of History and the Last Man*. New York: Free Press.

Furedi, F. (1992) *Mythical Past, Elusive Future: History and Society in an Anxious Age*. London: Pluto Press.

Furedi, F. (1997) *Culture of Fear: Risk-Taking and the Morality of Low Expectations*. London: Cassell.

Furedi, F. (2001a) 'Bullying: The British Contribution to a Social Problem', in Joel Best (ed.) *How Claims Spread: Cross National Diffusion of Social Problems*. New York: Walter de Gruyter

Furedi, F. (2001b) *Paranoid Parenting*. London: Allen Lane.

Furedi, F. (2002) *Culture of Fear: Risk-Taking and the Morality of Low Expectations: Revised Edition*. London: Continuum.

Furedi, F. (2004) *Therapy Culture: Cultivating Vulnerability in an Uncertain Age*. London: Routledge.

Furedi, F. (2005) *The Politics of Fear: Beyond Left and Right*. London: Continuum.

Furedi, F. and Brown, T. (1997) *Disconnected: Ageing in an Alien World*, London: Reconnecting.

Furlong, A. and Cartmel, F. (1997) *Young People and Social Change: Individualization and Risk in Late Modernity*. Buckingham: Open University Press.

Garland, D. (1985) *Punishment and Welfare: A History of Penal Strategies*. Aldershot: Gower.

Garland, D. (1996) 'The Limits of the Sovereign State'. *The British Journal of Criminology*, Vol. 36, No. 4, pp. 445–471.

Garland, D. (2002) *The Culture of Control: Crime and Disorder in Contemporary Society*. Oxford: Oxford University Press.

Garland, D., and Sparks, R. (2000) *Criminology and Social Theory*. Oxford: Oxford University Press.

Garside, R. (2004) *Crime, Persistent Offenders and the Justice Gap*. London: Crime and Society Foundation.

Giddens, A. (1991) *Modernity and Self Identity*. Cambridge: Polity Press.

Giddens A. (1994) *Beyond Left and Right: The Future of Radical Politics*. Cambridge: Polity Press.

Giddens, A. (1998) *The Third Way: The Renewal of Social Democracy*. Cambridge: Polity Press.

Gilling, D. (1999) 'Community Safety: A Critique'. *The British Criminology Conferences: Selected Proceedings*, Volume 2. London: The British Society of Criminology.

Glassner, B. (1999) *The Culture of Fear: Why Americans Are Afraid of the Wrong Things*. New York: Basic Books.

Goldson, B. (1997) 'Children in Trouble: State Responses to Juvenile Crime', in P. Scratton (ed), *'Childhood' in 'Crisis'*. London: UCL Press.

Goode, E. and Ben-Yehuda, N. (1994a) *Moral Panic: The Social Construction of Deviance*. Oxford: Blackwell Publishing.

Goode, E. and Ben-Yehuda, N. (1994b) 'Moral Panics: Culture, Politics, and Social Construction'. *Annual Review of Sociology*, Vol. 20, pp. 149–171.

Gordon, C. (1991) 'Governmental Rationality', in Graham Birchell, Colin Gordon and Peter Miller (eds.) *The Foucault Effect: Studies in Governmentality*. Chicago: University of Chicago Press.

Gould, P. (1999) *The Unfinished Revolution: How the Modernisers Saved the Labour Party*. London: Abacus.

Graef, R. (1992) *Living Dangerously: Young Offenders in Their Own Words*. London: Harper Collins.

Habermas, J. (1992) *The Structural Transformation of the Public Sphere*. Cambridge: Polity Press.

Hall, S., Critcher, C., Jefferson, T., Clarke, J., and Roberts, B.(1978) *Policing the Crisis: Mugging, the State and Law and Order*. London: Macmillan.

Hartless, J., Ditton, J., Nair, G. and Phillips, S. (1995) 'More sinned against than sinned'. *British Journal of Criminology*, Vol. 35, No. 1, pp. 114–133.

Harpham, G. (1999) *Shadows of Ethics: Criticism and the Just Society*. Durham, NC: Duke University Press.

Hayes, D. and Hudson, A. (1992) *Who Are the C2s?: A Social and Political Attitudes Survey, Basildon 1992*. Kent: Education and Work Research Group.

Hayes, D. and Hudson, A. (2001) *Basildon: The Mood of the Nation*. London: Demos.

Heartfield, J. (2002) *The 'Death of the Subject' Explained*. Sheffield: Sheffield Hallam University Press.

Heartfield, J. (2003) 'Capitalism and Anti-Capitalism'. *Interventions*, Vol. 5, No. 2, pp. 271–289.

Hernstein, R. and Murray, C. (1996) *The Bell Curve: Intelligence and Class Structure in American Life*. New York: Simon and Schuster.

Hewitt, J. (1998) *The Myth of Self Esteem: Finding Happiness and Solving Problems in America*. New York: St. Martin's.

Hillman, M., Adams, J. and Whiteleg, J. (1990) *One False Move . . . A Study of Children's Independent Mobility*. London: PSI Publishing.

Hillyard, P., Pantazis, C., Tombs, S., and Gordon, D. (eds.) (2004) *Beyond Criminology: Taking Harm Seriously*. London: Pluto Press.

Himmelfarb, G. (1995) *The Demoralization of Western Society*. London: St. Edmundsbury Press.

Hobsbawn, E. (1994) *The Age of Extremes: The Short Twentieth Century, 1914–1991*. London: Michael Joseph.

Hollin, C. (2002) 'Criminological Psychology' in *The Oxford Handbook of Criminology: Third Edition*. Oxford: Oxford University Press.

Holman, B. (1995) *Children and Crime: How Can Society Turn Back the Tide of Delinquency?* Oxford: Lion Publications.

Home Office (1991) *British Crime Survey*. London: HMSO.
Home Office (1992) *British Crime Survey*. London: HMSO.
Home Office (1995) *Anxieties about Crime: Findings from the 1994 British Crime Survey*. London: HMSO.
Home Office (1998) *Guidance Document of Crime and Disorder Act: Local Child Curfews*. London: HMSO.
Home Office (2003) *Home Office Statistical Bulletin*. London: Home Office.
Hough, M. and Mayhew, P. (1983) *The British Crime Survey: First Report*. London: HMSO.
Howard, P.K. (2002) *The Collapse of the Common Good*. New York: Ballantine Books.
Hunt, Alan. (1999a) *Governing Morals A Social History in Moral Education*. Cambridge; Cambridge University Press.
Hunt, Alan (1999b) 'Anxiety and Social Explanation: Some Anxieties About Anxiety'. *Journal of Social History*. Spring Edition.
Hunt, Arnold (1997) ' "Moral Panic" and Moral Language in the Media'. *The British Journal of Sociology*, Vol. 48, No.4, pp. 629–648.
Jacobs, K., Kemeny, J. and Manzi, T. (2003) 'Power, Discursive Space and Institutional Practices in the Construction of Housing Problems'. *Housing Studies*, Vol. 18, No. 4, pp. 429–446.
Jacoby, R. (1999) *The End of Utopia: Politics and Culture in an Age of Apathy*. New York: Basic Books.
Jameson, J. (2005) 'New Labour, Youth Justice and the Question of 'Respect'', in *Youth Justice*, Vol. 5, No.3, pp. 180–193.
Jeffs, T. and Smith, M. K. (1996) 'Getting the Dirtbags off the Streets'. *Youth and Policy*, Vol. 52, pp. 1–14.
Jenkins, P. (1992) *Intimate Enemies: Moral Panics in Contemporary Great Britain*. New York: Walter de Gruyter.
Jenkins, P. (1998) *Moral Panic: Changing Concepts of the Child Molester in Modern America*. New Haven: Yale University Press.
Jenkins, S. (1994) *Against the Grain*. London: John Murray.
Jenkins, S. (1995) *Accountable to None: The Tory Nationalisation of Britain*. London: Penguin.
Jenkins, P. (1996) *Pedophiles and Priests: Anatomy of a Contemporary Crisis*. Oxford: Oxford University Press.
Jones, G. (1987) 'Elderly People and Domestic Crime: Reflections on Ageism, Sexism, Victimology'. *British Journal of Criminology*, Vol. 27, No. 2, pp. 191–201.
Jones, T., Maclean, B. and Young, J. (1986) *The Islington Crime Survey*. Aldershot: Gower.
Jowells R., Curtice, J., Park, Alison., Brook, L., Ahrendt, D., and Thomson, K. (eds.) (1995) *British Social Attitudes: The 12th Report*. Dartmouth: Dartmouth Publishing Company.
Junger, M. (1987) 'Women's Experience of Sexual Harassment'. *British Journal of Criminology*, Vol. 27, No. 4, pp. 358–383.
Kaminer, W. (1993) *I'm Dysfunctional, You're Dysfunctional: The Recovery Movement and Other Self-Help Fashions*. New York: Vintage Books.
Kersten, J. (1996) 'Culture, Masculinities and Violence against Women'. *British Journal of Criminology*, Vol. 36, No. 3, pp. 381–395.
Killingbeck, D. (2001) 'The Role of Television News in the Construction of School Violence as a "Moral Panic" '. *Journal of Criminal Justice and Popular Culture*, Vol. 8, No. 3, pp. 186–202.
King, M. (1997) *A Better World for Children?: Explorations in Morality and Authority*. London: Routledge.

Labour Party (1993) *Partners against crime.*
Labour Party (1995) *A quiet life: Tough action on criminal neighbours.*
Labour Party (1996) *Tackling the causes of crime: Labour's proposals to prevent crime and criminality.*
Lasch, C. (1977) *Haven in a Heartless World.* New York: Basic Books.
Lasch, C. (1979) *Culture of Narcissism.* New York: Norton.
Lasch-Quinn, E. (2006) 'Secularism', in Dolan Cummings (ed.) *Debating Humanism.* Exeter: Societas.
Lash, S., Szerszynski, B. and Wynne, B. (1996) *Risk, Environment and Modernity: Towards A New Ecology.* London: Sage.
Lea, J. and Young, J. (1984) *What Is to Be Done about Law and Order?* Harmondsworth: Penguin.
Lee, E. (2001) 'Reinventing Abortion as a Social Problem: "Postabortion Syndrome" in the United States and Britain', in Joel Best (ed.) *How Claims Spread: Cross National Diffusion of Social Problems.* New York: Aldine de Gruyter.
Lee, E. (2004) *Abortion, Motherhood and Mental Health: Medicalizing Reproduction in the USA and Britain.* New York: Aldine de Gruyter.
Lemert, E.M. (1951) *Social Pathology: A Systematic Approach to the Study of Sociopathic Behaviour.* New York: McGraw-Hill.
Livingstone, S. and Bovill, M. (1999) *Young People New Media.* London: London School of Economics and Political Science.
Loseke, D. (1995) 'Writing Rights: The "Homeless Mentally Ill" and Involuntary Hospitalization', in *Images of Issues: Typifying Contemporary Social Problems.* New York: Walter de Gruyter.
Loseke, D. (1999) *Thinking about Social Problems: An Introduction to Constructionist Perspectives.* New York: Walter de Gruyter.
Luker, K. (1996) *Dubious Conceptions: The Politics of Teenage Pregnancy.* London: Harvard University Press.
MacArthur, B. (eds.) (1999) *The Penguin Book of Twentieth-Century Speeches: Second Revised Edition.* London: Penguin Books.
Maguire, M. and Pointing, J. (eds.) (1988) *Victims of Crime: A New Deal.* Milton Keynes: Open University Press.
Maguire, M., Morgan, R. and Reiner, R. (2002) *The Oxford Handbook of Criminology: Third Edition.* Oxford: Oxford University Press.
Malik, K. (1996) *The Meaning of Race: Race History and Culture in Western Society.* London: Macmillan.
Margo, J. and Dixon, M. (2006) *Freedom's Orphans: Raising Youth in a Changing World.* London: IPPR.
Marshall, G. (1998) *Dictionary of Sociology.* Oxford: Oxford University Press.
Marshall, K. (1982) *Real Freedom: Women's Liberation and Socialism.* London: Junius.
Mason, J. (1996) *Qualitative Researching.* London: Sage.
Matthews, R. and Young, J. (1986) *Confronting Crime.* London: Sage.
Maung, N.A. (1995) *Young People, Victimisation and the Police: British Crime Survey Findings on Experiences and Attitudes of 12 to 15 Year Olds.* London: HMSO.
McCabe, S. and Wallington, P. (1988) *The Police, Public Order and Civil Liberties: Legacies of the Miners' Strike.* London: Routledge.
McGallagly, J., Power, K., Littlewood, P. and Meikle, J. (1998) *Evaluation of the Hamilton Child Safety Initiative.* Crime and Criminal Justice Research Findings No. 24. Edinburgh: The Scottish Office Central Research Unit.
McMullan, J. (1996), 'The New Improved Monied Police: Reform, Crime Control, and the Commodification of Policing in London'. *British Journal of Criminology.* Vol. 36, No. 1, pp 85–108.

McRobbie, A. and Thornton, S.L. (1995) 'Rethinking "Moral Panic" for Multi-Mediated Social Worlds'. *The British Journal of Sociology*, Vol. 46, No. 4, pp. 559–574.

Measham, F., and Brain, K. (2005) '"Binge" drinking, British alcohol policy and the new culture of intoxication', in *Crime Media and Culture* Vol. 1, p. 262.

Mészáros, I. (1995) *Beyond Capital: Towards a Theory of Transition*. London: Merlin Press.

Milne, S. (1995) *The Enemy Within: The Secret War against the Miners*. London: Pan.

Mills, C. W. (1967) *The Sociological Imagination*. New York: Oxford University Press.

Mills, C. W. (1968) *Power Politics and People*. New York: Ballantine.

Moorcock, K. (1998) *Swings and Roundabouts*. Sheffield: Sheffield Hallam University.

MORI (2001) *Trust in Public Institutions*. London: Audit Commission.

Morris, N. (1970) *The Honest Politicians Guide to Crime Control*. Chicago: University of Chicago Press.

Morrison, K. (1995) *Marx Durkheim Weber: Formations of Modern Social Thought*. London: Sage.

Muncie, J. (1999) *Youth and Crime: A Critical Introduction*. London: Sage.

Nash, V. (2002) *Reclaiming Community*. London: IPPR.

New Oxford English Dictionary (1989) Oxford: Clarendon.

Nolan, J. (1998) *The Therapeutic State: Justifying Government at Century's End*. New York: New York University Press.

Nolan, J. (2001) *Reinventing Justice: The American Drug Court Movement*. Princeton, NJ: Princeton University Press.

NSPCC (2000) *Child Maltreatment in the United Kingdom: A Study of the Prevalence of Child Abuse and Neglect*. London: NSPCC.

O'Connor, W. and Lewis, J. (1999) *Experiences of Social Exclusion in Scotland Research Programme Research Findings No. 73*. Edinburgh: Scottish Executive.

O'Malley, C and Waiton, S. (2005) *Who's Antisocial: New Labor and the Politics of Antisocial Behaviour*. London: Academy of Ideas.

O'Malley, P. (1991) 'Legal Networks and Domestic Security', *Studies in Law, Politics and Society*, Vol. 11, pp. 171–190.

O'Malley, P. (1992) 'Risk, Power and Crime Prevention', *Economy and Society*, Vol. 21, pp. 252–275.

O'Malley, P. (eds.) (1998) *Crime and the Risk Society*: Aldershot: Ashgate.

Orr, J. (1997) 'Strathclyde's Spotlight Initiative'. In Norman Dennis (ed.) *Zero Tolerance: Policing a Free Society*. London: The IEA Health and Welfare Unit.

Oxford English Dictionary (1885) Oxford: Clarendon.

Pain, R. (1995) 'Elderly Women and Fear of Violent Crime: The Least Likely Victims? *The British Journal of Criminology*, Vol. 35, No. 4, pp. 584–598.

Pearson, G. (1983) *Hooligan: A History of Respectable Fears*. London: Macmillan.

Phillips, J. (1988) *Policing the Family: Social Control in Thatcher's Britain*. London: Junius.

Phipps, A. (1988) 'Ideologies, Political Parties, and Victims of Crime', in M. Maguire and J. Pointing (eds.) *Victims of Crime: A New Deal*. Milton Keynes: Open University Press.

Pitts, J. (1988) *The Politics of Juvenile Crime*. London: Sage Publications.

Pupavac, V. (2001) *Children's Rights and the New Culture of Paternalism*. Leicester: Perpetuity Press

Putnam, R. (2000) *Bowling Alone*. New York: Simon and Schuster.

Reber, A. (1995) *The Penguin Dictionary of Psychology: Second Edition*. Suffolk: Penguin.

Reece, H. (2003) *Divorcing Responsibly*. Oxford: Hart.

Reitan, E. A. (1997) *Tory Radicalism: Margaret Thatcher, John Major and the Transformation of Britain, 1979–1997*. Oxford: Rowman and Littlefield.

Revell, L. and Heartfield, J. (1996) *The Moral Impasse: The End of Capitalist Triumphalism*. London: Junius.

Richards, F. and Freeman, M. (1988) *Confrontation: The Third Thatcher Term*. London: Junius.

Riesman, D. (1961) *The Lonely Crowd*. New Haven, CT: Yale University Press.

Roberts, H. and Sachdev, D. (1996) *Young People's Social Attitudes*. London: Barnardos and Social Community Planning Research.

Rock, P. (1990) *Helping Victims of Crime: The Home Office and the Rise of Victim Support In England and Wales*. Oxford: Clarendon Press.

Roiphe, K. (1997) *Last Night in Paradise: Sex and Morals at the Century's End*. New York: Little, Brown and Company.

Rose, D. (1996) *In the Name of the Law*. London: Jonathan Cape.

Rose, N. (1996) 'The Death of the Social? Re-figuring the Territory of Government'. *Economy and Society*, Vol. 25, No. 3, pp. 327–356.

Rose, N. (1999) *Governing the Soul: The Shaping of the Private Self*. London: Free Association Books.

Rutherford, A. (1995) 'Signposting the Future of Juvenile Justice Policy in England and Wales', in Howard League for Penal Reform, *Child Offenders UK and International Practice*. London: Howard League.

Rutter, M. & Giller, H. (1983) *Juvenile Delinquents: Trends and Perspectives*. Harmonsworth: Penguin.

Rutter, M., Giller, H. and Hagell, A. (1998) *Antisocial Behaviour by Young People*. Cambridge: Cambridge University Press.

Rutter, M. and Smith, D. (eds.) (1995) *Psychosocial Disorder in Young People: Time Trends and Their Causes*. Chichester: John Wiley.

Sampson, R.J. (2001) 'Review of "Antisocial Behaviour by Young People"'. *Social Development*, Vol. 10, No. 1.

Schlesinger, P. and Tumber, H. (1993) 'Fighting the War against Crime: Television, Police and Audience'. *British Journal of Criminology*, Vol. 33, No. 1, pp. 19–32.

Schneider, G. (2003) *Conservatism in America since 1930: A Reader*. New York: NYU Press.

Scott, S. and Parkey, H. (1998) 'Myths and Reality: Anti-social Behaviour in Scotland'. *Housing Studies*, Vol. 13, No. 3, pp. 325–345.

Scraton, P. (1985) *The State of the Police*. London: Pluto.

Scraton P. (ed.) (1997) *'Childhood' in 'Crisis'?* London: UCL Press.

Seldon, A. and Hickson, K. (2004) *New Labour, Old Labour: the Wilson and Callaghan governments, 1974–79*. London: Routledge.

Sennett, R. (1986) *The Fall of Public Man*. London: Faber and Faber.

Sennett, R. (2004) *Respect: The Formation of Character in an Age of Inequality*. London: Penguin.

Silverman, D. (2000) 'Analysing Talk and Text', in Norman Denzin and Yvonne Lincoln's *Handbook of Qualitative Research: Second Edition*. London: Sage.

Simon, J. (1987) 'The Emergence of a Risk Society: Insurance, Law, and the State', *Socialist Review*, No. 95, pp. 61–89.

Smith, S. (1984) 'Crime in the News'. *British Journal Of Criminology*, Vol. 24, No. 3, pp. 289–295.

Smith, W. and Torstensson, M. (1997) 'Gender Differences in Risk Perception and Neutralizing Fear of Crime'. *British Journal of Criminology*, Vol. 37, No. 4, pp. 608–634.

Sommers, C. and Satel, S. (2005) *One Nation under Therapy: How the Helping Culture Is Eroding Self-Reliance*. New York: St. Martin's Press.

South Lanarkshire Council (1997a) *Focus on Hillhouse Scotland's First Citizens' Jury*. Hamilton: Chief Executives Service.

South Lanarkshire Council (1997b) *Information: Child Safety Initiative Launch*. Hamilton: South Lanarkshire Council.

South Lanarkshire Council (1998) *Access to Leisure and Entertainment: Findings from a Citizens' Jury*. Hamilton: South Lanarkshire Council.

Spector, M. and Kitsuse, J. (2001) *Constructing Social Problems*. New Brunswick, NJ: Transaction Publishers.

Springham, K. (1998) *Time To Go Home Says Who?* Glasgow: Scottish Human Rights Centre.

Squires, P. (1997) Gilling, D. (1999) 'Community Safety: A Critique'. *The British Criminology Conferences: Selected Proceedings*, Volume 2. London: The British Society of Criminology.

Squires, P. and Stephen, D. (2005) *Rougher Justice: Anti-social Behaviour and Young People*. Devon: Willan.

Stirling Council (1997) *Are You Getting Enough . . . Opportunity?* Stirling: Stirling Council Youth Services.

Summerfield, C. and Babb, P. (2003) *Social Trends No. 33*. London: The Stationary Office.

System 3 (1996) *South Lanarkshire Council Community Survey Final Report*. Hamilton: South Lanarkshire Council.

Taylor I. and Taylor L, (eds) (1973) *Politics and Deviance*. Harmondsworth: Penguin.

Thatcher, M. (1995) *The Downing Street Years*. London: Harper Collins.

Thompson, K. (1998) *Moral Panics*. London: Routledge.

Tilley, N. (2005) *Handbook of Crime Prevention and Community Safety*. Devon: Willan.

Tisdall, K. (2006) 'Antisocial Behaviour Legislation Meets Children's Services: Challenging Perspectives on Children, Parents and the State', in *Critical Social Policy*, Vol. 26, No. 1, pp. 101–120.

Truss, L. (2005) *Talk to the Hand: The Utter Bloody Rudeness of Everyday Life*. London: Profile Books.

Ungar, S. (2001) 'Moral Panic Versus the Risk Society: The Implications of the Changing Sites of Social Anxiety'. *British Journal of Sociology*, Vol. 52, Issue 2, pp. 271–292.

Valentine, G. (1996) 'Children Should Be Seen and Not Heard'. *Urban Geography*, Vol. 17, No.3, pp. 205–220.

Valentine, G. (1997) '"Oh Yes I Can." "Oh No You Can't": Children and Parents' Understanding of Kids' Competence to Negotiate Public Space Safely'. *Antipode*, Vol. 29, No. 1, pp. 65–89.

Valentine, G. and McKendrick, J. (1997) 'Children's Outdoor Play: Exploring Parental Concerns about Children's Safety and the Nature of Childhood'. *Geoforum*, Vol 28, No.2, pp. 219–235.

Van Dijk (1988) 'Ideological Trends within the Victim's Movement: An International Perspective', in M. Maguire and J. Pointing. (eds.) *Victims of Crime: A New Deal*. Milton Keynes: Open University Press.

Van Dijk, J. (1994) 'Crime and Victim Surveys'. *Paper Presented at the Eighth International Symposium on Victimology, Adelaide, South Australia, August 21–26*.

Victor, J.S. (1998) 'Moral Panic and the Construction of Deviant Behaviour: A Theory and Application to the Case of Ritual Child Abuse'. *Sociological Perspectives*, Fall, pp. 99–125.

Waddington, P.A.J. (1986) 'Mugging as a Moral Panic: A Question of Proportion', *British Journal of Sociology*, Vol. 37, No. 2, pp. 245–259.

Waddington, P.A.J. (2000) 'Orthodoxy and Advocacy in Criminology'. *Theoretical Criminology*, Vol. 4, No.1, pp. 93–111.

Wainwright, D. and Calnan, M. (2002) *Work Stress: The Making of a Modern Epidemic*. Buckingham: Open University Press.

Waiton, S. (2001) *Scared of the Kids: Curfews, Crime and the Regulation of Young People*. Sheffield: Sheffield Hallam University Press.

Waldron, D. (2005) 'Role-Playing Games and the Christian Right: Community Formation in Response to a Moral Panic.' *Journal of Religion and Popular Culture*, Vol. 9, Spring.

Wheway, R. and Millward, A. (1997) *Child's Play: Facilitating Play on Housing Estates*. Coventry: Chartered Institute of Housing.

Williams, R. (2004). *The Anxious City: British Urbanism in the Late 20th Century*. London: Routledge.

Wilkinson, H. and Mulgan, G. (1995) *Freedom's Children: Work, Relationships and Politics for 18–34 Year Olds in Britain Today*. London: Demos.

Wilkinson, L.T. (1964) *Social Deviance: Social Policy, Action and Research*. London: Tavistock.

Wilson, J. Q. (1975) *Thinking about Crime*. New York: Basic Books.

Wilson, J. Q. (1985) *Thinking About Crime: Revised Edition*. New York: Vintage.

Wolfe, A. (2005) *The Transformation of American Religion: How We Actually Live Our Lives*. Chicago: University of Chicago Press.

Young, J. (1971a) *The Drugtakers*. London: MacGibbon and Kee.

Young, J. (1971b) 'The Role of the Police as Amplifiers of Deviance, Negotiators of Drug Control as Seen in Notting Hill', in S. Cohen (ed.) *Images of Deviance*. Harmondsworth: Penguin.

Young, J. (1988a) 'Radical Criminology in Britain: The Emergence of a Competing Paradigm'. *British Journal of Criminology*, Vol. 28, No. 2, pp. 159–183.

Young, J. (1988b) 'Risk of Crime and Fear of Crime: A Realist Critique of Survey-based Assumptions', in M. Maguire and J. Pointing (eds.) *Victims of Crime: A New Deal*. Milton Keynes: Open University Press.

Young, J. (1999) *The Exclusive Society: Social Exclusion, Crime and Difference in Late Modernity*. London: Sage.

Young, M. (1991) *An Inside Job: Policing and the Police Culture in Britain*. Oxford: Clarendon.

Zedner, L. (2006), 'Policing before and after the Police: The Historical Antecedents of Contemporary Crime Control'. *British Journal of Criminology*, Vol. 46, No. 1, pp 78–96.

Zimring, F. (2000) *American Youth Violence*. New York: Oxford University Press.

Index

Lightning Source UK Ltd.
Milton Keynes UK
12 September 2009

143655UK00001B/37/P

9 780415 872720